Sustainable Development Goals and Income Inequality

Edited by

Peter A.G. van Bergeijk

International Institute of Social Studies, Erasmus University, The Hague, the Netherlands

Rolph van der Hoeven

International Institute of Social Studies, Erasmus University, The Hague, the Netherlands

 Edward Elgar
PUBLISHING

Cheltenham, UK • Northampton, MA, USA

Published by
Edward Elgar Publishing Limited
The Lypiatts
15 Lansdown Road
Cheltenham
Glos GL50 2JA
UK

Edward Elgar Publishing, Inc.
William Pratt House
9 Dewey Court
Northampton
Massachusetts 01060
USA

A catalogue record for this book
is available from the British Library

Library of Congress Control Number: 2017941892

This book is available electronically in the **Elgar**online
Social and Political Science subject collection
DOI 10.4337/9781788110280

ISBN 978 1 78811 027 3 (cased)
ISBN 978 1 78811 028 0 (eBook)

Typeset by Servis Filmsetting Ltd, Stockport, Cheshire

Contents

Contributors

Tony Addison UNU-WIDER, Helsinki

Giovanni Andrea Cornia University of Florence

Peter Edward Newcastle University Business School

Richard Jolly Institute of Development Studies (IDS), University of Sussex, Brighton

Malte Luebker Institute of Economic and Social Research (WSI), Dusseldorf

Deepak Nayyar Jawaharlal Nehru University (JNU), New Delhi

Andy Sumner Kings College, London

Peter A.G. van Bergeijk International Institute of Social Studies (ISS), Erasmus University, The Hague

Rolph van der Hoeven International Institute of Social Studies (ISS), Erasmus University, The Hague

Jan Vandemoortele Independent researcher (previously at UNDP and UNICEF)

Rob Vos International Food Policy Research Institute (IFPRI), Washington D.C. and International Institute of Social Studies (ISS), Erasmus University, The Hague

1. The challenge to reduce income inequality (introduction and overview)

Peter A.G. van Bergeijk and Rolph van der Hoeven

In September 2015 the General Assembly of the United Nations issued a statement on the 2030 Agenda for Sustainable Development (Post-2015 Development Agenda) and adopted the Sustainable Development Goals (SDGs). The SDGs are in a sense the successor of the Millennium Development Goals (MDGs), but are also quite distinct. The core business of the MDG agenda was the fight against extreme poverty and fostering social progress; the SDGs are more complex and more comprehensive as they aim at sustainable development – defined in a broad sense to include its environmental, economic and social dimensions. Also the SDG process itself is much more complex. In contrast to the preparation of the MDGs, which was mostly an internal affair of top officials of the United Nations (UN) and of development fora around the Organisation for Economic Co-operation and Development (OECD) and the Bretton Woods Institutions (Fukuda-Parr, 2014; Saith, 2006) the preparations for the Post-2015 Development Agenda and negotiations on the SDGs became massive, with involvement of all parts of the UN system, governments, scholars, non-governmental organizations, global philanthropists, foundations and enterprise representatives. A set of interagency activities in the UN and its specialized agencies was reflected, inter alia, in the report: *Realizing the Future We Want for All* (UN, 2012) that was the first main input to the consultations. The Open Working Group for the SDGs of the UN (OWG) agreed on a list of 17 goals. The process by which this list of 17 goals was drawn up included many national and global consultations which culminated in the report 'A Million Voices' (UNDG, 2013) and a report of a High Level Panel of eminent persons chaired by three heads of state (UN System Task Team on the Post-2015 Development Agenda, 2013). Indeed, Stewart (2015: 288) notes that it is a 'huge achievement to have plucked agreement out of a five-year maelstrom', although one can ask how many of the real poor had the opportunity to raise their voices on these issues.

Achieving agreement, however, has carried costs in terms of specificity and efficiency (*Economist*, 2015). The SDGs have been called a wish-list of unfocused and unattainable goals. At least four issues have been raised regarding the do-ability of the SDG project: inclusiveness in implementation, manageability, appropriate measurement and financial planning. Firstly, the idea of top-down management by (inter)governmental organization has been questioned and it has been argued that new actors for change should become part and parcel of the SDG process, including private firms, non-governmental organization and civic society (Hajer et al., 2015; Howard and Wheeler, 2015). In this sense, the SDG process itself will have to become much more inclusive in the implementation phase. Second, with 17 goals and 169 targets the process could very well become unmanageable (Stokstad, 2015) both analytically, politically and in terms of monitoring and review and of follow-up (Kindornay and Twigg, 2015). Effective policy will probably require prioritization of strategic (intrinsic and instrumental) targets (Pongiglione, 2015) and further analysis of the interdependencies in the network of targets underlying the 17 SDGs (Le Blanc 2015). A third important issue is the need to conceptually design, measure and connect the several hundreds of indicators (Hák, Janousková and Moldan, 2016) and to strengthen initiatives to increase international statistical comparability for SDG-related indicators that will be accessed both at a national and global level (Schoenmaker, Hoekstra and Smits, 2015). Fourth, an important issue is not only to set goals but also to find the financial means that are necessary to reach these goals (Sachs, 2015, Chapter 4 by Vos this volume). Financing was an issue for the MDGs, both in terms of the methodology that was deployed to arrive at the cost estimates and some of the underlying assumptions (including, for example, major efforts – in relative terms – by poor nations through domestic resource mobilization). A critical attitude towards the official and semi-official estimates is also warranted because they seem to be driven by what is possible from the perspective of donors (the largest estimate amounts to only 0.3 per cent of world GDP) rather than by what amounts should be made available. Still it can be observed that the estimates of the global financing needs increased as the end date for the MDGs came closer (Figure 1.1), reflecting that it became increasingly clear that more finance was necessary. Moreover, even against these modest estimates, globally funding actually fell short by a third (Development Finance International and Oxfam, 2015).

The MDGs were formulated in 2000 in the benign if not optimistic global economic context of the Great Moderation but the period covered by the

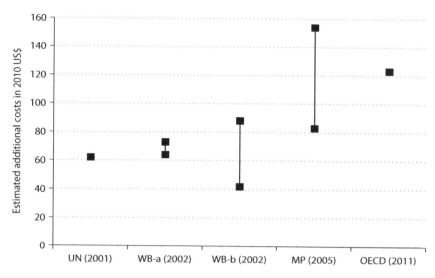

Notes:
Conversion to 2010 US$ based on US CPI.
UN: Report of the High-Level Panel on Financing for Development.
WB-a: Financing gap for a limited group of countries in Devarajan, Miller and Swanson (2002).
WB-b: Costs related to health, education and environment in Devarajan, Miller and Swanson (2002).
MP: Millennium Project.
OECD: Atisophon et al. (2011).

Source: Based on Atisophon et al. (2011, Table 1, p. 12 and Table 2, p. 15).

Figure 1.1 *(Semi) official global MDG cost estimates (billions of 2010 US$)*

MDGs ended in 2015 in the aftermath of the Great Depression, providing 'a grim future and rapid blurring of boundaries between the developed and developing contexts in terms of rising inequities and poverty' (Tiwari, 2015: 314). In this economic context, it will be even more difficult to reach productive employment, inclusive development and greater equality within and among nations. Some see no or only a very limited role for the SDGs that are 'still stuck in the straitjacket of existing structures, institutions and regimes, and therefore, the vision gets fragmented and remains at a low level of ambition' (Ghosh, 2015: 321).

This book discusses whether the SDGs have the potential to address the issues discussed above and recognize the need for transformative develop-ment. It zooms in on one of the most important questions of development today, *how to stem the growing (income) inequality in the world* (Palma, 2011; van der Hoeven, 2011; Vandemoortele, 2011; UNDP, 2013). The focus on this topic reflects the finding that the strongest hubs in the network of SDG targets occur for 'inequality, poverty and growth and employment (. . .that) all have links with 10 other goals or more' (Le Blanc, 2015: 179). Moreover, growing and persistent income inequality in many countries is an important subject that increasingly pervades in economic, social and environmental systems, and therefore warrants a study on its own. Indeed, the authors in this book provide additional reasons to focus on inequality and the potential role of SDGs in reducing inequality.

BROADENING THE DEVELOPMENT AGENDA FOR THE SDG WORLD

Richard Jolly (Chapter 2 this volume) argues that the future for development needs to be framed by five fundamental objectives: universalism, sustainability, human development, inequality and human rights, which are all embodied in the SDGs even if not always with deep commitment. He discusses three fundamental objectives in more depth: universalism, inequality and human development.

Universalism (SDGs apply to *all* countries) removes the long-standing weakness of development – that it was 'us' talking about the desirability of things happening in 'their' countries. This does not mean a total change of content and agenda but rather a broadening of the context and application of the SDG framework in recognition of the social and political complications which often constrain doing what 'we' (the experts) think is obviously desirable for 'them' (the developing world). Universalism may also help to strengthen the political economy analysis of the global strategy to reach sustainable development and the required policy actions. The principle of Universalism could bring more attention to comparative work regarding developed countries, with more attention to context and institutions – and long run changes – and perhaps to the political economy of policy proposals.

Jolly welcomes that inequality, after thirty years of virtual neglect in international economic policy has at last been put centre stage. The opportunity of working on inequality must not be missed, because the forces of reaction will not remain side-lined for long, even though the extremes of income inequality within countries are at unprecedented levels. Already the reductions of Gini coefficients in the majority of Latin America countries are being reversed and the triumphs of conservative governments in Europe, notably in Britain and the Netherlands among others, show the many ways in which right-wing policies can be presented to appeal to electorates. Inequality must be analysed in a multidimensional manner and brought into mainstream policy. Wilkinson and Pickett (2009) demonstrate that inequality has a major impact on mental illness, child and adult mortality, obesity, educational performance, teenage births, homicide, imprisonment rates, levels of trust and social mobility. The common factor behind these many and widespread repercussions of inequality, is stress.

Jolly recalls that the human development paradigm has its own stimulating richness and subtleties, but that it needs to be pursued within Sen's framework of capabilities, functionings and choices. He wonders, however, why human development is so rarely part of mainstream work, either in the teaching of development or as a frame for policy analysis and policy making. This neglect of human development contains a clear message, namely that human development theory, techniques and applications need to be integrated into development teaching as well as into policy studies and consultancies. This would be an important step towards offsetting the narrow applications of neo-liberal economic teaching and policy making and the narrowness of austerity policies being promoted across Europe today. It is illogical and absurd to think that one can restore balance to a country's economy by unbalancing the lives of its people.

Jolly's five objectives relate not only to development studies but to country-by-country implementation, as already set out in the SDGs. The UN's Committee on Development Policy (CDP), has made important recommendations with respect to the SDGs, about the need for improved global governance, and for a more relevant and robust system and approach for monitoring progress towards the SDGs over the next 15 years. The CDP has also underlined the importance of ensuring that the SDGs are adapted to the national context of each country with a process of democratic consultation involving civil society as well as national parliaments.

FROM MDGs TO SDGs: CRITICAL REFLECTIONS ON GLOBAL TARGETS AND THEIR MEASUREMENT

Jan Vandemoortele (Chapter 3 this volume) provides a critical reflection on the precursors of the SDGs, the MDGs that had 2015 as target date. It is difficult to develop a counterfactual to the MDGs and it is therefore difficult to attribute developments since 2000 to success or failure of the MDGs. Positive points are that the MDGs helped to demystify 'development' for the general public and that the MDGs emphasized the striving towards as much as the achieving of global targets. However unintended consequences of the MDGs included the way the MDGs have been developed and formulated, especially their lack of an underlying development theory, how they have been operationalized, how they have been implemented and how this has led to a distortion in setting development priorities for structural change.

Strengths of the SDGs are getting the message to the public at large and the consultation processes by which the SDGs were developed and conceived, resulting in a broader set of areas of concern and on linking global goals towards national targets. But the SDGs are not fully inclusive, in particular because of their formulation in absolute numbers that in practical terms reduce the universality and in reflecting an old world view. For example nutrition issues are dominated by malnutrition and not by obesity.

For Vandemoortele the SDGs are not yet a universal agenda or an equitable agenda. He recommends that the implementation of the SDGs must start at the country level, whereby each and every country – developing and developed alike – selects and adapts those targets that are most relevant to the national context. At the global level, three actions are required. First, the way of aggregating the global narrative needs to change. With the MDGs, this was mostly driven by global statistics and world maps with off-track countries coloured in red. With the SDGs, the global assessment needs to pay more attention to how global targets make a difference at national and sub-national levels. Second, the choice of indicators must help remedy some of the flaws in the formulation of the SDGs. The inclusion of the Palma ratio, for instance, can fix target 10.1 about inequality. This ratio measures the income share of the top 10 per cent divided by the income share of the bottom 40 per cent. The inclusion of body mass indices can fix the target on nutrition, which ignores the growing challenge of being overweight or obese. Third, one of the few truly universal targets in the SDGs cannot be left orphaned. It concerns bullet 1.2 – *By 2030, reduce at least by half the proportion of men, women and children of all ages living in poverty in all its dimensions according to national definitions.* While the global narrative is already focusing on extreme poverty and hunger – which are not universal targets – the question arises who will be championing target 1.2? Who will compile the register of national definitions? By addressing these aspects, the considerable time and efforts invested in the SDG negotiations by countless stakeholders are likely to bear some fruit. But member states do not seem always ready to accept indicators that cover relevant, but politically sensitive, dimensions of sustainable and equitable development.

FROM BILLIONS TO TRILLIONS: TOWARDS REFORM OF DEVELOPMENT FINANCE AND THE GLOBAL RESERVE SYSTEM

Rob Vos (Chapter 4 this volume) argues that there are many Global Public Goods (GPGs) elements in the SDG agenda. First, achieving sustainable development is a GPG in itself. Other global public goods include sustainable food security, preserving biodiversity, oceans, ecosystems, and so on, preserving a stable climate, treatment of communicable diseases and other global health issues, and stable and well-regulated international financial markets. Safeguarding these GPGs should also contribute to greater reducing international inequality. Providing these GPGs will require a stronger global partnership and much more development finance than currently available. This is acknowledged in Agenda 2030 and by SDG17, but this is little progress from the much-criticized MDG8 and its poor delivery track record. Furthermore, the AAAA – Addis Ababa Action Agenda of the third Financing for Development Conference, agreed in July 2015 just before the adaptation of the SDGs in September 2015 – seems a step backwards from the Monterrey Consensus, achieved at the first conference on Financing for Development in 2002. In Addis Ababa, no major new commitments for strengthening and widening the global partnership for development were made: no significant additional funds were pledged, no new directions for a multilateral trading system consistent with the SDGs were agreed upon or even discussed, and likewise systemic problems underlying repeated international financial instability were not even on the agenda.

The only positive outcomes were the establishment of an infrastructure fund (public–private partnership financing) and the agreement on a 'technology facilitation mechanism'. The implementation of Agenda 2030 may turn out to be shorthanded because of a weak global partnership, leaving many of the deficiencies in global governance mechanisms unresolved[1] and the risk of leaving Agenda 2030 grossly underfinanced. Ways to leverage vast new resources for sustainable development finance are revamping the global reserve system and simultaneously addressing the key weaknesses of that system to bring greater international financial stability.

According to World Bank (2015) several trillions are needed to meet the global challenges that are at the centre of the SDG agenda. While several initiatives for new sources of innovative finance, such as new international taxes, could add to existing development assistance, these would not measure up to the required trillions. The current problems of the global reserve system (asymmetric adjustments, Triffin dilemma caused by the dominance of the dollar, and excess reserve accumulation causing a deflationary bias to the world economy) need to be fixed. Excess reserves and new and regular issuance of Special Drawing Rights (SDRs) by the IMF could be leveraged for long-term finance for investments in sustainable development. The establishment of new multilateral development banks, such as the New Development Bank established by the BRICS countries and the Asia Infrastructure Investment Bank founded upon China's initiative are partial responses in this direction that have already been put in motion. More is needed, however, to live up to the challenge and Vos argues that opportunities are there by going at the heart of the global reserve system.

GLOBAL INEQUALITY AND GLOBAL POVERTY SINCE THE COLD WAR: HOW ROBUST IS THE OPTIMISTIC NARRATIVE?

Peter Edward and Andy Sumner (Chapter 5 this volume) discuss how the growth in global consumption since the end of the Cold War in 1990 has impacted on the co-evolution of global inequality and poverty. It is often suggested that this era of growth has led to a dramatic reduction in global poverty and to the emergence of both a new global middle class and a more equal world. They argue that this dominant and optimistic narrative on globalization since the Cold War is considerably more methodologically fragile than it at first seems. Edward and Sumner contest this mainstream view and constructed a Growth, Inequality and Poverty model (GrIP) driven by consumption, output and distribution trends, taking into account various definitions of inequality and poverty as well as various methods to make use of old and new purchasing power parity rates.

Further, Edward and Sumner suggest that this has implications for the UN goal to end global poverty by 2030. The fall in inequality is almost exclusively attributable to the effect that the rise of China has had on between-country inequality. Changes in global inequality across the rest of the world are much more modest. Much heralded falls in global poverty have raised the consumption of the poorest, but the extent to which that is the case depends on where one draws the global poverty line as at the lower end of the global distribution a change of just 10 cents can remove 100 million people from global poverty headcounts. If one takes instead the average poverty line for all countries (a more genuinely global poverty line) of \$5 per day poverty headcounts have hardly changed since the Cold War. Meanwhile, the numbers living at risk of sliding back into poverty (between \$1.90 and \$10 a day) grew by 1.6bn, compared to a rise of 1.1bn in the numbers living above this level, and around half of those living above this level saw their share of global consumption fall. Edward and Sumner suggest therefore that the dominant or optimistic narrative, of falling poverty and an emerging 'middle class' largely free from the threat of poverty, disguises both considerable growth in the size of the 'global precariat' living in conditions that most in the developed world would consider to be well below 'middle class' and an erosion of the financial security of a significant proportion of those living at higher consumption levels.

IS LATIN AMERICA'S RECENT INEQUALITY DECLINE PERMANENT OR TEMPORARY?

Giovanni Andrea Cornia (Chapter 6 this volume) challenges the idea that a recession by definition increases inequality. In the first decade of the twenty-first century various Latin American countries saw declines in income inequality. These declines in inequality were the result from changes in the political regimes towards the left or the centre, from deliberate policy changes as well as from changes in international conditions. Policies that helped to reduce inequality included a rise in secondary education of low-middle class children, labour market policies that included a rise in the minimum wages greater than in average wages, improved collective bargaining, especially in Southern Cone countries and a formalization of informal jobs, changes in tax policies, that included a rising tax/GDP ratio, more progressive taxation, more attention in public expenditure towards the poor, including social transfers in the form of social pensions and Conditional Cash transfers. Furthermore prudent macro policy (counter-cyclical fiscal/monetary policy, low deficits, low inflation, reduced external debt) contributed also to a decline in inequality.

Cornia poses the question whether the declining trend of income inequality in Latin America at the beginning of the new millennium did continue after the 2008 financial crisis and the ensuing decline in primary commodity prices. Cornia argues that from 2008 to 2012 the decline in inequality in Latin America on average continued though at a slower pace, but that 2013 showed on average a rise in inequality in Latin America, with more countries having an increase in the Gini ratio of inequality than those with a decline. Inequality went down during the sharp crisis of 2009, thanks to Keynesian policies that sustained domestic consumption and redistribution in face of falling exports. He attributes the increase in inequality in 2013, and possibly 2014 and 2015 to changes in political regimes leaning to the right, a halting of the progressive policies applied in the previous decades because of slowdown in GDP (which he labels 'political stress') leading to failing government approval rates. Further factors are that over 2009–2012 redistribution and the Gini fall benefitted only the poor (and no longer also the middle class, as it had happened over 2003–2009), causing an electoral shift by the middle-class in favour of centre-right regimes;[2] and that serious domestic policy mistakes were made (such as repressed inflation). But he sees no abandonment of the successfully applied macro model, nor dramatic changes in the labour market policies or in the public expenditure/GDP ratio, though with reduced fiscal space because of external conditions. A preliminary regression analysis shows that in the period 2003–2008 rising exports for different categories of exporters in Latin America were related to a decline in the Gini ratio, however in the 2009–2011 and 2012–2013 periods falling exports were only in mineral exporters negatively correlated with the income inequality, that is, a drop in exports caused a rise in inequality for this group of countries.

Cornia concludes that after the structural adjustment programmes in the 1980s and fully fledged liberalization in the last decade of last century, Latin American countries were affected by strong dependency on global markets, and that as in the EU, lasting global recessions inevitably impact on growth, balance of payments, government revenue, and possibly inequality, but that after 2008, inequality continued to fall until 2012 thanks to strong initial conditions and policy commitments. However, in 2013 there were the first clear signs that inequality stopped falling (50 per cent falls and 50 per cent rises). Cornia foresees that changes in the terms of trade and in exports might affect future Gini as the 'redistributive institutions' put in place in the 2000s may be more difficult to finance. This is key especially in nine mineral exporting countries. With deteriorating growth in 2014–2015, inequality might be inevitably affected cyclically – but not structurally. A structural change in Gini trend will depend on a new wave of elections. A deepening of the 2000s reforms (in the field of taxation, education and industrial policy) could help in combating the effects of the world crisis on income inequality. Despite the unparalleled inequality improvements recorded over 2002–2012, Latin America remains together with Southern Africa the region with the highest inequality in the world. The battle for a more egalitarian society needs therefore to go on.

THIRTY YEARS IN AFRICA'S DEVELOPMENT: FROM STRUCTURAL ADJUSTMENT TO STRUCTURAL TRANSFORMATION?

Tony Addison (Chapter 7 this volume) reviews 15 years of MDGs and previews the 15-year time span of the SDGs, and emphasizes the importance of 'structure'. The era of structural adjustment preceding (and still partially dominating) the era of the MDGs advanced a rather simple theory of structural change: the main driver was relative price incentives guiding the market to efficient outcomes. Addison recalls that the role of the state in that era was to stand back, lightly regulate (if at all), protect private property rights, and provide public goods including infrastructure. In this model, inequality might show a modest rise in the middle-stage of development but was ultimately to be contained as economies moved from low- to middle-income status, thereby providing more opportunity for all. Inclusive growth would follow almost automatically, and poverty reduction with it. But we have arrived at a point, in the era of the SDGs, at which Africa has yet to achieve the level and speed of structural transformation that is required. The last decade's super-cycle in commodities seems to be over, dangerously exposing the weakness of posting categories like the 'African lions' and their undiversified growth model. Moreover, African policy makers have yet to absorb the implications for investment in their extractive industries of what real progress on international climate change agreements will mean for the demand for Africa's exports of fossil fuels (oil and coal).

In the 1980s achieving structural change appeared to be a straightforward process, and one to be largely driven by market mechanisms. But at the onset of the SDGs that structural change has not occurred, which illustrates the weakness of relying on market mechanisms alone (despite their importance), and points to the need for better models of state and enterprise cooperation suitable for Africa's economies. Such cooperation is inherently political, and to be effective, as well as transparent, it must mesh with the democratic politics of each country. The old forms of state and enterprise cooperation that characterized the one-party systems of post-independence Africa, and which degraded into unproductive rent-seeking (and sometimes fed into violent conflict) are not viable for today's democracies. Nor are they capable of delivering integration with the global economy in ways that facilitate national structural transformation.

Today's policy agenda implied by the SDGs is subtle. Raising farm productivity; creating clusters of high value-added manufacturing and services; managing natural resource wealth in the public interest; making the right infrastructure choices; constructing financial systems that facilitate diversified economies; achieving inclusive urbanization; and adapting to climate change are challenges with no easy answers. The development states that Africa needs to create must have a deep knowledge of what the private sector is capable of achieving. Then high-value synergies of private and state action can be identified and acted upon – while ensuring that business operates within a framework of supporting regulation that protects the public interest. These are indeed great challenges for the international system and African people and their governments.

POVERTY, EMPLOYMENT AND INEQUALITY IN THE SDGs: HETERODOX DISCOURSE, ORTHODOX POLICIES?

Malte Luebker (Chapter 8 this volume) recalls that employment and labour issues were entirely absent from the initial set of MDGs in 2000, and that only in 2005, somewhat hastily, a new target 1B was added to address this oversight with a rather simple underlying narrative: growing labour productivity, if combined with an expansion of wage employment, should help to end working poverty and thus poverty in general. The absence of references to labour institutions was regrettable: the MDGs fell short of the understanding of poverty, employment and inequality that was reached a century earlier, when Rowntree (1901) wrote his inquiry into the social conditions of the wage-earning classes of York, he could not help but wander off into the 'larger questions bearing upon the welfare of human society' and recognized that the 'legislation affecting the aggregation or the distribution of wealth' was part of the wider social problem causing poverty (Rowntree, 1901: 145). Changing the word 'land' into 'world', and updating the statistics, one of his closing sentences still rings true today: 'That in this land of abounding wealth, during a time of perhaps unexampled prosperity, probably more than one-fourth of the population are living in poverty, is a fact which may well cause great searching's of heart' (Rowntree, 1901: 304).

Luebker argues that more than a hundred years later it's about time to address the distribution of income and wealth. He therefore welcomes that the 2030 Agenda for Sustainable Development makes ample reference to employment and inequality. Goal 8 is devoted to 'Promote sustained, inclusive and sustainable economic growth, full and productive employment and decent work for all' and expands on two familiar themes, productivity and employment, while adding labour rights as a new element. While the proliferation of goals and targets prompts cynics (and a few non-cynics) to dismiss the SDGs as an unattainable wish-list without focus, the more nuanced treatment of labour arguably presents a worthwhile advance in attaining a wider set of progressive policies concerned with addressing rising inequalities.

However goal 8, if this goal is taken on its own, might not deliver on its promise of sustained, inclusive and sustainable economic growth. It is silent about labour market institutions. In their absence, productivity growth may not translate into higher wages for workers and hence the formula '*productivity* + *employment* = *inclusive and sustainable growth*' will not work its magic. Examples for this are abound, including from Asia, which are discussed in Chapter 8. The result of such a disconnect between wages and productivity is a shift in the functional distribution of income at the expense of labour, leading to increasing inequality the very opposite of inclusive growth heralded in the preamble of the SDGs.

To achieve a more equitable growth path, Luebker argues that goal 10 of the SDGs provides some useful advice on the role of fiscal, wage and social protection policies to reduce inequalities of outcome and to achieve faster income growth for the poorest – in other words, to achieve growth with redistribution. While the SDGs are strong on some policies that have direct impact on the primary and secondary distribution of incomes, they fail to mention strengthening institutions to give workers a voice and a meaningful stake in development. Luebker argues that labour rights need to encompass the right to freedom of association. There is only an indirect reference to this in the 2030 Agenda, which invokes the Universal Declaration of Human Rights (which includes the right to form and join trade unions).

CAN CATCH UP REDUCE INEQUALITY?

Deepak Nayyar (Chapter 9 this volume) observes that, during the past 25 years, there has been a significant increase in the share of developing countries in world output, manufacturing and trade. This catch up, in aggregates, has been driven by economic growth. But the process is characterized by uneven development and emerging divergences. There is an exclusion of regions, of countries within regions, of regions within countries, and of people, leading to increasing divergences within the developing world. Asia led the process, while Latin America stayed roughly where it was, and Africa experienced regress. He identifies 14 countries (eight in Asia, four in Latin America and two in Africa, the so-called Next-14 or N14) which have led the catch up and whose experience provides insights or lessons for others. Nayyar attributes development outcomes in these countries to initial conditions, enabling institutions and supportive governments. National strategies, development policies and economic institutions in the post-colonial era that differed across countries laid the foundations. The creation of a physical infrastructure and the spread of education in society were critical elements. The role of the state in evolving policies, developing institutions and making strategic interventions, whether as a catalyst or a leader, was also central to their process of catch up. But rapid economic growth was not always transformed into meaningful development that improved the well-being of ordinary people. Absolute poverty declined. Yet poverty persisted. The underlying reason was that economic inequality increased almost everywhere, particularly in the N14.

Despite constraints, developing countries must ensure that the benefits of catch up are distributed in a far more equal manner between people and regions within countries. Unless growth improves the living conditions of people, it will not be possible to sustain economic growth in the long run. Thus, poverty eradication, employment creation and inclusive growth are an imperative. This is the only sustainable way forward, because it enables developing countries to mobilize their most abundant resource, people, for development, and reinforce the process of growth through cumulative causation (insofar as people provide resources on the supply side and create markets on the demand side).

Nayyar sketches reasons why other developing countries could follow the N14 and sustain high growth – large populations, demographic characteristics, and low wages – but recognizes that their potential might not be realized because of country-specific internal and external constraints. In terms of internal constraints, Nayyar emphasizes the two-way interaction between development and institutions, economic and social, as well as missing control mechanisms to deal with market failure and government failure. He would like to see a Karl Polanyi type of great transformation in the N14 and in the countries that follow in their footsteps. As to external constraints, the recent economic crisis could slow down but would not halt the catch up process. However, a faster development of alternative, non-fossil, energy sources, in the quest for sustainable development is important. The end of the first decade of the twenty-first century could be a turning point which suggests the beginning of profound changes in the balance of economic and political power in the world, in which countries either could cooperate better in a multi-polar world or where reluctance of the dominant powers to acknowledge reality could halt the process of economic and social progress. The rising tensions and the slow progress, or even regress, in global governance and economic cooperation since 2010 (stalled reform of Bretton Woods, lack of coordination of economic policies) show that global cooperation is not an automatic or assured outcome but needs to be pursued vigorously.

Nayyar formulates two interlinked hypotheses. Economic growth (catch-up) is essential for reducing inequality (between and within countries), but at the same time it will be unsustainable without reducing inequality (within countries). He concludes that catch up can reduce inequality. If it does not, there will be no catch up.

CAN THE SUSTAINABLE DEVELOPMENT GOALS STEM RISING INCOME INEQUALITY IN THE WORLD?

In the last chapter, Rolph van der Hoeven reviews processes of growing income inequality and what kind of challenges these pose for the post 2015 development agenda and the SDGs. He discusses what the drivers are for often growing income inequality, concentrating on the functional income distribution between capital and labour and the increasing share in many countries of the rich (top 1 per cent of the income curve). It is important to concentrate on the distribution of income between capital and labour as this drives personal income distribution. He relates growing functional income inequality to recent developments in the labour markets among others caused by globalization. He observes that *the decline of the labour share has not halted or been reversed after the financial crisis and also does not attest to the sometimes-heard thesis that the financial crisis did hit capital owners harder than ordinary workers and their families.* The share of the top 1 per cent is increasing in almost all developing countries, a consequence of the declining labour share and of greater inequality between wages themselves.

Van der Hoeven then reviews the process leading to and the outcome of the MDGs, arguing like other authors in this volume, that neglecting inequality was a great oversight of the MDGs. The SDGs in contrast do refer to reducing inequality, but van der Hoeven judges the compromise text of goal 10 on inequality and its major target too weak to be meaningful for proper implementation. He also deplores that an earlier proposal to use the Palma ratio to capture income inequality had not been retained in the final wording in goal 10 of the SDGs. He furthermore refers to the outcome of the conference on Financing for Development in July 2015 where in its final Addis Ababa Action Agenda several proposals were not retained, that could have led to greater command of national resource by developing and emerging countries, to achieve the necessary structural change and to reducing national income inequality. He argues therefore that on the basis of a first reading of the SDGs, and by judging how inequality was treated at the conference on Financing for Development one could say that the SDGs, in the way they have been currently formulated and how international agreement is reached, can as yet not be regarded as a powerful instrument to reduce inequality.

However, van der Hoeven argues that another issue that came to the fore during the preparation of the SDGs is the active involvement of civil society. Action by civil society, supported by some governments, did manage that the SDGs are now embedded in the Human Rights Declaration as well as in the other international instruments relating to human rights and international law, and that a follow-up and review process should be an integral part of the SDGs. Here van der Hoeven still sees opportunities to give more concrete attention to inequality in the SDGs. The Statistical Commission of the UN, in consultation with all stakeholders did set in 2016 verifiable indicators towards the targets of the SDGs, while member states are encouraged to develop national strategies, which will be part of a review process coordinated by the High Level Political Forum on Sustainable Development, based on SDG progress reports. These review processes will not only be informed by governments and international agencies, but also by civil society. They thus pose a continued and future challenge to put issues of inequality at the forefront of development policy. At various passages in the SDGs and in the Addis Ababa Action Agenda many lofty words have been said about reducing inequality.

Active involvement of civil society can thus call governments and the UN system to task on growing national and international income inequalities and demand measures which go beyond the formulation of some of the vaguely formulated goals and targets, but which do correspond to the general language of the SDGs and the Post-2015 Development Agenda. This could then form the basis of a global social contract (van der Hoeven, 2011) for an effective development partnership.

Elements of such a global social contract should include first the *right to development* especially the economic, social and cultural rights and the basic elements thereof in the form of non-discrimination, participation and accountability. Second, the contract should include *the introduction of a global social floor*, which is financially possible, but where currently political will is lacking. Third, *a revitalized form of global governance*, where the coherence, at national and international level between social, economic and environmental sustainable policies, is strengthened, thus allowing developing countries to strive for necessary structural transformation. This could take the form of a Global Economic Coordination Council. Deliberations at the council need not only to be based on current statistics of GDP and other economic phenomena, but also need to include alternative measures of development such as the HDI, greening economic progress and special attention in all measures to the bottom 40 per cent of the population in relation to the top 10 per cent of the population. As Ghosh (2015: 328) concludes: 'These are clearly ambitious goals, which probably require international political economy conditions that are unlikely to be met at present. But, that should not blind us to their necessity. Only a global new deal can help build the levels of trust needed to tackle shared problems and broaden the scope for effective development partnerships.'

CONCLUDING REMARKS

All authors underline the seriousness of persistent high and/or growing inequality in many countries and see the absence of any concern for inequality in the MDGs as a great omission. The challenge that most countries are faced with is to reduce income inequality. Although the SDGs contain a goal to reduce inequality (goal 10) the target related to this goal is wholly insufficient as it relates only to progress of the bottom 40 per cent of the population. In phrasing the target in this fashion there is no sensible indicator to attest the growing importance of the growing cleavage between income of work and income of capital and the income of super rich (the top-1 per cent) which manifest themselves in much more visible form in emerging and in developed countries. Yet it is important to give attention to the behaviour of the rich, as ignoring their ascendency will put the social fabric under strain, as shown in some Latin American and other countries, as well as in many developed countries. If the burden of domestic financing of the SDGs falls on the middle class, they may well not accept such a redistributive scheme, especially in times when economic growth, because of absence of international coordination, is faltering. The contributors favour, therefore, the use of the Palma ratio to monitor progress of the inequality goal of the SDGs and to suggest national policy measures to stem growing income inequality. Several argue that the Palma ratio, despite the fact that it was not mentioned in the final formulation of the SDGs, ought to be part of national reviews on progress on SDGs, especially under pressure from civil society.

National income inequality is also circumscribed by the international context in which countries find themselves. The formulation of SDG 17 on international partnership is weak on issues of improved global governance. Also the Addis Ababa Action Agenda (the outcome of the third conference on financing for development in 2015), although mentioning the necessity of an improved international financial framework, improvement in tax collection, reduction of illicit capital outflows and avoiding tax payments by multinational enterprise in developing countries, failed to make a bold international institutional framework guiding the SDGs. Thus many developing countries are still deprived of, or need to develop more strongly, a sufficient domestic resource base to undertake redistributive measures and to finance the SDGs.

NOTES

1. See, for example, Alonso, Cornia and Vos (2013) and Alonso and Ocampo (2015).
2. Edward and Sumner (2015) argue that the Gini ratio is misleading because top incomes have not fallen, implying that the rich get richer and that especially the upper middle incomes were taxed to pay for the poor, leading to a drop in the Gini ratio. They argue therefore for the use of the Palma ratio as an indicator and to give special attention to the behaviour of the rich and their plight to contribute to national poverty reduction.

REFERENCES

Alonso, J.A. and J.A. Ocampo (eds) (2015), *Global Governance and Rules for the Post-2015 Era*, London: Bloomsbury Academic.
Alonso, J.A., G.A. Cornia and R. Vos (eds) (2013), *Alternative Development Strategies for the Post-2015 Era*, London: Bloomsbury Academic.
Atisophon, V., J. Bueren, G. De Paepe, C. Garroway and J.-P. Stijns (2011), Revisiting MDG Cost Estimates from a Domestic Resource Mobilisation Perspective, *OECD Development Centre Working Paper 306*, Paris: OECD.
Devarajan, S., M.J. Miller and E.V. Swanson (2002), Goals for Development: History, Prospects, and Costs, *Working Paper 2819*, Washington, DC: World Bank.
Development Finance International and Oxfam (2015), Government Spending Watch Report 2015: Financing the Sustainable Development Goals: Lessons from government spending on the MDGs.
Economist (2015), Unsustainable Goals, *Economist*, 28 March.
Edward, P. and A. Sumner (2015), Philanthropy, Welfare Capitalism or Radically Different Global Economic Model: What Would It Take to End Global Poverty within a Generation Based on Historical Growth Patterns? *Working Paper 413*, Washington, DC: Center for Global Development, http://www.cgdev.org/publica tion/end-global-poverty-within-generation-historical-growth (accessed 12 June 2017).
Fukuda-Parr, S. (2014), Global Goals as a Policy Tool: Intended and Unintended Consequences, *Journal of Human Development and Capabilities: A Multi-Disciplinary Journal for People-Centered Development*, 15(2–3), 118–131.
Ghosh, J. (2015), Beyond the Millennium Development Goals: A Southern Perspective on a Global New Deal, *Journal of International Development* 27, 320–329.
Hajer, M., M. Nilsson, K. Raworth, P. Bakker, F. Berkhout, Y. de Boer, J. Rockström, K. Ludwig and M. Kok (2015), Beyond Cockpit-ism: Four Insights to Enhance the Transformative Potential of the Sustainable Development Goals, *Sustainability*, 7, 1651–1660.
Hák, T., S. Janousková and B. Moldan (2016), Sustainable Development Goals: A Need for Relevant Indicators, Ecological Indicators, 60, 565–573.
Howard J. and J. Wheeler (2015), What Community Development and Citizen Participation Should Contribute to the New Global Framework for Sustainable Development, *Community Development Journal*, 50(4), 552–570.
Kindornay, S. and S. Twigg (2015), *Establishing a Workable Follow-up and Review Process for the Sustainable Development Goals*, Report, London: ODI.

Le Blanc, D. (2015), Towards Integration at Last? The Sustainable Development Goals as a Network of Targets, *Sustainable Development*, 23, 176–187.

Palma, G. (2011), Homogeneous Middles vs. Heterogeneous Tails and the End of the Inverted-U: It is All About the Share of the Rich, *Development and Change*, 42(1).

Pongiglione, F. (2015), The Need for a Priority Structure for the Sustainable Development Goals, *Journal of Global Ethics*, 11(1), 37–42.

Rowntree, B.S. (1901), *Poverty: A Study of Town Life*, London and New York: Macmillan.

Sachs, J.D. (2015), Goal-based Development and the SDGs: Implications for Development Finance, *Oxford Review of Economic Policy*, 31, 268–278.

Saith, A. (2006), From Universal Values to Millennium Development Goals: Lost in Translation, *Development and Change*, 37(6), 1167–1199.

Schoenmaker, N., R. Hoekstra and J.P. Smits (2015), Comparison of Measurement Systems for Sustainable Development at the National Level, *Sustainable Development*, 23, 285–300.

Stewart, F. (2015), The Sustainable Development Goals: A Comment, *Journal of Global Ethics*, 11(3), 288–293.

Stokstad, E. (2015), Sustainable Goals from UN Under Fire, *Science*, 347(6223), 702–703.

Tiwari, M. (2015), Looking Back to Move Forward: the MDGs and the Road to Post-2015, *Journal of International Development*, 27, 313–319.

UN (2012), *Realizing the Future We Want for All*, New York: UN.

UNDP (2013), *Humanity Divided: Confronting Inequality in Developing Countries*, New York: UNDP.

United Nations Development Group (UNDG) (2013), *A Million Voices, the World We Want, a Sustainable Future With Dignity For All*, New York: UNDG.

UN System Task Team on the Post-2015 UN Development Agenda (2013), *Statistics and Indicators for the Post-2015 Development Agenda*, New York: United Nations, http://www.un.org/en/development/desa/policy/untaskteam_undf/UNTT_MonitoringReport_WEB.pdf (accessed 12 June 2017).

van der Hoeven, R. (ed.) (2011), *Employment, Inequality and Globalization: A Continuous Concern*, London: Routledge.

Vandemoortele, J. (2011), The MDG Story: Intention Denied, *Development and Change*, 42(1).

Wilkinson, R. and K. Pickett (2009), *The Spirit Level: Why More Equal Societies Almost Always Do Better*, London: Allen Lane.

World Bank (2015), *From Billions To Trillions: Transforming Development Finance Post-2015 Financing For Development: Multilateral Development Finance* Development Committee 2 April 2015, Washington: World Bank.

2. Broadening the development agenda for the SDG world

Richard Jolly

Do development studies have a future? The death of development studies has long been predicted – and a few have even disputed whether it should even have been born. Wasn't economic development already enough? In contrast, in this chapter I argue that development studies is not only as much needed today as at any previous time but that its perspectives and multidisciplinary approach can serve as a priority to replace the narrow economism of neo-liberal orthodoxy. Moreover the agenda of development studies should be broadened to encompass countries in all parts of the world. The adoption of the SDGs, the Sustainable Development Goals, by all 193 countries of the UN in September 2015, as universal goals has already set the stage for the application of a development approach throughout the world, focused on human objectives and human rights in a way which draws on development experience of countries in all parts of the world.

Development studies will in the future need to be framed by five fundamental objectives: universalism, sustainability, human development, reducing inequalities and human rights (Figure 2.1). All five are embodied in the SDGs, but especially the first, which represents a game-changing advance as well as a formal political endorsement, internationally and nationally.[1] Although with varying levels of commitment, all the world's countries have accepted the SDGs. The goals have gained extra legitimacy because their formulation and adoption is the culmination of a worldwide

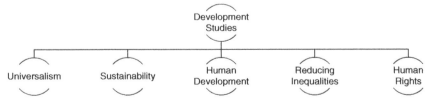

Figure 2.1   Five fundamental objectives embodied in SDGs

process of participation. Taken together, the SDGs represent a fundamental change to the development agenda as it has taken shape in the years after the Second World War.

These changes in perspectives hold challenges for the academic and research community, as well as for governments. Even for those in research and teaching, changing the frame of reference for development may be more difficult than imagined. After a lifetime of working in a world separated into developed and developing countries, researchers and teachers in development studies will need to move from a world of North and South, of catch-up and poverty reduction, of donors and aid to a one-world planet where we are all in it together, human priorities are universal and realpolitik must grapple with the hard issues of inequalities on the doorstep as well as in the world at large.

Thomas Kuhn in *The Structure of Scientific Revolutions*[2] argued that new theories only get adopted by the younger generation. Older scientists cling to outmoded theories and have the vested interests of their careers causing them to remain implacably opposed to the new. The physicist Max Planck put it more starkly: 'A new scientific truth does not triumph by convincing its opponents and making them see the light, but rather because its opponents eventually die, and a new generation grows up that is familiar with it.'[3]

Clinging to the old has recently been subject to empirical testing. In a 2015 paper entitled 'Does Science Advance One Funeral at a Time?'[4] a group of researchers at the National Bureau of Economic Research identified more than 12,000 'elite' scientists from different fields, judging elite status by criteria based on funding, number of publications, and whether they were members of the National Academies of Science or the Institute of Medicine. Searching obituaries, the team found 452 who had died before retirement. They then looked to see what happened in the fields from which these celebrated scientists had unexpectedly departed, by analysing publishing patterns.

What they found confirmed the truth of Planck's maxim. Junior researchers who had worked closely with older elite scientists, authoring papers with them, published less. In contrast, newcomers to the same field were less likely to cite the work of deceased eminents, and published more. The articles by these newcomers were more substantive and influential and attracted a high number of citations. It was this group which moved the whole field along.

In spite of this warning about the outmoded ideas of older persons, I have no intention of stopping at this point. I press ahead, in the hope that in the less scientific field of development, long experience and a willingness to speak out may trump any conservatism of sticking to the tramlines of previous work. So I proceed to elaborating the five principles which I believe should guide development studies in the future.

FIRST, UNIVERSALISM[5]

In my view, universalism means a broadening of context and application, though by no means a total change of content and agenda. Development studies will be more concerned, as Emanuel de Kadt once put it, with 'development in our own back yard'.[6] It will also mean that development experts will use approaches and techniques developed in and for developing countries and apply them in and for developed countries. This is what Dudley Seers demonstrated in his own work during the last decade of his life, when he largely abandoned work on developing countries for a succession of studies on 'underdeveloped Europe'.[7]

For some development specialists (though by no means all), this may also encourage a welcome change of attitude – no longer lording it over others as experts but relating to those in policy positions with more understanding, recognizing the social and political complications which often constrain doing what experts recommend as obviously desirable. Mark Mazower in his description of visiting economists from the World Bank and IMF showed what too often has happened:

> Most of the economists in the IMF had little interest in history, nor in the other social sciences. Its staffers were mostly male, and almost entirely economists, trained in American and English universities. Entering the IMF and the World Bank in the 1980s, they were rational-expectations revolutionaries, who based their prescriptions on in-house templates couched in the language of the highly formalized mathematical models that the profession was coming to prize.[8]

Recognizing development as a universal challenge may help strengthen the focus on the political economy of strategy and policy action – and raise awareness of the difficulties and complications of such strategy. Again, Mazower has some biting words:

> Practitioners [of neo-liberal economics] . . . existed in a state of more or less total ignorance of the cultures, languages or institutions of the countries they had been told to cure, having been trained, as many economists still are, to believe that this ignorance – being a matter of 'exogenous variables' – did not matter.[9]

What might a more universal agenda mean for research and teaching? Bringing together analysis of so-called developing countries with analysis of so-called developed countries would broaden the understanding of development in both approaches. It would direct more attention to comparative work in developed countries, with more focus on context and institutions, long-run changes and on the political economy of policy proposals. In the UK today, one is often appalled at the narrow national framing of public debate on economic policy, endlessly focused on UK national issues, so little on the experience and policy approaches of countries elsewhere in Europe, let alone of countries beyond. As a major example, austerity in Europe today is discussed with little reference to the devastating two decades of experience of austerity in the more than fifty countries of Latin America and sub-Saharan Africa from 1980 to 2000. The short publication, *Be Outraged*,[10] analysed the problems of austerity in Europe today with a much broader approach. For every policy alternative proposed, *Be Outraged* gave examples of how that policy was already being implemented in some developing country. A key message was that the North now needs to learn from the South.

For teaching development in many institutions in developed countries, a universal approach would deal with one of the curious and long-standing weaknesses, namely, that students from the South are brought to the North to learn about the problems and policy conclusions for their own countries in the South. Students complained about this on the MPhil course which Dudley Seers taught in 1975–1976. Dudley's response was to take his students to Scotland to analyse what would be the consequences of the recent discoveries of North Sea oil. Dudley also got policy makers from Norway and Venezuela to share their experiences. The study visit was written up as an IDS Communications paper with Seers and the students as co-authors.[11]

SECOND, SUSTAINABILITY

Lessons from countries with lower levels of per capita income would also broaden the number of country examples of alternatives and priorities for tackling sustainability. Sustainability in poorer countries involves structural and technological changes to achieve reasonable living standards at lower levels of GDP per capita, lower levels of resource use (especially of physical materials) with lower impacts on the environment. Although many developing countries have not yet achieved reasonable living standards for all, their middle classes have in a number of cases demonstrated sustainable living standards with much less environmental damage. Costa Rica is one such example and arguably also Barbados and Sri Lanka.

Of course, the elites in many developing countries are already well embarked on the high consumption patterns already established in the developed countries. But it could be very revealing to analyse the many households satisfying their basic needs in a broad sense and achieving reasonable levels of welfare, happiness, mobility and security at only a fraction of the resource use in much richer countries.

One critical issue of sustainability is often misunderstood in more populist arguments about living within the resource limits of the planet. Will long-run sustainability mean zero growth of GNP? In my view, zero growth of GNP, even as conventionally measured, is not a necessary condition for achieving a sustainable balance in the use of scarce resources. Sustainability does not imply a stagnant society or even zero growth of GDP, but keeping the use of scarce resources and the negative externalities of production within tight and sustainable boundaries. This is especially necessary in a world where population is still growing and living standards are growing much more rapidly. The possibility of achieving growing consumption within sustainable boundaries will depend on the development and application of new technologies, often technologies yet to be developed – and thus a shift in the focus of science and technological effort. These very elements imply growing GNP, not a stagnant one – though, of course, they raise questions about what sort of growth and they certainly mean an end to higher rates of growth GNP being taken as a better sign of successful policy than lower rates.

Sustainability in lifestyles and living standards will mean a shift in consumption patterns away from ever greater consumption of material goods and mobility, towards more services and leisure. Here the challenges are no longer of economic satisfaction but more of lifestyles – about which Keynes wrote brilliantly in the 'Economic Consequences for Our Grandchildren':[12]

> Thus for the first time since his creation man will be faced with his real, his permanent problem – how to use his freedom from pressing economic cares, how to occupy the leisure which science and compound interest will have won for him, to live wisely, agreeably and well. . .Yet there is no country and no people who can look forward to the age of leisure and abundance without a dread. For we have been trained too long to strive and not to enjoy. It is a fearful problem for the ordinary person, with no special talents, to occupy himself, especially if he no longer has roots in the soil or in custom or in the beloved conventions of a traditional society.

Keynes went on:

> To judge from the behaviour and the achievements of the wealthy classes today in any quarter of the world, the outlook is very depressing! For these are, so to speak, our advance guard – those who are spying out the promised land for the rest of us and pitching their camp there. For they have most of them failed

disastrously, so it seems to me – those who have an independent income but no associations or duties or ties – to solve the problem which has been set them. I feel sure that with a little more experience, we shall use the bounty of nature quite differently from the way the rich use it today, and will map out for ourselves a plan of life quite otherwise than theirs.

Today, 85 years from when Keynes was writing, we have much more experience, and, indeed, experience from many quarters of the world. The growth of per capita incomes in the developed countries anticipated by Keynes has broadly been realized, but not the reductions in the working hours of labour, in spite of initial reductions until the 1960s along the trends Keynes predicted.[13] The balance of work and leisure has changed but largely through the increases of labour-saving household equipment, saving hours of drudgery in the home, though with some but still not major changes in the balance between the time spent by women and men in household work.

The main change however is the rise of consumer society, among most of the population in developed countries and increasing proportions among the middle classes in the urban areas of developing countries. Fashions in clothing, music, films and media have now spread globally – and are consciously promoted by global corporations. Television has been a major force for extending ideas and lifestyles for half a century, and in the last 20 years, the spread of mobile phones and smartphones has connected people in all parts of the world in unprecedented ways. Some of these have given even poor people access and raised awareness with many links which are positive for their economic and social opportunities and welfare. The longer run impacts are less clear, though they will be both positive and negative.

THIRD, HUMAN DEVELOPMENT

The discussion of sustainability and new lifestyles leads directly to human development (HD). The HD paradigm presents a broader and more flexible frame for development analysis and policy than the neo-liberal economic paradigm, more open to future possibilities, with its own stimulating richness and subtleties. It needs to be pursued within the framework of capabilities, functionings and choices as so brilliantly elaborated and analysed by Amartya Sen, now also backed up by many others like Martha Nussbaum, Des Gasper, Ingrid Robeyns and Sakiko Fukuda-Parr.[14] The fact that some 140 countries have produced their own national human development reports is a further example of its widespread application.

Yet some key questions need answering. Have the perspectives of HD been sufficiently stretched and elaborated for analysing the possibilities and opportunities presented in countries which become ever richer in income? So far, the priorities of policy analysis in human development have mostly focused on the implications for poorer people and poorer countries in the world. Is it not time for the HD approach to illuminate the options and needs of those at the richest end of the spectrum? This would also be a very appropriate focus for some of the National Human Development Reports in the very high human development group of countries.

There are related questions. Why is it that HD is so rarely part of mainstream work, either in the teaching of development or as a frame for policy analysis and policy making, even among the UN agencies? UNDP itself loves the Human Development Report as a brilliant document which each year guarantees headlines round the world. But the UNDP, let alone other UN agencies, has rarely adopted human development as a frame for its own programmes, let alone as a frame for international policy or advocacy for humane global governance.[15]

For the ISS, the IDS and other development institutions, this respectful neglect of human development contains a clear message. Human development theory, techniques and applications need to be brought in from the cold. Human development needs to be made part of development teaching as well as policy studies and consultancies. This would be an important and constructive step towards offsetting the narrow applications of neo-liberal economic teaching and policy making – and the narrowness of austerity policies being promoted across Europe today. As Mahbub ul Haq put it in the 1990 HD Report, it is short-sighted to think that one is restoring balance to a country's economy by unbalancing the lives of its people.[16] Human development analysis would also be a frame for better considering the special problems of different categories of people, especially today of older people and how to strengthen their capabilities for the choices and opportunities that make sense in the later stages of life.

FOURTH, INEQUALITY

After thirty years of virtual neglect in international economic policy – in spite of many calls for it to be recognized as of major importance – inequality has at last been put centre stage, thanks especially to the work of Piketty[17] and colleagues and the econometric work of Berg and Ostry[18] of the IMF.

This window of opportunity for working on inequality must now not be missed, because the forces of reaction will not remain sidelined for long, in spite of the extremes of income inequality within countries being at unprecedented levels. Already the dramatic reductions of Gini coefficients in the majority of Latin America countries, as shown by Andrea Cornia[19] and by Luis Felipe Lopez Calva and Nora Lustig,[20] are being slowed or reversed.

The work by Richard Wilkinson and Kate Pickett[21] is also an important reminder that inequality must be analysed in a broader and multidimensional manner and brought into mainstream policy in many areas of action. The *Spirit Level* shows ten dimensions of well-being where inequality has a major impact, namely: mental illness, child and adult mortality, obesity, educational performance, teenage births, homicide, imprisonment rates, levels of trust and social mobility. Wilkinson increasingly believes that the common factor behind these many and widespread repercussions of inequality is stress – and is a reminder that the future universal agenda of human development must encompass a wide range of multidisciplinary work.

Tony Atkinson, in *Inequality: What Can Be Done*[22] identifies the broad range of actions which can help to reduce inequality, drawing on experience between the world wars and especially during and after the Second World War until the late 1970s. Over these periods, the Gini coefficients and other indicators of inequality were sharply reduced in the UK and in the US. This leads Atkinson to list 15 proposals for reducing substantively the extent of inequality, the first three of which are less often cited in the literature of inequality but were found to be important in the experience he reviewed:

1. Changing the direction of technological change, to encourage innovation in a form which increases the employability of workers and emphasizes the human dimension of service provision.
2. Shifting the balance of power among stakeholders by (a) introducing an explicitly distributional dimension into competition policy, (b) ensuring a legal framework which allows trade unions to represent workers on level terms and (c) establishing a Social and Economic Council, where one does not exist, for bringing into public policy the concerns of social partners and other NGOs.
3. Setting by governments an explicit target for preventing and reducing unemployment and underpinning this target with guarantees of public employment at the minimum wage to all who seek it.

Atkinson's other proposals are more conventional – establishing a national pay policy, a more progressive income tax with rates increasing to 65 per cent on the highest income, a broadening of the tax base (with an earned income discount applied to the first tranche of earnings), taxation of receipts of inheritance and *inter vivos* gifts, and a proportional or progressive tax on property (with valuations at least every five years).

Equally important and for the long-run more fundamental, Atkinson made other proposals focused on sustainable efforts to end poverty and establish young people in remunerative work. These included substantial child benefit paid to all children but taxed as income, national saving bonds with a guaranteed real savings rate and a maximum holding per person, a minimum capital endowment paid to all persons reaching adulthood, a public investment authority to enable the state to build up holdings in investment and property and a participation income at national level, complementing existing social protection or a renewal of social insurance. He also included an explicitly global dimension that rich countries should raise their target for ODA to 1 per cent of GNP.

Such measures are bold and far reaching, though as Atkinson argues, some more feasible than many realize. Many elements in the package would be reinforcing of other measures and none are such that the whole package must be rejected if one is not acceptable. On the other hand, the importance of Atkinson's analysis is that he shows by analysis and historical examples that if the upward trends in inequality are to be reversed, not merely slowed or temporarily halted, a range of such bold measures are essential.

FIFTH, HUMAN RIGHTS

Since the creation of the UN, attention to human rights and actions to take them seriously at national and international level have increased decade by decade. These have moved from the Declaration of 1948, the Covenants of the 1960s, the Conventions on elimination of all forms of discrimination against women (CEDAW) in the 1970s and on the Rights of the Child (CRC) in the 1980s to the creation of the Office of the High Commissioner of Human Rights in 1993.

The challenge now is to ensure action country-by-country. Here the Rights Based Approach to Development (HRABD) articulated by the UN in the late 1990s provides a frame, though one which is frequently misunderstood, even by countries which count themselves as strong supporters. Fulfilling the various rights and conventions in each country is obviously the fundamental objective. But how countries move to implementation is often ignored. The three points often neglected or misunderstood in the HRABD are the need for (1) fulfilling human rights in the *processes* of implementing them; (2) helping claimants to articulate their own claims; and (3) strengthening duty bearers to realize and fulfil their duties. Even when the goals of a country are broadly aligned with human rights, as are the SDGs globally, these three points in carrying them forward may often be neglected.

To give substance to these neglected dimensions, it may be useful to quote the instructions which UNICEF gave to their field offices in explaining how a rights-based approach should operate with respect to children:

> Children as right-holders have claims against those with obligations to ensure the fulfilment of those rights. Children whose rights remain unfulfilled have claims against those with obligations to act. Parents, communities, CSOs, governments and others have resulting duties. At the same time, parents and other duty bearers also may have other unfulfilled rights, for instance due to poverty, and have claims on resources themselves. Vulnerability and exclusion are manifestations and causes of the lack of capacities within families, communities and government and others to fulfil children's rights. The human rights of children and women are particularly threatened in situations of instability and crisis.[23]

ROLES FOR THE UN

These five priorities relate not only to development studies but to country-by-country implementation, as already set out in the SDGs. To achieve this, countries will need strong international support as well as national action in the years ahead, from institutions of development studies, as well as by governments and the UN and other international organizations, especially those of the Bretton Woods Institutions. The UN's important roles have already been defined as encouraging countries to formulate their own priorities among the SDGs as a frame for implementation of policies and for monitoring their progress and reporting internationally.

The UN's Committee on Development Policy (CDP) has also made more specific recommendations with respect to the SDGs.[24] These have emphasized the need for ensuring that the SDGs are adapted to the national context of each country with a process of democratic consultation involving civil society as well as national parliaments. National commitments and action are part of creating an enabling environment for sustainable development worldwide.

All this requires an accountability framework which is inclusive, transparent, and participatory through a bottom-up process. States will need to make public their commitments and the CDP proposes that the UN Regional Commissions should organize a peer review process for regularly assessing progress. The statistical priority is not to develop yet more international data systems but to strengthen national statistical offices and efforts. All this would feed into the global UN process, involving the new High Level Political Forum mandated by the General Assembly and the Economic Development Cooperation Forum of ECOSOC.

CONCLUSIONS

The stage has been set through the SDGs for a fundamental shift in the focus and content of development studies, with major implications for development teaching and research in institutions like the ISS and IDS. I summarize them in terms of six key priorities:

1. Universality – broadening teaching and research to apply development thinking and research from developing countries to problems in the so-called developed counties – and vice versa.
2. Sustainability – including analysis of consumption and lifestyle patterns in both richer and poorer countries in relation to priorities for achieving sustainability within countries and on a regional and global basis.
3. More use of the paradigm of Human Development, including its applications to human security and humane global governance.
4. Wider multidisciplinary applications of work on inequality throughout the whole range of human development concerns, policies and actions.
5. Focusing on human rights in relation to the SDGs in all countries, especially to support and assist the process of democratic setting of priorities at all levels of policy making and implementation.
6. Providing professional assistance in the processes of review, monitoring and accountability of the SDGs, especially by support of regional peer reviews of progress and assisting assessments of progress in high-level UN fora.

Broadening the agenda does not mean the death of development studies but their renewal and revival. The shift of focus and broadening of coverage can enliven and energise the next generation of committed development professionals. It can be a great advance. It will remove the long-standing weakness of development – that it was experts in the North talking about the desirability of things happening in other people's countries in the South. It can truly bring development home, to all countries and to the world.

NOTES

1. This point has also been argued by many others and from different points of view, including P.A.G. van Bergeijk, *Earth Economics* (Cheltenham, UK and Northampton, MA, USA, Edward Edgar Publishing) 2014 and in the interview of Robert Wade on the global financial crisis, *Development and Change*, 40(6), 1153–1190.
2. Thomas K. Kuhn, *The Structure of Scientific Revolutions* (Chicago, University of Chicago Press) 1962.
3. Max Planck, *Scientific Autobiography and Other Papers* (New York, Philosophical Library) p. 33.
4. Pierre Azoulay, Christian Fons-Rosen and Joshua S. Graff Zivin, *NBER Working Paper No 21,788*, December 2015.
5. I use universalism in the UN sense of covering all countries worldwide. Some social scientists have suggested that universalism is a Western concept and necessarily carries a Western bias. I try to avoid this.
6. Much quoted at the time in IDS, but I am not sure whether ever written down.
7. For instance, Dudley Seers et al., *Underdeveloped Europe: Studies in Core–Periphery Relations* (Hassocks, Harvester Press) 1979.
8. Mark Mazower, *Governing the World: The History of an Idea* (London, Allen Lane) 2012, p. 353.
9. Mark Mazower, *Governing the World: The History of an Idea* (London, Allen Lane) 2012, pp. 353–354.
10. Richard Jolly et al., *Be Outraged: There are Alternatives* (London, OXFAM) 2012 and available on the OXFAM website, http://oxfamilibrary.openrepository.com/oxfam/bitstream/10546/224184/1/bk-be-outraged-210512-en.pdf.
11. MPhil Faculty and Students, 'North Sea Oil: the Application of Development Theories', *IDS Communications 121* (Brighton, IDS) 1977.
12. John Maynard Keynes, *Essays in Persuasion* (London and Basingstoke, Macmillan) p. 328.
13. Robert Skidelsky and Edward Skidelsky, *How Much is Enough: the Love of Money and the Case for a Good Life* (London, Allen Lane) 2012 review Keynes' remarkable essay against the present economic and social situation.
14. See, for examples, articles in the *Journal of Human Development and Capabilities* (Abingdon, Routledge).
15. These issues are explored in Hirai Tadashi, Flavio Comim and Richard Jolly, 'Why does the HDR gather interest and praise – but so few universities use HD for teaching and research?' (forthcoming).
16. UNDP, *Human Development Report 1992* (Oxford, Oxford University Press) p. 34.
17. Thomas Piketty, *Capital in the 21st Century* (Cambridge, Harvard University Press) 2014.
18. Andrew G. Berg and Jonathan D. Ostry, 'Inequality and unsustainable growth: two sides of the same coin?', *IMF Discussion Note* (Washington, IMF) 2011.
19. Giovanni Andrea Cornia has written or edited a succession of books on the reductions of inequality in Latin America, one of the most recent being Giovanni Andrea Cornia (ed.) *Falling Inequality in Latin America* (Oxford, Oxford University Press) 2014.
20. Luis Felipe Lopez Calva and Nora Claudia Lustig (eds), *Declining Inequality in Latin America: A Decade Of Progress?* (Washington, Brookings Institution Press) 2010.
21. Richard Wilkinson and Kate Pickett, *The Spirit Level: Why More Equal Societies Almost Always Do Better* (London, Allen Lane) 2009.
22. Anthony B. Atkinson, *Inequality: What Can Be Done* (Cambridge, Harvard) 2014. The 15 proposals are elaborated chapter by chapter and summarized on pages 237–239.
23. UNICEF, *Programme Policy and Procedure Manual*, 6, para 7 (New York, UNICEF).
24. United Nations, Economic and Social Affairs, Committee for Development Policy: *The United Nations Development Strategy Beyond 2015* (New York, United Nations) 2012. The CDP has issued subsequent reports, available on its website www.un.org/en/development.

3. From MDGs to SDGs: critical reflections on global targets and their measurement

Jan Vandemoortele

INTRODUCTION

After more than two years of intergovernmental negotiations, the UN member states agreed on 'Agenda 2030' and the associated SDGs – the Sustainable Development Goals (UN, 2015). The SDGs are often described as transformative and universal, but these adjectives are unwarranted. It is true that, conceptually, the development agenda has become more holistic. Agenda 2030 covers more areas of concern than did the Millennium Declaration (UN, 2000). Its formulation process was participative and consultative and more attention was paid to the link between global goals and national targets. These are commendable aspects, which make the SDGs a better framework than the Millennium Development Goals (MDGs). Yet, the SDGs fall short of representing a transformative and universal agenda that addresses inequality.

Before scrutinising the SDGs in some detail, the chapter starts with a brief discussion about the often neglected but essential question: What is the purpose of setting global targets? It then examines whether the SDGs are fit for purpose, given the defining challenges the world is facing today. Doubt is cast about the fittingness of their basic premise, as well as about their supposedly universal nature and alleged focus on inequality. The chapter also points to some omissions and technical oddities. Since the SDGs constitute a political agreement, the chapter surveys the multilateral context in which they were fashioned. The chapter examines the choice of indicators for tracking Agenda 2030. As the SDGs experience a slow and arduous take-off at the country level, a two-pronged approach is suggested to help turn them into a useful and practical instrument.

PURPOSE OF GLOBAL TARGET SETTING

As the debate got underway about the SDGs, one would have expected that the first point on the agenda would have been: Why do we need new global targets? This point was not discussed, however. Its omission has affected the content of Agenda 2030 because stakeholders hold quite divergent views and opinions about the meaning and purpose of global targets. In the absence of an open and honest discussion about the sense and nonsense of global target setting, some widespread misconceptions and misinterpretations have persisted.

The purpose of numerical global targets is not to impose specific benchmarks upon member states. Essentially, global targets are meant to help accelerate progress – through public pressure and political accountability – yet their applicability can only be judged within the country-specific context. As good servants but bad masters, global targets always need to be tailored to the national situation. The World Summit for Children emphasised this point: 'These [global] goals will first need to be adapted to the specific realities of each country [. . .] to ensure their technical validity, logistical feasibility, financial affordability and to secure political commitment and broad public support' (UNICEF, 1990: paragraph 6).

Vietnam and Cambodia feature among the countries that adapted the MDGs to the local context. In the former, they were translated into the VDGs – the Vietnam Development Goals – which were more ambitious than those set at the global level. The latter issued the CDGs – the Cambodia Development Goals – which put the bar considerably lower than the global target and added a numerical target for removing landmines. The global discourse, however, has shown little interest in such adaptation at the country level. It has almost exclusively focused on global statistics and world maps that coloured off-track countries in red.

Contrary to what some believe, global targets are not meant to replace human rights treaties, to change the meta-narrative about development, or to justify the imposition of specific policy prescriptions onto national government. Such misconceptions have led to rather sterile criticisms of the MDGs. Many a human rights advocate faulted the MDGs for their negative externalities. But they were never intended to supplant existing human rights instruments; they simply introduced intermediate stepping stones towards the gradual realisation of human rights, in the form of numerical and time-bound targets. Similarly, many observers accused them of fostering the Washington consensus. Yet, it would be naive to think that a simple list of targets could have brought about a change in the dominant development narrative.

It can be argued that the MDGs helped to demystify 'development' for the wider public, journalists and teachers. By stressing non-money-metric outcomes such as mortality, illiteracy and hunger, they underscored that development involves much more than economic growth. They also emphasised that sectoral interdependencies are important. The latter point is crucial for taking the understanding of development beyond sectoral isolationism, which is widespread among specialists. As a WHO experts group states, 'much of the improvement in health has occurred in areas that are not usually considered to be within the health sector' (WHO 2010: 1). Little else can be expected from global targets. They are certainly not meant to repeat and include everything.

MANY ITEMS, FEW TARGETS

The realm of the SDGs is far more comprehensive than that of the MDGs. Since they cover more areas of concern, it is normal that they contain more goals than the original MDGs (17 versus 8), as well as more targets (169 versus 18) and more indicators (232 versus 48). They also need considerably more words than the MDGs (5,000 versus 300). But more is not necessarily better. Several items on the SDG-list are too fuzzy and too woolly to qualify as targets.

To be verifiable, a target needs three key elements: (1) a numerical outcome, (2) a specific deadline, and (3) a clear concept. Three SDG-targets are highlighted to illustrate those elements. Item 3.1 – *By 2030, reduce the global maternal mortality ratio to less than 70 per 100,000 live births* – is a valid target. Its domain is well-defined; it includes a deadline as well as a numerical outcome. Item 17.2 – *Developed countries to implement fully their ODA commitments, including the commitment by many developed countries to achieve the target of 0.7 per cent of ODA/GNI* – omits the deadline. This is not surprising given that rich countries still fail to keep the promise, nearly half a century after they first made it. Item 16.5 – *Substantially reduce corruption and bribery in all their forms* – lacks all three elements. It does not contain a numerical outcome, the deadline is omitted and it is conceptually fuzzy. There is no agreed definition or objective metric for corruption. Stiglitz describes campaign contributions in his country as 'corruption, American-style' (Stiglitz, 2015: 171). It is doubtful whether the intended purpose of item 16.5 is to bring about campaign finance reform in the USA.

Instead of setting numerical outcomes, many items of Agenda 2030 use vague language, such as 'substantially reduce' or 'substantially increase', 'support and strengthen', 'progressively improve', and 'achieve higher levels of'. Such objectives lack numerical precision for unambiguous monitoring. Several also fail to set a specific deadline. When they do, it is mostly for the year 2030, although the years 2020 and 2025 inexplicably crop up for some targets.

The majority of the 169 items do not cut it as verifiable targets. The International Council for Science, in collaboration with the International Social Science Council reviewed the 169 items from a scientific point of view. The report card is rather harsh (ICSU and ISSC, 2015). It concludes that more than half of the SDGs need to be reformulated to add a minimum level of specificity, and that nearly a fifth are best thrown out because they are either redundant or too ambiguous (Figure 3.1).

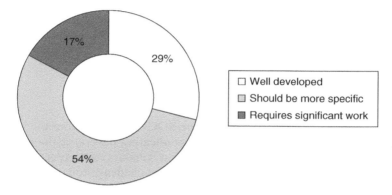

Source: ICSU and ISSC (2015: 6).

Figure 3.1 A scientific assessment of the 169 items mentioned under the SDGs

A few passages suffice to illustrate that many SDGs lack clarity and precision. Item 4.7, for instance, aims to *ensure, by 2030, that all learners acquire the knowledge and skills needed to promote sustainable development.* Item 5.4 seeks to *recognize and value unpaid care and domestic work.* Item 7.1 reads, *ensure, by 2030, universal access to affordable, reliable and modern energy services.* None of these items offer conceptual clarity or a numerical outcome. A key part of Agenda 2030 is goal 13 – *Take urgent action to combat climate change.* The first three items under that goal read as follows: 13.1 *Strengthen resilience and adaptive capacity to climate-related hazards*; 13.2 *Integrate climate change measures into national planning*; and 13.3 *Improve education on climate change mitigation.* Whilst not unimportant, it is a moot question whether work on resilience, planning and education can be considered as 'urgent' action.

When eliminating the items that lack either a numerical outcome, a specific deadline or conceptual clarity, the 169 items end up comprising fewer than 30 verifiable targets. It is noteworthy that the latter are not dissimilar from the MDGs. They cover similar concerns, that is, poverty and hunger, child and maternal mortality, hunger, unsafe drinking water. Thus, the SDGs are not quite the paradigm shift or the transformative agenda as some argue.

The SDGs violate a key lesson learnt from the MDGs, namely that their relative success resulted from the three 'Cs': clear, concise and computable. It would be hard to claim that 169 items represent a concise agenda, their formulation uses unclear and fuzzy language and most items cannot be objectively measured. The latter will create leeway and latitude for subjective assessments in the future. Obviously, the architects of Agenda 2030 have not heeded the UN's advice that 'experience of the MDGs has shown that data will play a central role in advancing the new development agenda' (UN, 2014: 7).

POVERTY BUT NOT INEQUALITY

Apart from violating the three 'Cs', the SDGs also start from the wrong premise. Agenda 2030 postulates that 'eradicating poverty is the greatest global challenge' (UN, 2015: 1). Yet, most scholars and experts do not believe that poverty constitutes the key global challenge today. That view, they argue, is no longer valid because of the significant rise in inequality that has occurred within most countries over the past three to four decades. The key global challenge now is extreme inequality.

Shiller puts it quite categorically, 'The most important problem we are facing now today, I think, is rising inequality' (quoted in Dorling, 2014: 1). Stiglitz argues, 'we are paying a high price of our inequality—an economic system that is less stable and less efficient, with less growth, and a democracy that has been put into peril' (Stiglitz, 2012: xii). Many other voices could be added to the choir, including those of Wilkinson and Pickett (2010), Galbraith (2012), UN (2013), UNDP (2013), Dorling (2014), Piketty (2014), and Atkinson (2015). Nevertheless, Agenda 2030 puts extreme poverty at the centre and pledges several times that 'no one will be left behind' (UN, 2015: 1, 3, 7, 12, 31).

In most countries, progress, although respectable, has seen a systemic bias against the least well-off people. Despite the considerable progress achieved during the MDG-era across the world, the evidence shows that in most countries, it has bypassed the people at the bottom of the social ladder (Minujin and Delamonica, 2003; Moser, Leon and Gwatkin, 2005; Reidpath et al., 2009; WHO, 2008; Wilkinson and Pickett, 2010). The mantra 'Leave No One Behind' may seem self-evident, but it is not innocuous because it shrouds the challenge of extreme inequality, which has become a major obstacle for addressing extreme poverty.

The SDGs pay only superfluous attention to inequality. Two comments are warranted regarding goal 10 – *Reduce inequality within and among countries*. First, it ranks in tenth position. Ranking does matter because it reflects the relative importance of the objective. As with the MDGs, poverty and hunger remain in first and second position, respectively. Inequality is not among the top three or top five priorities. Concern about this topic comes much later, suggesting that it is not quite a top priority.

Second, and more importantly, the relevant target is formulated in such a way that it does not truly address inequality. The aim of target 10.1 is to *progressively achieve and sustain, by 2030, income growth of the bottom 40 per cent of the population at a rate higher than the national average*. This formulation cannot claim to deal with inequality because it covers only a segment of the population. To genuinely address inequality, it should encompass the entire income spectrum, not just the poorest segment. Atkinson insists, 'One of the themes of this book is that we need to consider the distribution as a whole' (Atkinson 2015: 183). Even if the bottom 40 per cent would see their income grow at a faster rate than the rest of society, the absolute income gap between them and the top 10 per cent is unlikely to narrow. By focusing on the bottom 40 per cent, target 10.1 essentially addresses poverty, not inequality.

It is perfectly possible for a country to achieve faster income growth for the bottom 40 per cent and, at the same time, witness an increase in inequality. Such a scenario – based on income transfers from the next 50 per cent but leaving the top 10 per cent unaffected – is not hypothetical, given that several countries are witnessing a hollowing out of the middle class and a virtual secession of the top 10 per cent. In other words, meeting target 10.1 does not necessarily mean a decrease in inequality. Yet, stakeholders and observers repeatedly assert that the SDGs address inequalities. The then head of UNDP, for example, stated, 'Reducing inequalities is at the heart of the new development agenda the world has committed to achieving by 2030' (UNDP, 2016).

The head of UNICEF wrote, 'the world has made tremendous progress in reducing inequities' (UNICEF, 2015: i). But such careless use of terminology confounds poverty with inequality; two concepts that are related yet different. Essentially, poverty is about insufficiency whilst inequality is about hierarchy. Hierarchy implies unequal power relations, for example, between male and female, adult and child, dominant and minority groups (in terms of language, race or religion), privileged and disadvantaged, affluent and destitute. Such unequal relations invariably lead to domination and discrimination, even exclusion and abuse.

The problem with inequality is not that some individuals have more money and wealth than others; it is that highly unequal societies lose the commitment to treat citizens equally (Swift, 2001). Hierarchy leads to discrimination – think, for instance, about gender inequality. It is over-simplistic, therefore, to put concerns about inequality down to either envy or greed. The significance of high inequality is not purely economic or financial, it is primarily to be understood as influencing political processes and psychosocial perceptions. High inequality corrodes societal values, including empathy. It becomes a barrier to mutual respect between social groups.

The SDGs' failure to adequately address inequality is not due to a technical mistake but driven by a political narrative that dodges, if not contests, the fact that extreme inequality is a defining challenge of our time. Therefore, political correctness demanded that Agenda 2030 focus on extreme poverty and hunger rather than on extreme inequality. The slogan 'Leave No One Behind' is little more than a shrewd construct to mask the refusal of world leaders to accept that extreme inequality is one of the most pressing challenges the world is facing today. Yet, addressing extreme inequality will almost automatically eliminate extreme poverty.

GLOBAL DEAL, BUT NOT A UNIVERSAL AGENDA

It is common to hear that the SDGs are universal. Agenda 2030 reiterates this point as many as nine times (UN, 2015: 1, 3, 6, 13, 31, 32). Universality is seen as a major achievement, for it supposedly moves the discourse beyond the North–South split, which was so characteristic of the MDGs. However, to be universal – to be truly a 'one-world' agenda – Agenda 2030 needs to apply to all countries in a similar manner. Upon closer examination, however, the SDGs do not pertain to all countries in similar ways. They represent a global deal – containing a set of performance targets for developing countries and a few delivery targets for developed nations – rather than a universal agenda.

The MDGs were not universal either. The targets about extreme poverty, hunger, primary education, child and maternal mortality, and safe drinking water did not apply to developed countries. To a large extent, this remains true for the SDGs. Most of the verifiable targets in Agenda 2030 relate to the developing world, especially the least developed countries. The very first target is not universal in scope because it defines extreme poverty in terms of living on less than $1.25 per day. The second goal – about hunger – is not universal either although it could have been formulated as a universal goal had it included overweight. But only underweight is mentioned, which is remarkable given that current trends indicate that the world will see, within the time frame of Agenda 2030, more overweight children than underweight ones. The fact that a quarter of today's obese children in the world live in Africa underscores the universal nature of the problem.

It is mindboggling that the development agenda for the next 15 years omits such a serious threat to public health in most countries – rich and poor alike. Experts refer to overweight and obesity as an epidemic or a tsunami, because they cause diabetes, stroke, hypertension, cardiovascular disease, cancer, dementia and depression. Significantly, the World Health Organization issued its first *Global Report on Diabetes* (WHO, 2016a), showing that the global prevalence of diabetes has nearly doubled since 1980 – driven by the unrelenting rise in overweight and obesity across the world. It is, therefore, beyond belief that Agenda 2030 does not even mention the issue, let alone setting a numerical target about it. An agenda that sidesteps this challenge cannot claim to be universal in scope. Some argue that target 2.2 – *end, by 2030, all forms of malnutrition* – implicitly refers to overweight and obesity, but it refers only to *stunting and wasting in children under 5 years of age*.

It would be naive to think that the omission is simply an oversight; it is intentional. Breastfeeding is another area that is omitted by the SDGs. Developed nations are not ready and willing to commit to specific, numerical and time-bound targets for human development that apply within their border. This pre-empts a truly universal agenda. In addition, most governments are reluctant to adequately regulate the food industry with the aim of drastically reducing sugar consumption (Taubes, 2016). Hence, it is politically more convenient to focus the SDGs on ending hunger.

Thus, the claim that the SDGs represent a universal agenda that applies to all countries in a similar way is simply untenable. Nonetheless, it is frequently reiterated. On 25 September 2015, the day the UN General Assembly formally adopted Agenda 2030, the UN Secretary-General hailed the SDGs for their universal nature (UN News Centre, 2015). Other leaders followed suit. The CEO of the UK network for international development organisations, for instance, wrote on that day, 'The SDGs represent a marked departure from their predecessors–the MDGs–due to their universality' (Jackson, 2015).

SOME ODDITIES

The SDGs also contain some oddities of a more technical nature. Most of the verifiable targets set absolute benchmarks, contrary to relative ones which were set by the MDGs. Relative benchmarks aim for a percentage change, for example, the MDGs targeted to reduce the child mortality rate by two thirds. The SDGs, by contrast, aim for absolute benchmarks, for example, an under-five mortality rate of 25 per 1,000 live births. Relative and absolute benchmarks are both incomplete as each assesses progress from a particular angle. If taken separately, they can lead to misleading interpretations. Arguably, a combination of relative and absolute benchmarks constitutes the best guarantee against possible biases in setting global targets. Yet, that counsel has not been followed. The SDGs, when they set numerical outcomes, mostly adopt absolute benchmarks. In the end, they are likely to lead to unfair and misleading assessments, particularly for the least developed countries. As with the MDGs, the narrative is likely to persist that Africa will be missing the targets. Hence the quip 'Africa is not missing the target, you are missing the point' (Vandemoortele, 2009: 355).

Another noticeable aspect of the SDGs is that some targets are collective (set for all countries together) whilst others are set for all countries individually. Collective targets are to be achieved at the global level, but not necessarily by every country. Target 3.1 – *to reduce, by 2030, the global maternal mortality ratio to less than 70 per 100,000 live births* – is such a target. It can be achieved globally even when several countries will end up with a ratio above 70 because other countries will have a ratio below that level. By contrast, target 3.2 – *with all countries aiming to reduce under-five mortality to at least 25 per 1,000 live births, by 2030* – must be achieved by all countries individually. It is not clear why the SDGs set some targets collectively while others are country-specific.

Another oddity is target 3.6 – *to halve, by 2020, the number of global deaths from road traffic accidents*. This collective target is placed under the health goal as if it had anything to do with healthcare. It is inconceivable that the intention is to focus on curative health by keeping those injured in road traffic accidents alive, rather than to reduce such accidents in the first place.

Another target worth mentioning, this one in a positive sense, is item 10.c which aims to *reduce, by 2030, to less than 3 per cent the transaction costs of migrant remittances and eliminate remittance corridors with costs higher than 5 per cent*. A remittance is money earned by a migrant worker that is sent to the country of origin. Remittances account for hundreds of billions of dollars annually and represent an economic lifeline for countless families. They are also important macro-economically for several countries. Bringing down transaction costs on remittances is a concrete way of improving wellbeing for millions of people. Item 10.c is a valid target and is valuable too, although it is not clear why it is shown under the goal regarding inequality.

A FRAGMENTED WORLD

It appears, thus, that the SDGs constitute a mixture of high-minded ideals and noble intentions, several omissions and a few oddities, the whole sprinkled with a few verifiable targets. This raises the question why so much time and effort devoted to defining the Post-2015 Agenda has yielded such a convoluted outcome. Part of the answer rests with the aim of setting out a holistic agenda through a participatory approach. Yet, the main reason why the outcome is deficient in so many ways can be attributed to the current multilateral context, which is radically different from the days when the MDGs saw the light of day.

The MDGs took root in the post-Cold War era, which was characterised by strong multilateralism and a widespread sense of optimism. However, the 'New World Order' – a term used by the US President in his 1991 address to the UN General Assembly – did not materialise. Instead, a fundamental change gradually unfolded in the world, namely the emergence of the global South. New intergovernmental forums and international institutions have been established to reflect this change, for example, BRICS, G-20, NDB (New Development Bank), AIIB (Asian Infrastructure Investment Bank). To some extent, this fundamental change poses a challenge to the West, which has traditionally dominated global fora and international organisations. Consequently, the Western lens is no longer the only one through which the world is perceived and interpreted. Whilst developed countries cling to the old worldview of the 'Age of the West', developing countries perceive a new world order in which they will play a chief role. As a result, the North–South divide has widened and deepened. The schism has come to characterise most global debates – be it on development, climate change or trade.

The implication of this divide is that debates at global summits have become exceedingly arduous, yielding precarious outcomes that are seldom groundbreaking. The quest for international consensus has gradually turned into dissensus. The year 2015 saw this repeated at four different world summits: finance for development (in Addis Ababa), sustainable development (in New York), climate change (in Paris) and global trade (in Nairobi). International agreements increasingly serve to mask profound disagreements among member states. The community of nations has become too fragmented to adopt global targets that are clear, concise and computable. Hence the fuzzy and convoluted nature of the SDGs.

Not only has multilateralism weakened, the role played by different actors at the UN has changed too. Apart from the member states, there are three other important players: the UN secretariat, civil society and the private sector. The UN secretariat has not played an assertive role in shaping Agenda 2030. It limited itself to that of convenor and provider of technical inputs. Despite the deep divide among member states, its leadership refrained from taking bold and creative initiatives to give meaning and substance to the intergovernmental debate. This was quite different from UN leadership shown earlier, for example by Jim Grant at UNICEF who orchestrated the World Summit on Children in 1990 and by Kofi Annan who convened the Millennium Summit in 2000. Dag Hammarskjöld contrasted two concepts for the world body: either as a 'static conference machinery' or as a 'dynamic instrument for an organised world community' (Lipsey, 2013: 448). The UN leadership has opted for the former in recent years, rather than the latter.

Civil society organisations saw their role greatly enhanced, especially at the various world summits of the 1990s. Although they actively participated in the discussions about the SDGs, their influence was diminished by the growing insistence on the part of government representatives regarding their sovereign role – emblematic of the growing sense of nationalism in many a country. In comparison with the MDGs, global corporations, on the other hand, played a more prominent role in shaping Agenda 2030 (Quintos, 2014). The UN Global Compact, for instance, states, 'A new paradigm in development thinking is recognizing the centrality of private enterprise in pursuit of the development agenda' (UN Global Compact, 2014: 3). Member states show an increased readiness to involve the corporate and private sector in discussions and activities about development. Public–private partnerships are proliferating and many aid projects are being contracted out. The controversial negotiations at the World Health Assembly about the framework for engagement with non-state actors reflect the same trend (WHO, 2016b); with some speaking of a corporate takeover (GPF, 2015).

In short, the SDGs emerged from a context of debilitated multilateralism, characterised by a deepening North–South divide, a stronger sense of national sovereignty among government representatives, aloof leadership throughout the United Nations, diminished influence of civil society organisations and greater leverage of global corporations and big philanthropists. This context is radically different from the one that prevailed when the MDGs saw the light of day. To a large extent, it explains why the SDGs lack clarity and real ambition.

UNFITTING INDICATORS

In such a fragmented world, it is only natural for member states to find it hard to formulate a bold and inspiring agenda with clear and concrete targets. One would expect, however, that the selection of indicators for monitoring Agenda 2030 would be easier. After all, indicators are not as politically charged as targets. Still, it would be a mistake to assume that choosing indicators is purely a technical matter. After all, statistics do shape the way in which people perceive the world. Therefore, they are often used – and abused – to influence public perceptions.

Statistics are frequently manufactured as ammunition in political battles. Although meant to describe and explain reality in an objective manner, statistics often serve to manage public perceptions. As they get amplified in the echo chambers of mainstream media, they end up shaping public opinion. As Best points out, 'people who bring statistics to our attention have reasons for doing so' (Best, 2001: 7). Fioramonti argues that numbers are used 'to control, albeit without giving the impression of control; designed to rule, without coercion' (Fioramonti, 2014: 206).

The UN Statistical Commission adopted a global indicator framework for monitoring Agenda 2030 (UN, 2016). A closer look at the 232 indicators suggests that politics also swayed that exercise. Two examples illustrate this. The indicator selected for item 16.5 – *substantially reduce corruption and bribery in all their forms* – is 'the percentage of persons who had at least one contact with a public official, who paid a bribe to a public official, or were asked for a bribe by these public officials, in the previous 12 months'. This indicator is problematic, for three reasons.

First, it is not based on objective and direct observation but on subjective interpretation and flawed memory. A recall period of 12 months inevitably reduces the accuracy of people's response. Second, it purposely associates corruption solely with public officials, pretending it does not exist in the private sector. Volkswagen's 'dieselgate' and the 'Libor' and 'Forex' scandals are just some recent examples that corruption and cheating are not the monopoly of the public sector. Transparency International recently reported on widespread corruption in the pharmaceutical sector (TI, 2016). Akerlof and Shiller point out that 'each of the three economic contractions in the United States involved corruption scandals' (Akerlof and Shiller, 2009: 29); caused by corporate malfeasance, not by corrupt public officials. They refer to the Savings and Loans Association fiasco in 1990–91, the Enron scandal in 2001, and the subprime mortgage debacle in 2008. The selected indicator for monitoring item 16.5 is biased, because it will shape people's perceptions that public officials are inherently corrupt and that further privatisation is needed.

Third, the focus on so-called petty corruption leaves aside grand and systemic corruption, which mostly takes the form of tax avoidance and tax evasion. Research shows that 'Trade misinvoicing is the primary measurable means for shifting funds out of developing countries illicitly.

Over the ten-year time period of this study, an average of 83.4 per cent of illicit financial outflows were due to the fraudulent misinvoicing of trade' (Kar and Spanjers, 2015: vii). Another study confirms the magnitude of the problem and argues that tax evasion and capital flight are the main motives for massive over-invoicing of exports observed across countries (UNCTAD, 2016). In other words, petty corruption by public officials is not the main challenge in this area, as the proposed indicator would suggest.

The indicator for monitoring corruption is not the only one that is problematic. The other example is the one chosen for monitoring extreme poverty – below $1.25 per day, expressed in purchasing power parity (PPP). It is likely to be the one that will be mentioned most frequently, despite it being highly problematic. Deaton's comment that 'PPP comparisons rest on weak theoretical and empirical foundations' (Deaton, 2010: 5) casts serious doubt on the accuracy of global poverty estimates. Atkinson describes the estimates on extreme poverty as 'numbers about which there is considerable uncertainty' (World Bank, 2017: xv–xvi). Reddy and Lahoti explain that 'under the current method, data on Japanese real-estate prices may impinge on whether a household in India is deemed to be living in extreme poverty or not' (Reddy and Lahoti, 2016: 115).

Essentially, the problem with the statistics on global poverty is that they are manufactured, based on estimates rather than on direct observation. One can determine through direct observation whether a child is stunted or not (by relating height to age), but one cannot say through direct observation whether that same child lives below the international poverty line or not. The latter requires lots of additional information (on household income, household size and composition, imputed rent of owner-occupied dwelling, consumption of own-produced food, prices of consumer goods, PPP values, and so on). Obtaining such information frequently requires proxies and assumptions that are subject to large margins of error.

For example, the latest poverty estimates indicate a steep drop for Pakistan, with extreme poverty plummeting from 59 per cent in 1990 to a mere 6 per cent in 2013 (World Bank, 2016). But this astonishing achievement is not reflected by other indicators. According to the country's nutrition survey, stunting did not decrease over that period. In fact, it increased slightly from 42 per cent in both 1985–1987 and 2001 to 44 per cent in 2011 (Aga Khan University, 2013: 59). The Demographic and Health Survey of 2012–2013 finds that 'nationally, 45 per cent of children under age 5 are stunted' (NIPS and ICF, 2013: 165). In other words, data for Pakistan make it obvious that the global poverty statistics are highly problematic, if not flawed altogether.

When sharp and contradictory differences occur between manufactured statistics and those obtained through direct observation (as for stunting), one should use the former with great caution. However, they are often taken at face value, even in academic journals, and so become accepted wisdom. The more frequently they are repeated, the more credence they are given. Kahneman explains how it works: 'A reliable way to make people believe in falsehoods is frequent repetition, because familiarity is not easily distinguished from truth' (Kahneman, 2011: 62). Such numbers fall under the category of 'facts by repetition'. Passas adds, 'a large proportion of conventional wisdom guiding policy is unfortunately not founded on solid evidence but reflects perceptions shaped by superficial, incomplete, or wrong information, which has been repeated and regarded as accurate in scholarly and policy documents' (Passas, 2012: 256).

The indicators selected for monitoring extreme poverty and corruption are both developed at the World Bank, which is also the institution that generates the relevant data. Some argue that they are designed to yield statistics that reinforce the dominant economic narrative – that is 'policy-based evidence-making'. What can be said with certainty is that statistical rigor rests not only upon the competence of the institution that designs the indicator and produces the data, but also on its disinterested nature.

Measurability, of course, is not everything. The maxim 'Not everything that counts can be counted' implies that several aspects of development cannot be readily quantified. Admitting so is not a sign of feebleness but an honest acceptance that statistical alchemy cannot turn qualitative information into reliable quantitative data. Schumacher writes, 'To measure the immeasurable is absurd and constitutes an elaborate method of moving from preconceived notions to foregone conclusions' (Schumacher, 1973: 38). Therefore, several dimensions of development are not fit for quantitative target setting. For those where it is fitting to set numerical targets, a degree of objective measurability must be maintained because solid and objective data offer the ultimate defence against false claims that are based on fake evidence and alternative facts. Piketty ends his hefty bestseller with the sentence, 'Refusing to deal with numbers rarely serves the interests of the least well-off' (Piketty, 2014: 577).

NEXT STEPS

When setting global targets, some difficult choices must be made. On the one hand, they should be clear and concise; on the other hand, they should reflect the complexity of development. The two objectives are mutually exclusive; an agenda cannot be comprehensive and concise. The MDGs opted for clarity and conciseness, whilst the SDGs err on the side of complexity and comprehensiveness. None quite manages to strike a judicious balance. Overall, the SDGs represent a better framework than the MDGs because they significantly widen the scope of the development agenda and raise important issues, such as inequality, birth registration, corruption, migration, social protection, violence against women – albeit that many get covered half-heartedly or poorly.

The complexity and the ambiguous language of Agenda 2030 make for a difficult storyline – with too many competing priorities. The traction of the SDGs at the country level has been underwhelming so far. Some crucial steps need to be taken before their potential can become reality. Foremost, stakeholders must show a readiness to go beyond appearances, half-truths and falsehoods about the SDGs (Vandemoortele, 2016). Once that crucial step is taken, considerable work remains to be done at the national and the global level.

At the national level, all countries – rich and poor alike – must select and adapt those items that are most relevant to their national context. Agenda 2030 foresees this step: 'Targets are defined as aspirational and global, with each government setting its own national targets guided by the global level of ambition but taking into account national circumstances' (UN, 2015: 13). However, this is frowned upon by many, for two reasons.

First, they believe that it will lead to cherry-picking and watering down. But the risk only exists if the task of selecting and adapting global targets is assigned to government alone. Here, Agenda 2030 is clearly mistaken. A selection process controlled by government will inevitably result in a national agenda that is narrow in scope and low in ambition. It is vital to adopt a participatory process, involving the social partners, civil society, academics, and other relevant stakeholders.

The second objection is that it will muddle international comparability and blur the global narrative about the SDGs. Indeed, if countries pursue different aspects of Agenda 2030, for which different aims and possibly different metrics will apply, aggregation and global monitoring will become difficult, if not impossible. However, given their comprehensive nature, the SDGs cannot be interpreted as a one-size-fits-all agenda. A list of 169 woolly targets does not make a focused agenda. Adaptation and selection are imperative. It means that the monitoring of the SDGs will have to be done in a radically different way than was the case with the MDGs. This will require more imagination and inventiveness, as well as the use of qualitative information besides quantitative data.

Intergovernmental organisations – such as the United Nations, African Union, European Union, Organisation of American States, Arab League, Association of Southeast Asian Nations – have a role to play here. Yet, none has taken adequate steps so far to encourage and support their member states to select and adapt the SDGs to a manageable list of priorities tailored to the domestic situation. Neither have they proposed novel ideas and methods for monitoring and aggregating country-level performances into a meta-narrative. The European Commission has released two documents regarding the implementation of Agenda 2030 (EC, 2016a; EC, 2016b). Apart from reiterating existing positions, they do not bring new ideas to the table for implementing and monitoring the SDGs (Vandemoortele, forthcoming).

At the global level, the important and urgent step to be taken is to select fitting indicators to help remedy some of the flawed targets. For example, target 10.1 regarding inequality can be readily fixed by including the Palma ratio, that is, the income share of the top 10 per cent divided by that of the bottom 40 per cent (Palma, 2011). Sadly, the proposed indicator framework does not mention it. The body mass index (BMI) is a practical and straightforward way of monitoring target 2.2 – *to end all forms of malnutrition* – that would include overweight and obesity too. However, the proposed indicator framework covers only stunting and wasting and omits BMI. A modest step forward is the inclusion of indicator 2.2.2: 'prevalence of malnutrition (weight for height >+2 or <-2 standard deviation from the median of the WHO Child Growth Standards) among children under 5, disaggregated by type (wasting and overweight)'.

Those who argue that indicators such as the Palma ratio and BMI would change the meaning of the agreed targets need look no further than the indicator selected for target 1.2 – *reduce at least by half, by 2030, the proportion of people living in poverty in all its dimensions according to national definitions*, which is the 'proportion of the population living below the national poverty line'. The proposed indicator significantly changes the meaning of the target by making the money-metric dimension supplant all others.

Unfortunately, member states do not seem ready to accept indicators that reveal politically sensitive dimensions of reality. They are yet to show a willingness to accept indicators that reflect reality to the fullest, instead of sticking to those that capture only the most convenient aspects. It seems that they do not want to measure what is really important. Hence the question: Do we dare to measure what we want, or do we meekly accept what those who rule want us to measure?

REFERENCES

Aga Khan University (2013) *The National Nutrition Survey 2011: Pakistan.* In collaboration with the Pakistan Medical Research Council and the Cabinet Division of the Government of Pakistan. Islamabad: Aga Khan University.

Akerlof, G. and R. Shiller (2009) *Animal Spirits: How Human Psychology Drives the Economy, and why it Matters for Global Capitalism*. Princeton, NJ: Princeton University Press.

Atkinson, A. (2015) *Inequality: What Can Be Done?* Cambridge, MA: Harvard University Press.

Best, J. (2001) *Damned Lies and Statistics: Untangling Numbers from the Media, Politicians and Activists*. Berkeley: University of California Press.

Deaton, A. (2010) Price Indexes, Inequality, and the Measurement of World Poverty. *American Economic Review*, 100(1): 5–34.

Dorling, D. (2014) *Inequality and the 1%*. London: Verso.

EC (2016a) *Next Steps for a Sustainable European Future: European Action for Sustainability*. Brussels: European Commission.

EC (2016b) *Proposal for a New European Consensus on Development: Our World, Our Dignity, Our Future*. Brussels: European Commission.

Fioramonti, L. (2014) *How Numbers Rule the World: The Use and Abuse of Statistics in Global Politics*. London: Zed Books.

Galbraith, J. (2012) *Inequality and Instability: A Study of the World Economy Just Before the Great Crisis*. Oxford: Oxford University Press.

GPF (2015) *CSOs Voice Concerns Over Corporate Takeover of WHO*. New York: Global Policy Forum. https://www.globalpolicy.org/component/content/article/270-general/52761-csos-voice-concerns-over-corporate-takeover-of-who. html (accessed 12 June 2017).

ICSU and ISSC (2015) *Review of Targets for the Sustainable Development Goals: The Science Perspective*. Paris: International Council for Science (ICSU).

Jackson, B. (2015) *Bringing the Goals Home: is the UK Government Ready for the SDGs?* https://www.devex.com/news/bringing-the-goals-home-is-the-uk-government-ready-for-the-sdgs-86981 (accessed 12 June 2017).

Kahneman, D. (2011) *Thinking, Fast and Slow*. London: Penguin Books.

Kar, D. and J. Spanjers (2015) *Illicit Financial Flows from Developing Countries: 2004–2013*. Washington, DC: Global Financial Integrity.

Lipsey, R. (2013) *Hammarskjöld: a Life*. Ann Arbor, MI: The University of Michigan Press.

Minujin, A. and E. Delamonica (2003) Mind the Gap! Widening Child Mortality Disparities. *Journal of Human Development*, 4(3): 396–418.

Moser, K., D. Leon and D. Gwatkin (2005) How Does Progress towards the Child Mortality Millennium Development Goal Affect Inequalities between the Poorest and the Least Poor? Analysis of Demographic and Health Survey Data. *British Medical Journal*, 33(1): 1180–1183.

NIPS and ICF (2013) *Pakistan Demographic and Health Survey 2012–13*. Islamabad and Calverton: National Institute of Population Studies [Pakistan] and ICF International.

Palma, J. (2011) Homogeneous Middles vs. Heterogeneous Tails, and the End of the "Inverted-U": It's All About the Share of the Rich. *Development and Change*, 42(1): 87–153.

Passas, N. (2012) Terrorist Finance, Informal Markets, Trade and Regulation: Challenges of Evidence Regarding International Efforts, in C. Lum and L. Kennedy (eds) *Evidence-Based Counterterrorism Policy*. New York: Springer, pp. 255–279.

Piketty, T. (2014) *Capital in the Twenty-First Century*. Cambridge, MA: The Belknap Press of Harvard University Press.

Quintos, P. (2014) *The Post-2015 Corporate Development Agenda Expanding Corporate Power in the Name of Sustainable Development.* IBON International and Campaign for Peoples Goals. http://www.cetri.be/IMG/pdf/the20post-203e50.pdf (accessed 12 June 2017).

Reddy, S. and R. Lahoti (2016) $1.90 a Day: What Does It Say? The New International Poverty Line. *New Left Review,* 97(1): 106–127.

Reidpath, D., C. Morel, J. Mecaskey and P. Allotey (2009) The Millennium Development Goals Fail Poor Children: The Case for Equity-Adjusted Measures. *PLoS Med,* 6(4).

Schumacher, E. (1973) *Small is Beautiful: Economics as if People Mattered.* London: Sphere Books.

Stiglitz, J. (2012) *The Price of Inequality.* London: Allen Lane.

Stiglitz, J. (2015) *The Great Divide: Unequal Societies and What We Can Do About Them.* New York: W.W. Norton & Co.

Swift, A. (2001) *Political Philosophy: a Beginners' Guide for Students and Politicians.* Cambridge: Polity Press.

Taubes, G. (2016) *The Case Against Sugar.* New York: Knopf.

TI (2016) *Corruption in the Pharmaceutical Sector: Diagnosing the challenges.* Berlin: Transparency International. http://www.transparency.org.uk/publica tions/corruption-in-the-pharmaceutical-sector/ (accessed 12 June 2017).

UN (2000) *Millennium Declaration.* New York: United Nations.

UN (2013) *Inequality Matters.* Report on the World Social Situation 2013. New York: Department of Economic and Social Affairs, United Nations.

UN (2014) *The Millennium Development Goals Report 2014.* New York: United Nations.

UN (2015) *Transforming our World: the 2030 Agenda for Sustainable Development.* Document A/RES/70/1. New York: United Nations. http://www.un.org/ga/search/view_doc.asp?symbol=A/RES/70/1&Lang=E (accessed 12 June 2017).

UN (2016) *Report of the Inter-agency and Expert Group on Sustainable Development Goal Indicators.* Document E/CN.3/2016/2/Rev.1. New York: Statistical Commission, United Nations.

UN Global Compact (2014) *The Role of Business and Finance in Supporting the Post-2015 Agenda.* New York: United Nations. https://www.unglobalcompact.org/docs/news_events/9.6/Post2015_WhitePaper_2July1 4.pdf (accessed 12 June 2017).

UN News Centre (2015) *UN Adopts New Global Goals, Charting Sustainable Development for People and Planet by 2030.* http://www.un.org/apps/news/story.asp?NewsID=51968#.Vw8-iWOO7Vo (accessed 12 June 2017).

UNCTAD (2016) *Trade Misinvoicing in Primary Commodities in Developing Countries: The Cases of Chile, Cote d'Ivoire, Nigeria, South Africa and Zambia.* Document UNCTAD/SUC/2016/2. Geneva: United Nations Conference on Trade and Development.

UNDP (2013) *Humanity Divided: Confronting Inequality in Developing Countries.* New York: United Nations Development Programme.

UNDP (2016) *Helen Clark: Keynote Speech on Combating Inequalities and Achieving the Sustainable Development Goals.* http://www.undp.org/content/undp/en/home/presscenter/speeches/2016/04/13/helen-clark-keynote-speech-on-combating-inequalities-and-achieving-the-sustainable-development-goals.html (accessed 12 June 2017).

UNICEF (1990) *Plan of Action for Implementing the World Declaration on the*

Survival, Protection and Development of Children in the 1990s. New York: United Nations Children's Fund.

UNICEF (2015) *For Every Child, a Fair Chance: The Promise of Equity.* New York: United Nations Children's Fund.

Vandemoortele, J. (2009) The MDG Conundrum: Meeting the Targets Without Missing the Point. *Development Policy Review*, 27(4): 355–371.

Vandemoortele, J. (2016) *SDGs: The Tyranny of an Acronym?* http://impakter.com/sdgs-tyranny-acronym/ (accessed 12 June 2017).

Vandemoortele, J. (forthcoming) *The EU and the Implementation of the SDGs: So Much To Do Yet So Little Time Left.* Report prepared for the International Institute for Democracy and Electoral Assistance. Stockholm: IDEA.

WHO (2008) *Closing the Gap in a Generation: Health Equity Through Action on the Social Determinants of Health.* Geneva: Commission on Social Determinants of Health, World Health Organization.

WHO (2010) *Report of the World Health Organization Expert Working Group on Research and Development Financing.* Geneva: World Health Organization.

WHO (2016a) *Global Report on Diabetes.* Geneva: World Health Organization.

WHO (2016b) *Framework of Engagement with Non-State Actors.* Document A69/6. http://apps.who.int/gb/ebwha/pdf_files/WHA69/A69_6-en.pdf (accessed 12 June 2017).

Wilkinson, R. and K. Pickett (2010) *The Spirit Level. Why Equality is Better for Everyone.* London: Penguin Books.

World Bank (2016) *PovcalNet: An Online Analysis Tool For Global Poverty Monitoring.* http://iresearch.worldbank.org/PovcalNet/home.aspx (accessed 12 June 2017).

World Bank (2017) *Monitoring Global Poverty: Report of the Commission on Global Poverty.* Washington, DC: World Bank.

4. From billions to trillions: towards reform of development finance and the global reserve system

Rob Vos

CAN WE LIVE UP TO THE CHALLENGE?

The sustainable development goals (SDGs) of the 2030 Agenda for Sustainable Development aim to meet the dual challenge of overcoming poverty and protecting the planet. They aim, in part, to complete the unfinished business of previous agenda set up around the Millennium Development Goals (MDGs). The SDGs go much further, however, as they also seek to address pervasive global inequalities and making sure development takes place within planetary boundaries. These dimensions turn the new agenda into a transformative one, as existing development pathways are bound to step beyond the limits of ecosystems. The trodden pathways are also unlikely to correct the pervasive global inequalities.

Transformative change of global ramifications will be intrinsically challenging, requiring courageous policy shifts. The 17 SDGs are a reflection of the complexity and interconnectedness of the global challenges of the twenty-first century. Accordingly, courageous policy shifts are not just needed at the national level, but a new balance will have to be found between international rules setting and the provisioning of global public goods (such as a fair trading system and financial and climate stability), on the one hand, and the creation of the space needed by nations and societies to determine their own destiny, on the other. Several recent studies have laid out possible directions to establish such a balance (see for example, Vos and Montes, 2013a; Alonso, Cornia and Vos, 2013; and Alonso and Ocampo, 2015). While much more modest in scope than these contributions, this chapter is ambitious enough to suggest a paradigm shift in the thinking about development finance.

It argues that a number of global public goods aspects of the new agenda warrant new, global financing mechanisms. More in particular, it focuses on one proposal that revives an old idea of using global liquidity, the IMF's special drawing rights (SDRs), to leverage new long-term development finance (see, for example, Haan, 1971). The analysis suggests that the potential for doing so is vast, providing ample funding to finance development needs, especially investments that contribute the global public goods provisioning, such as climate protection. Doing so would contribute simultaneously to the delivery of another global public good, namely, greater global financial stability. It would reduce (if not eliminate) reliance on a single national currency (the United States dollar) as the world's reserve currency, thereby overcoming the deflationary and instability biases underlying the current international monetary system.

Leveraging SDRs, as argued in this chapter, could yield as much as US$1 trillion per annum additional resources in development finance. While significant, the proposed mechanism should be seen as but one step in the direction of necessary reforms to development finance mechanisms and the global financial system. There are no precise estimates of the financing requirements to underpin implementation of the new development agenda, as action plans towards its implementation still need to unfold and any estimate of financing needs could be a moving target. Even so, some new estimates of the possible costs have been put on the table which all suggest the discourse on development financing needs should shift from 'billions to trillions' (IMF, World Bank and regional multilateral development banks, 2015).

This chapter focuses on one proposal to make this quantum leap. However, the magnitude of resource mobilization by leveraging international liquidity is perhaps not the most important aspect of this proposal. Rather, this would be the use of truly global means to finance the global public goods associated with delivery on the new development agenda. It would constitute a shift away from the traditional way of looking at development finance, namely one of donor–recipient and, mostly, North–South relations. The global partnership as defined through the eighth goal of the MDG agenda represented a continuation of the traditional development finance architecture. This turned out to be the case despite the attempts of Monterrey Consensus of 2002 to look beyond hammering on compliance by donor countries on their commitment of delivering 0.7 per cent of their gross national income (GNI) in official development assistance (ODA). The Monterrey Consensus formed the start of the Financing for Development (FFD) process to underpin delivery on the MDG agenda and, looking beyond ODA, called for improved domestic resource mobilization, a fair trading system, and new, innovative development finance mechanisms, as well as pervasive reforms to the international financial system (including of the global reserve system). The FFD follow-up to underpin the SDG agenda, enshrined in the Addis

Ababa Action Agenda (AAAA), emphasized similar lines of action, but left out any action concerning reform of the global financial system, thereby constituting a step backwards.

This chapter argues to take a further step forward. The remainder of this chapter is organized as follows. The next section identifies the global public goods components of the SDG agenda and provides a brief review of recent estimates and projections of the finance needs that would be associated with delivery on those components. Section 3 describes some recent trends in available development finance, how those match up to the estimated financing needs. The relative contributions made by new, innovative forms of international finance for development over the past 15 years are also reviewed in that light. Section 4 discusses first how increased use of SDRs would underpin a more stable and equitable global reserve system, addressing fundamental flaws of the current system. The section subsequently describes the ways through which this essentially monetary reform measure could be used to leverage long-term development finance. Section 5 concludes with an assessment of the political feasibility of the proposal.

FROM BILLIONS TO TRILLIONS TO FINANCE GLOBAL PUBLIC GOODS

Global Public Goods

The 2007–2008 food price crisis, the 2008–2009 global financial crisis, the avian flu, Ebola, and other global health pandemics, and the threat of climate change have increased awareness of an increased prevalence of externalities and cross-border social and economic spill-overs among countries, regions and the world at large. The specific domain in the literature referred to as global or international public goods has emerged from those externalities.

In the economics literature, public goods are defined as those that share two rare qualities: non-excludability and non-rivalry. This means, respectively, that when provided to one party, the good is available to all and its consumption by one party does not reduce the amount available to the others. The term global public goods is used for 'goods' which are non-rivalrous and non-excludable for the world at large, as opposed to a public good which exists in just one national area. Knowledge or a stable climate are often given as examples of global public goods. Externalities associated with such public goods (or 'bads' as in the case of climate change) spread beyond national borders (regionally or globally). There are challenges to the classical definition of public goods, which also apply to global public goods (see, for example, Stiglitz, 1999; Kaul, Grunberg and Stern, 1999; Kaul, Concei, Le Goulven and Mendoza, 2003). This is not the place to go into these. The analysis below accepts the general notion of global public goods.

The new sustainable development agenda explicitly deals with improving the provision of some global public goods considered crucial for development. Such considerations were part of goal 8 of the MDG agenda – global partnership for development – as well as the goals for health (treating transmissible diseases) and environmental sustainability (protection of biodiversity). In the 2030 Agenda, the presence of goals related to the provision of global public goods is broader and they are part of many of the SDGs. That is the case, for example, of 'correct trade restrictions in agricultural markets' in the goal about achieving food security and some have argued that the objective of achieving global food security contains relevant international public good aspects, for instance, where food insecurity has been found to induce conflicts with trans-border consequences (Vos, 2015). Components most clearly related to public goods (national, regional, and global) form part of the environmental goals, linked with obtaining a sustainable management of water, ensuring a sustainable use of the oceans, seas, and marine resources, protecting the sustainable use of territorial ecosystems, building resilient infrastructure, making cities and human settlements resilient and sustainable, and taking actions against climate change.

Alike in the case of the MDGs, the 2030 Agenda dedicates a goal to 'strengthen the means of implementation and revitalize the global partnership for sustainable development'. This goal, SDG 17, is in line with goal 8 of the MDGs. Apart from a few relevant inclusions on the need to 'strengthen domestic resource mobilization', it includes support for improving domestic capacity for tax and other revenue collection, to 'enhance international cooperation on and access to science, technology and innovation', and stresses the need to promote the 'development, transfer, dissemination and diffusion of environmental sound technologies to developing countries on favourable terms'. The references to the need to increase international aid are retained from the MDG agenda, including the target of providing 0.7 per cent of donor-country GNI in ODA to developing countries.

Global economic stability is an example of a critical trans-border public good that no one single country can deliver. In the context of a strongly interconnected global economy, measures to ensure that the international economic system is resilient in the face of shocks are of central import-ance. Strengthening global financial and economic stability requires better coordination of regulatory policies across countries, coupled with closer dialogue among national policy makers to ensure that spill-over effects of national policies on other countries are appropriately factored into national policy setting.

SDG Financing Needs

No precise estimates of financing requirements are available. Determining them is extremely difficult to begin with. Not only because the implementation plans for following through on the 2030 Agenda are yet to unfold, but also because the need for resources will be a moving target, dependent on the speed of progress with implementation and on how global economic conditions evolve. The impacts of climate change cannot be determined with certainty, but climate projections suggest that they will become increasingly adverse over time. While targets to stabilize the climate, as laid down in the Paris Agreement of December 2015 (UNFCCC, 2015), have a longer time horizon (2050) than those of the 2030 Agenda, action needs to commence now. Delays in implementation of the agenda would increase the cost of action, assuming it is not yet too late (see, for example, Stern, 2014).

Nonetheless, recently various estimates of the possible costs have been put on the table. All point in the direction of additional investment requirements of more than a trillion per year. The Global Commission on the Economy and Climate Change (NCE, 2014) estimates that, over the next 15 years, the global economy will require an estimated US\$89 trillion for climate change action alone. These resources would be needed for infrastructure investments across cities, energy and land-use systems worldwide, and US\$4.1 trillion in incremental investment for the low-carbon transition to keep within the internationally agreed limit of a 2°C rise in global temperatures from pre-industrial averages. In a report on transitioning to green economies, the United Nations (2011) estimated that for developing countries additional financing needs for climate change mitigation and adaptation in developing countries would average between US\$140 billion and US\$175 billion per annum during 2010–2030, plus additional upfront investments of between US\$265 billion and US\$565 billion in the first years of the period to jumpstart transformations for emission reductions and a further US\$30 billion to US\$100 billion per annum for adaptation. When also including investments to provide (clean) energy for all, end hunger and making food systems sustainable, and improve forest resource management, the same UN report estimates the cost of incremental investments in sustainable development to be made in developing countries could average about US\$1.1 trillion per year in the coming decades. These estimates are presented in Table 4.1, after updating the estimated

Table 4.1   Estimates of required incremental investment levels for sustainable development

	Aims and assumptions	Incremental investment requirements	Of which: in developing countries
		(annual; 2000–2050; billions of 2010 US$)	
Climate change mitigation: Energy supply	Stabilize greenhouse gas concentrations to limit warming to <2°C (with at least 50 per cent probability)	1,000	600
Climate change mitigation: Energy end-use efficiency	Significant end-use efficiency increase and greenhouse gas stabilization to <2°C	800	480
Climate change adaptation (mostly in agriculture)	Minimum investments in securing livelihoods, assuming successful mitigation	105	105
Agriculture and food security	Increasing agricultural yields to ensure global food security without further expanding agricultural land	265	265
Total (per annum)		2,172	1,452

Source: Adapted from United Nations (2012: Table VI.3). Data for agriculture and food security are from FAO, IFAD and WFP (2015).

cost to end hunger from a more recent estimate by FAO, IFAD and WFP (2015). Including the latter, the estimate for a central estimate from a range of projections would bring incremental investment requirements for developing countries to near US$1.5 trillion per annum.

Schmidt-Traub and Sachs (2015) provide an often-cited estimate of total cost incremental investments to support achievement of the SDGs in developing countries at between US$1.5 billion and US$2.5 billion per annum during 2015–2030. Their (preliminary) estimates cover incremental investment needs to meet the goals for health, education, food security, access to modern energy, universal access to water and sanitation, protection of biodiversity, large infrastructure, climate change mitigation and adaptation, as well as improved data for SDG monitoring.[1] According to

Schmidt-Traub and Sachs, about half of the required resources would need to be leveraged from private (commercial) sources, including by changing incentive structures. The other half of these resources should come from (domestic and international) public finance sources.

In line with these estimates, the IMF, the World Bank and all regional multilateral development banks recommended to the Development Committee of the Bretton Woods Institutions that the discourse on development financing should shift its value from 'billions to trillions' (IMF, World Bank and regional multilateral development banks, 2015).

THE CHANGING LANDSCAPE OF DEVELOPMENT FINANCE

Changing Finance

The global development landscape has changed since the MDGs were adopted in 2000. The five emerging countries grouped in the BRICS (Brazil, Russia, India, China and South Africa) now account for roughly the same share of global GDP (about one-third) as the major high-income economies grouped in the G7. At the same time, inequality within many countries is on the rise and there is a growing gap between the richest and poorest countries, with some of the poorest countries caught in a 'poverty trap'.

The past decade has seen significant increases in the level of financial flows to developing countries from OECD-DAC countries (Figure 4.1). This reflects the growing importance of international private finance, particularly increased flows to middle-income countries in the form of foreign direct investments, bonds and syndicated bank lending with at least five years of maturity, and private philanthropy, such as from foundations and NGOs. Not featured in the graph are two important sources of external finance to developing countries that have increased significantly over the past two decades: remittances (currently estimated at over US$500 billion per annum, almost four times the level of ODA) and official financing from the BRICS (for which insufficient consistent data are available). ODA flows reached US$132 billion in 2015, but their pattern has been uneven and donor commitments to provide at least 0.7 per cent of GNI in ODA have never been within reach. ODA to Africa has declined in real terms over the last several years. If all OECD-DAC countries were to meet their long-standing commitment to set aside 0.7 per cent of their gross national income (GNI), annual ODA levels would more than double (UN-MDG Gap Task Force 2008–2015).

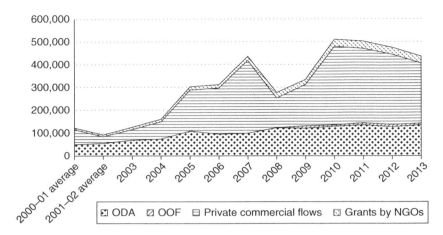

Notes: Refers to net financial flows originating from OECD-DAC member countries.
ODA = Official development assistance; OOF = other official flows. Private commercial
flows include direct foreign investment, export credits, bonds and other commercial
portfolio investments in developing countries. Grants by NGOs include contributions from
private foundations.

Source: OECD-DAC.

Figure 4.1   *Financial flows to developing countries, 2000–2013 (millions of US$)*

A diverging pattern of development finance architecture has emerged
across countries at different stages of development (Figure 4.2). ODA
remains a significant source of finance for low-income countries, fragile
states and those in conflict. While the share of ODA in overall external
financing for upper middle-income countries is relatively small – they
now rely primarily on private flows (FDI and bonds) – they nonetheless
receive 40 per cent of ODA grants. Beyond the financial flows depicted
in Figure 4.1, domestic resource mobilization has increasingly become
a key source for funding national development plans. Relatively strong
growth in many developing countries during the 2000s has lifted domestic
resource mobilization through taxes to US$7.7 trillion in 2012 (IMF,
World Bank and regional multilateral development banks, 2015). That
is, developing country treasuries currently receive over US$6 trillion
more each year than in 2000 helping lower aid dependency and raising
creditworthiness of many countries. Further strengthening of domestic
revenue collection will be needed to underpin implementation of the 2030
Agenda. However, increasing revenue mobilization remains a challenge for
many governments, particularly in low-income countries. Moreover, some

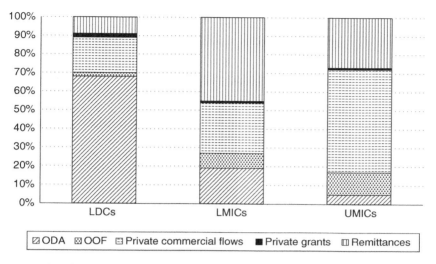

ODA OOF Private commercial flows ■ Private grants Remittances

Notes: See Figure 4.1 for definition of types of flows. LDCs = least developed countries; LMICs = lower-middle-income countries; and UMICs = upper middle-income countries.

Source: OECD-DAC.

Figure 4.2 Composition of financial flows to developing countries, 2012 (in per cent)

of the recent revenue gains in low-income countries reflect increased global demand for natural resources, and remain as volatile as commodity prices.

Hence, in a post-2015 world, traditional ODA and domestic resource mobilization are likely to remain important to finance development efforts of low-income countries. However, they unlikely will be enough to finance efforts that meet the global ambitions of the SDGs. Mobilizing larger amounts of private resources, such as foreign direct investments, bond issuance, and financing from institutional investors, for investments in inclusive and sustainable development, likely will be challenging. The challenge – against a backdrop of cautious market investment – will be to shift current development financing and invest-ment patterns. The global public goods nature of important elements of sustainable development efforts by low and middle-income countries warrant considering new, innovative sources of finance mobilized through global channels.

Innovative Finance for Provisioning of Global Public Goods

In 2001, a United Nations High-Level Panel on Financing for Development, chaired by the former President of Mexico, Ernesto Zedillo, recommended a number of strategies for the mobilization of resources to fulfil the commitments made in the UN Millennium Declaration that laid the foundations for the MDG agenda (United Nations, 2001). The Panel made a strong case for tapping international sources of financing for the provisioning of global public goods, including for the prevention of contagious diseases, research for the development of vaccines and agricultural crops, combating climate change, and preservation of biodiversity. These recommendations received follow-up in the Monterrey Consensus on Financing for Development in 2002.[2]

The call for studying the potential of using SDR's for development purposes did not get much response (however, see section 4 below). Other forms of innovative global financing mechanisms were proposed. Some of those have been put in practice, since the late 1990s. In 2012, the United Nations undertook a thorough review of these initiatives, as well as other major proposals (United Nations, 2012). The review found that most initiatives have been used to help finance new global health programmes and some to finance programmes for climate change mitigation and adaptation. The review concluded that global health funds have been effective in immunizing millions of children and providing treatments for AIDS and tuberculosis to millions of people in the developing world, but did not yield much additional development finance. In all, an estimated US$5.8 billion in health financing and US$2.6 billion in financing for climate and other environmental protection programmes have been managed through such mechanisms since 2002. Much of the funds for these innovative mechanisms have been mobilized through 'securitization' of existing ODA commitments; thus not adding new resources. In fact, while difficult to estimate, probably only a few hundred million dollars have been added annually (Figure 4.3).

Innovative financing for climate change is still incipient. Total resources raised for this purpose through innovative financing mechanisms (excluding an unquantifiable amount of debt-for-nature swaps over the last 25 years) amount to a mere US$1 billion between 2000 and 2012 (United Nations, 2012). About US$168 million was raised by the Adaptation Fund from a 2 per cent tax on transactions under the Clean Development Mechanism, and US$841 million from Germany's auctions of permits under the EU Emission Trading Scheme, channelled through its International Climate Initiative.

Two mechanisms in particular are expected to generate substantial

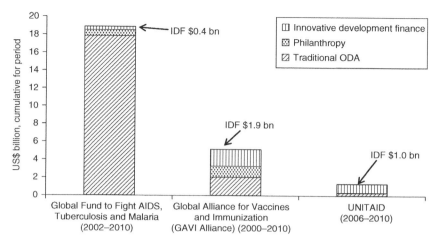

Source: United Nations (2012: Figure O.2).

Figure 4.3 Global health funds: only small share comes from additional innovative sources of development finance (IDF) (billions of US$; cumulative amounts for period)

resources for climate change programmes in the next few years. First, from 2013, the European Union is to auction carbon emissions allowances, which will generate an estimated US$20 billion–US$35 billion in annual revenues; some countries have indicated their intention to allocate half for climate change programmes (although inasmuch as this includes domestic programmes, much less is likely to be devoted to programmes in developing countries). Germany was expected to channel 15 per cent of its revenue (or an estimated US$500 million per year) to international climate-related programmes from 2013. The United Nations report estimated that if all European Union members do the same, over US$5 billion per year would become available for international climate financing from auctioning European Union emission allowances (United Nations, 2012: ix). To date, however, international credits funded from the auction have been much less than anticipated, owing to low and volatile auction prices (European Commission, 2015).

Second, for some time it was envisaged that the Reducing Emissions from Deforestation and Forest Degradation plus Conservation (REDD+) initiative, which has hitherto operated essentially as a coordinating mechanism for conventional multilateral and bilateral aid projects, should evolve into an innovative mechanism based on carbon trading. This step was finally taken at the Paris Agreement on climate change action (December 2015), the outcome of COP21. Article 6 of the Paris Agreement creates a new carbon trading mechanism for the mitigation of GHG emissions and to finance sustainable development investments. Countries generating so-called REDD credits will be able to either keep the credits to offset their own emissions from fossil fuels, or sell the REDD credits to countries that can use them to offset GHG emissions. Neither of these options reduces global GHG emissions, because in both cases the reduction in emissions from forests would be offset against continued emissions from fossil fuels. Yet, sales of credits could yield funds for sustainable investments. The new auction mechanism is to come into effect no sooner than 2020, however.

In short, existing mechanisms for innovative finance for global public goods are, as yet, limited. Other options may need to be considered. Considerable attention has been given to new forms of international taxation, such as a global carbon tax, a tax on international financial transactions and even a global billionaire's tax (United Nations, 2012). The next section, however, revives the idea of a link between the creation of international money in the form of SDRs and development finance and, more specifically, to link a truly international source of funding to the provisioning of GPGs.

INTERNATIONAL RESERVE ASSET CREATION TO BOOST FINANCE FOR DEVELOPMENT AND GLOBAL PUBLIC GOODS

Special Drawing Rights as a Reserve Asset

The immediate post-war period was marked by the creation of the International Monetary Fund (IMF) and the International Bank for Reconstruction and Development (IBRD) (both in 1944) and the United Nations Organization (in 1945). It is often regarded as the time when international economic cooperation reached its peak. The special circumstances of the time, with many of the countries involved in the creation process having being exhausted by the Second World War, while still living in the shadow cast by the Great Depression of the 1930s. In the 1930s, the 'beggar-thy-neighbour' policies of most governments – entailing the use of currency devaluations to increase the competitiveness of a country's export products and reduce balance-of-payments deficits – worsened national deflationary spirals, which resulted in plummeting national incomes, shrinking demand, mass unemployment, and an overall decline in world trade (Vos and Montes, 2013b: 7–8).

To overcome the weaknesses embedded in the pre-war international monetary system, a system of fixed exchange rates was introduced with the US dollar as the reserve currency and with the dollar pegged to the price of gold. Short-run balance-of-payment difficulties would be overcome by IMF loans. The new system would facilitate stable currency exchange rates, and a country with payment deficits would not have to induce a cut in national income to bring it to a level low enough for import demand to finally fall within that country's means. The agreement made no provisions for the creation of international reserves. While central banks could settle international payments imbalances between countries in gold or any acceptable currency, the dollar served as the main official reserve currency. This meant that the United States gained – and largely still gains – the 'seigniorage' benefit of providing the world's international currency.[3]

However, the supply of dollars put into international circulation depended on the US balance of payments. The world could thus face periods of 'dollar shortage' and periods of 'dollar glut'. During the latter, some governments converted some of their growing dollar reserve holdings into gold, reducing the US stock of gold and ultimately forcing the United States in 1971 to break the gold link, which in turn, after some years of failed negotiations, led to the end of the fixed exchange-rate system.

The conflict of interest between short-term domestic and long-term international objectives for countries whose currencies serve as global reserve currencies is known as the Triffin dilemma. This dilemma was first identified in the 1960s by former IMF economist Robert Triffin (Triffin, 1960; 1968). Countries running a balance-of-payment deficit would require an inflow of US dollars, thus requiring the United States to run an external surplus. If the latter would not be seen to serve the short-term macroeconomic interest of the reserve country, deficit countries would have to cut back on spending to correct their external deficit. John Maynard Keynes had anticipated this asymmetry in the need for external adjustment and concluded that this put a deflationary (if not a recessionary) bias into the global economy (Keynes, 1943; see also Ocampo, 2015). To overcome this bias, Keynes advocated the use of a global reserve currency called bancor, as part of his proposal for the post-war monetary system. His proposal did not make it at the time. The IMF's SDRs come closest to this concept of global liquidity, but have not been adopted widely enough to replace the dollar as the global reserve currency.

The SDR was created in 1969 to help assure an adequate and internationally managed global supply of international liquidity. The original intention was that countries should increasingly substitute SDRs for dollars as an international reserve asset and gradually make the SDR the principal reserve asset of the international monetary system. That did not happen.

After the first allocation of 9 billion SDRs in 1970–1972, which represented about 8 per cent of non-gold reserves in the final allocation year, a second allocation of 12 billion SDRs was made in 1979–1981, reaching about 6 per cent of reserves in 1981 (Boughton, 2001: 929). None were issued thereafter until 2009. A decision had been reached in 1997 to make a special allocation that would have doubled overall holdings and bring countries that had not been IMF members when the earlier allocations were made up to par with other members, but it was not implemented until 2009.

As a result, the SDR has played only a minor role as a reserve asset for settling obligations between central banks or with IMF and a limited number of other official institutions. The 'rediscovery' of the SDR in 2009 as part of the G20 response to the global financial crisis led to agreement to issue 161 billion SDRs (equivalent to US$250 billion) and approval of the overdue allocation of 21.5 billion SDRs (US$33 billion) decided upon in 1997. The agreement raised the stock of SDRs to about 4 per cent of non-gold reserves. Table 4.2 shows the impact on the allocation of SDR holdings by major country groupings. The new issuance of SDRs lifted SDR allocations to low-income countries from SDR 0.3 billion to SDR 3.6 billion and for middle-income countries from SDR 3.3 billion to

Table 4.2   SDR allocations by selected country groups according to the level of income, 1970–2009

	Allocations (in millions of SDRs)			Allocation to each group (% of total allocation)		
	1970–72	1979–81	2009	1970–72	1979–81	2009
High income: OECD	6,818	7,956	114,905	73.8	66.2	62.9
United States	2,294	2,606	30,416	24.8	21.7	16.7
Japan	377	514	11,393	4.1	4.3	6.2
Others	4,147	4,837	73,095	44.9	40.3	40.0
High income: non-OECD	41	363	10,797	0.4	3.0	5.9
Gulf countries	1	286	8,835	0.0	2.4	4.8
Excluding Gulf countries	40	77	1,962	0.4	0.6	1.1
Middle income	2,144	3,359	53,347	23.2	28.0	29.2
China	0	237	6,753	0.0	2.0	3.7
Excluding China	2,144	3,122	46,594	23.2	26.0	25.5
Low income	230	338	3,604	2.5	2.8	2.0
Total allocations	9,234	12,016	182,653	100.0%	100.0%	100.0%

Source: Erten and Ocampo (2012) based on IMF data.

SDR 53 billion. The developing country share remained at just below one-third, however, with high-income countries getting the bulk of the increase, with only slight shifts in the shares since the first days of the creation of SDRs.

So far, the 2009 SDR allocation has remained a one-time event. The question is whether SDRs will be issued more regularly in the future. The original aim in creating an international reserve currency remains worthwhile and should be pursued, even though the attraction of the SDR as a monetary asset has been limited by design. In particular, central banks are not able to use the SDR directly in foreign exchange market interventions because there are no private holders of SDRs. But, even if the SDR never becomes a private asset, it retains value as a usable reserve asset for settling inter-central bank claims as long as governments can freely swap SDRs for hard currencies and this is guaranteed by IMF rules. Moreover, experience shows that developing countries have used their SDR allocations more intensively than developed countries for balance-of-payments financing, both historically and during the current crisis (Erten and Ocampo, 2012: 10–11).

Not only could the IMF issue SDRs on a regular basis, as originally intended, but it could also skew allocations in favour of developing countries. For example, a revised allocation formula could take account of the fact that developing economies tend to have a larger demand for reserves relative to GDP than developed economies (Erten and Ocampo, 2012: 6).

Changing the SDR allocation formula would constitute a significant political undertaking, as it will require an amendment to the IMF Articles of Agreement. Amending the Articles, like decisions for a general SDR allocation under existing rules, requires an 85 per cent approval of member votes, giving the United States an effective veto. Indeed, United States support of regular SDR allocations would require that it exhibit a measure of global solidarity, as the seigniorage embodied in the new SDRs would be effected largely at the expense of a seigniorage no longer accruing to the United States. Nevertheless, such a change could significantly strengthen the international monetary system, which is an imperative that all IMF member countries support.

Regular SDR allocations would strengthen the international financial safety net and reduce developing country needs for 'self-insurance' against global economic shocks. Since the Asian financial crisis of the late 1990s, many developing countries have been accumulating official reserves to provide a buffer against any future shocks. In many cases, reserve holdings have risen well beyond needs, minimum import needs and short-term debt repayment needs and to significant shares of GDP. As shown in Figure 4.4, reserve holdings for developed countries have decreased as a share of GDP,

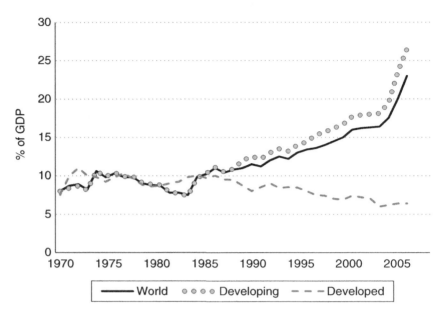

Note: Data refer unweighted cross-country averages of international reserves (minus gold) as a share of GDP for 24 developed economies and 154 developing economies.

Source: Based on IMF data and estimates in Pina (2015).

Figure 4.4   International reserve holdings as percentage of GDP, 1970–2009

while increasing steadily in developing countries to reaching over 25 per cent on average by 2009. Such large reserve holdings hedge against external shocks, but also imply that significant shares of developing country savings are kept in generally low-return liquid financial assets. As such, they add to the deflationary bias of the international monetary system.

The Commission of Experts, appointed by the President of the General Assembly in 2008 (the so-called Stiglitz Commission) to provide recommendations on responses to the global financial crisis, also recommended new issuance of SDRs on a regular basis, as part of farther-reaching proposals for international financial reform and thus gradually replace the global reserve system based mainly on the dollar with one based on an international currency (the SDR) (United Nations, 2009: Chapter 5). The Commission proposed annual allocations of between US$150 billion and US$300 billion of the international currency, so as to render it unnecessary for countries to impart a deflationary bias in the growth of global demand by running balance-of-payments surpluses in order to mobilize the foreign exchange to add to official reserves. Based on the revision of country shares in IMF quotas, this implies an increase of developing and emerging economy SDRs worth US$101–169 billion. If the allocation instead favoured developing countries raising their share to, say, two-thirds, they would receive between US$160 billion and US$270 billion worth of SDRs.

SDR as Financing for Development[4]

Perhaps the earliest proposal for mobilizing international funds for development that did not 'belong' to any set of tax payers was the so-called SDR link. Linking SDR issuance to long-term development finance, as proposed here, is not a new idea. It was the subject of multilateral discussion in the early 1970s, but was never agreed upon. In principle, the SDR has no direct link to development finance. However, the fact that an SDR allocation serves to create real purchasing power for the holder receiving the allocation has led numerous authors to ask whether that purchasing power could be captured for development or the financing of global public goods (see, for example, Haan, 1971; Ocampo, 2011), although none of these have gained much political traction either. Developed countries have typically opposed the link, fearing that there would be pressure for excessive and inflationary issues of SDRs.

The possible development financing functions of SDRs allocated to developed countries should be clearly separated from their role in increasing the reserves of developing countries, as discussed above. A more recent proposal by two IMF economists envisaged the use of SDRs for the financing of actions towards climate change mitigation and adaptation. Bredenkamp and Pattillo (2010) proposed the creation of a multilateral 'Green Fund' whose equity capital could be drawn from the 2009 allocation of SDRs, most of which had gone to developed countries, as also indicated above. However, given that equity shares with volatile prices do not normally qualify as a reserve asset and assuming that retaining reserve asset status was important, Bredenkamp and Pattillo further proposed that any shareholder should have the guaranteed ability to sell its shares to other shareholders at par. The proposal did not recommend spending the SDRs, but rather to float bond issues backed by SDRs (and thus backed, in effect, by the governments of major developed countries). The proposal suggested a leverage ratio of 10 to 1, such that US$1 trillion in bonds could be issued backed by US$100 billion in equity shares, once the Green Fund would have reached full size. Clearly, this leveraging is the proposal's main attraction, given the large investment resources needed to address climate change. The Green Fund would collect market-based interest payments from at least some of its borrowers, which it would then use to pay its bondholders. As low-income countries could not afford such loans, the Fund would also receive additional annual contributions from donors to enable it to underwrite its concessional activities (as is largely the case for the concessional loan facilities of IMF). The authors envisaged that substantial annual donor revenues would be needed, which according to their proposal might be mobilized from a carbon tax or some other international environmental revenue source. The proposal did not make it, however, to the IMF's executive board for consideration.

In the aftermath of the global financial crisis several other authors also proposed using SDRs to purchase long-term assets, although without earmarking these to a specific fund or a global public good as has been endorsed by some authors (see, for instance, Birdsall and Leo, 2011; Erten and Ocampo, 2012), as well as the Stiglitz Commission (United Nations, 2009). Others, including a UN high-level advisory group on climate financing, expressed reservations to such proposals (for example, United Nations, 2010: para. 89).

The attraction for proponents resides in the ability to tap the large pool of 'unused' SDRs, in order to invest them, for example, in equity shares in the Green Climate Fund, as noted above, in multilateral institution bonds, or in a new multilateral development fund. Through regular substantial SDR allocations, at least US$100 billion in development financing could potentially be raised per year (to leverage US$1 trillion, if a 10:1 leverage ratio is deemed acceptable). The proposal assumes that IMF would allocate between US$240 billion and US$400 billion worth of SDRs each year, of which about US$144 billion–US$240 billion worth of SDRs would be allocated to developed countries, and of which US$100 billion to US$200 billion would likely remain unutilized and it would thus be deemed unnecessary to maintain this sum as a reserve. This way, the 'seigniorage' from regular issuance of SDRs would no longer accrue as much to the international reserve currency countries, but would be allocated for use in part by the international community in favour of developing countries.

A major objection to this proposal could be that it violates the principles underlying SDRs, namely that these were created solely for transactions of a monetary nature (like transactions between central banks). Leveraging them in such a way as to expose their holder to risks of illiquidity would distort the purpose for which they were created. The question, then, is how much risk would be involved, which points to the need for careful design of the financial instrument in order to maintain its reserve nature. The counterargument is that leveraging 'idle' SDRs, as proposed here, is similar to the practice engaged in by a fair number of countries which have moved excess foreign currency reserves into sovereign wealth funds, where the liquidity and risk characteristics of specific assets in the fund determine whether or not to declassify those assets as reserve holdings even though they are held by the central bank. As proposed here, the IMF would be allowed to use the SDRs that are not utilized by member states, and treat them as 'deposits' to leverage the purchase of bonds from multilateral development banks, which would then finance development or global public objectives. This way the 'development link' in SDR allocations avoids being treated as a fiscal transaction, also argued by Ocampo (2011) and the Stiglitz Commission (United Nations, 2009).

Changing the SDR allocation formula would constitute a significant political undertaking, as it requires an amendment to the IMF Articles of Agreement. Amending the Articles, like decisions for a general SDR allocation under existing rules, requires 85 per cent of member votes in favour for approval. This gives the United States an effective veto. Indeed, US support for regular SDR allocations would imply a measure of global solidarity, as the seigniorage embodied in the new SDRs would be largely at the expense of seigniorage no longer accruing to the United States. Nevertheless, such a change would result in a significant strengthening of the international monetary system. SDRs would remain a reserve asset, but their additional availability, arranged through international coordination, could reduce the need for individual developing countries to set aside foreign-exchange earnings in reserve holdings of their own as a form of self-insurance against global market shocks.

CONCLUSIONS

The many global public goods elements in the new international development agenda – the 2030 Agenda for Sustainable Development – warrant considering a larger role for global sources of funding to underpin the global partnership for development. The global public good aspects notion is also acknowledged in the 2030 Agenda for Sustainable Development under SDG17. Yet, the ambitions of SDG17 do not seem to live up to the ambitions of the rest of the agenda. In fact, it constitutes little progress from the much criticized MDG8 and its poor delivery track record. Furthermore, the Addis Ababa Action Agenda of the third Financing for Development Conference agreed in July 2015 just before the adaptation of the SDGs in September 2015 is in at least one way a step backwards from the Monterrey Consensus, achieved at the First Conference on Financing for Development in 2002 (United Nations, 2015). In Addis Ababa, no major new commitments for strengthening and widening the global partnership for development were made. No significant additional funds were pledged, and no new directions for a multilateral trading system consistent with the SDGs was agreed upon or even discussed. And, as a clear step backwards, systemic problems underlying repeated international financial instability were not even on the agenda.

In short, implementation of the 2030 Agenda may turn out to be shorthanded because of a weak global partnership, leaving many of the deficiencies in global governance mechanisms unresolved and the risk of leaving the required development efforts grossly underfinanced. Turning to the latter issue, the analysis of this chapter suggests that vast amounts of new resources for sustainable development finance could be generated by revamping the global reserve system and, simultaneously, addressing the key weaknesses of that system to bring greater international financial stability.

Building on related recent proposals, this chapter proposed reviving the old idea of using international liquidity, the IMF's SDRs, to leverage new development financing. Regular issuance of SDRs would help resolve the Triffin dilemma by gradually phasing out the use of the US dollar as the major reserve currency. It would strengthen the international financial safety net to deal with balance-of-payments crises and reduce the need for developing countries to take out 'self-insurance' against external shocks by accumulating vast amounts of their own reserves. This will take the international community some way in providing the global public good of global financial stability, while eliminating the deflationary bias on global economic growth implied by the present international monetary system. By using idle SDRs to leverage new development finance, the provisioning of other global public goods (like a stable climate or improved global public health) can be underpinned with better funding.

Political hurdles are yet to be taken. The same that prevented earlier proposals in this direction to take hold, in particular political consent of the United States, which retains veto power regarding SDR issuance in the IMF. In addition, proper mechanisms for the allocation of the new finance would need to be defined, as well as deeper reforms of IMF's voice and quota structure to give greater voice to low-income countries. However, the global agreement reached on the transformative 2030 Agenda should provide enough political leverage for moving towards a much stronger global partnership by tackling a long-standing systemic flaw in the international monetary system to help ensure the implementation of the 2030 Agenda will not fall short of resources.

NOTES

1. Schmidt-Traub (2015) provides further details on how the estimates were derived, mentioning they should be interpreted with caution given the tentative nature of the estimate. The publication contains a slight revision from the Sachs–Schmidt-Traub estimates, but remains in the same order of magnitude.
2. Paragraph 44 of the Consensus stated, inter alia, that "[i]n that regard, we agree to study, in the appropriate forums, the results of the analysis requested from the Secretary-General on possible innovative sources of finance, noting the proposal to use special drawing rights allocations for development purposes. We consider that any assessment of special drawing rights allocations must respect the International Monetary Fund's Articles of Agreement and the established rules of procedure of the Fund, which requires taking into account the global need for liquidity at the international level" (United Nations, 2003: 16).
3. 'Seigniorage' refers to the difference between the value of money and the cost to produce and distribute it, or, put differently, it is the profit from money creation.
4. This sub-section draws on research undertaken by the author and colleagues when at the UN Department of Economic and Social Affairs, in preparation for the *World Economic and Social Survey 2012: In Search of New Development Finance* (United Nations, 2012).

REFERENCES

Alonso, José Antonio and José Antonio Ocampo (eds) (2015), *Global Governance and Rules for the Post-2015 Era*, London: Bloomsbury Academic.

Alonso, José Antonio, Giovanni Andrea Cornia and Rob Vos (eds) (2013), *Alternative Development Strategies for the Post-2015 Era*, London: Bloomsbury Academic.

Birdsall, Nancy and Benjamin Leo (2011), 'Find me the money: financing climate and other global public goods', CGD Working Paper, No. 248 (April), Washington, DC: Centre for Global Development.

Boughton, James (2001), *Silent Revolution: The International Monetary Fund, 1979–1989*, Washington, DC: International Monetary Fund.

Bredenkamp, Hugh and Catherine Pattillo (2010), 'Financing the response to climate change', IMF Staff Position Note, No. SPN10/06, Washington, DC: International Monetary Fund (25 March).

Erten, Bilge and José Antonio Ocampo (2012), 'Building a stable and equitable global monetary system', DESA Working Paper No. 118 (ST/ESA/2012/DWP/118), New York: United Nations Department of Economic and Social Affairs, http://www.un.org/esa/desa/papers/2012/wp118_2012.pdf (accessed 13 June 2017).

European Commission (2015), *Carbon Market Report 2015*, COM (2015) 576, Annex 1, Brussels: European Commission, http://ec.europa.eu/clima/policies/strategies/progress/docs/com_2015_576_annex_1_en.pdf (accessed 13 June 2017).

FAO, IFAD, and WFP (2015) *Achieving Zero Hunger: the Critical Role of Investments in Social Protection and Agriculture*, Rome: Food and Agriculture Organization of the United Nations http://www.fao.org/3/a-i4951e.pdf (accessed 22 June 2017).

Haan, Roelf (1971), *Special Drawing Rights and Development*, Leiden: Stenfert Kroese.

IMF, World Bank, and regional multilateral development banks (2015), 'From billions to trillions: transforming development finance', Development Committee Discussion Note DC2015-02, Washington DC: Development Committee (April).

Kaul, Inge, Isabelle Grunberg and Marc A. Stern (eds) (1999), *Global Public Goods: International Cooperation in the 21st Century*, New York, Oxford: Oxford University Press (for UNDP).

Kaul, Inge, Pedro Conceição, Katell Le Goulven, and Ronald U. Mendoza (eds) (2003), *Providing Global Public Goods: Managing Globalization*, New York, Oxford: Oxford University Press (for UNDP).

Keynes, John M. (1943), *The Keynes Plan*. Reproduced in J. Keith Horsefield (ed.) (1969), *The International Monetary Fund 1945–1965: Twenty Years of International Monetary Cooperation. Vol. III: Documents. International Monetary Fund*, Washington, DC: IMF, pp. 3–36.

NCE (2014), *Better Growth, Better Climate: The 2014 New Climate Economy Report*, London and Washington DC: The Global Commission on the Economy and Climate, http://www.newclimateeconomy.net (accessed 14 August 2017).

Ocampo, José Antonio (2011), *Reforming the International Monetary System*, 14th WIDER Lecture, Helsinki: UNU-WIDER.

Ocampo, José Antonio (2015), 'Reforming the international monetary and financial architecture', in José Antonio Alonso and José Antonio Ocampo (eds), *Global Governance and Rules for the Post-2015 Era*, London: Bloomsbury Academic, pp. 41–72.

Pina, Gonçalo (2015), 'The recent growth of international reserves in developing economies: a monetary perspective', *Journal of International Money and Finance*, 58: 172–190 (November).

Schmidt-Traub, Guido (2015), 'Investment needs to achieve the sustainable development goals: understanding the billions and trillions', SDSN Working Paper Version 2, Paris and New York: Sustainable Development Solutions Network (12 November), http://unsdsn.org/wp-content/uploads/2015/09/151112-SDG-Finan cing-Needs.pdf (accessed 13 June 2017).

Schmidt-Traub, Guido and Jeffrey Sachs (2015), 'Financing for sustainable development: implementing the SDGs through effective investment strategies and partnerships', SDSN Working Paper, Paris and New York: Sustainable Development Solutions Network (18 June), http://unsdsn.org/wp-content/uploads/2015/04/150619-SDSN-Financing-Sustainable-Development-Paper-FINAL-02.pdf (accessed 13 June 2017).

Stern, N. (2014), 'Growth, climate and collaboration: towards agreement in Paris 2015', Policy Paper December 2014, Centre for Climate Change Economics and Policy, Grantham Research Institute on Climate Change and the Environment.

Stiglitz, Joseph E. (1999), 'Knowledge as a global public good', in Inge Kaul, Isabelle Grunberg and Marc A. Stern (eds), *Global Public Goods: International Cooperation in the 21st Century*, New York: Oxford University Press, pp. 308–325.

Triffin, Robert (1960), *Gold and the Dollar Crisis: the Future of Convertibility*, New Haven: Yale University Press.

Triffin, Robert (1968), *Our International Monetary System: Yesterday, Today, and Tomorrow*, New York: Random House.

UNFCCC (2015), *Adoption of the Paris Agreement*, Conference of the Parties (COP) 21, Paris 30 November – 11 December 2015, FCCC/CP/2015/L.9/Rev.1,

Paris: United Nations Framework Convention on Climate Change, https://unfccc.int/resource/docs/2015/cop21/eng/l09r01.pdf (accessed 13 June 2017).

UN-MDG Gap Task Force (2008–2015) *The Global Partnership for Development*, Report of the MDG Gap Task Force, New York: United Nations (various issues).

United Nations (2001), *Recommendations of the High-level Panel on Financing for Development*, Report to the United Nations General Assembly, A/55/1000, New York: United Nations, http://www.un.org/en/ga/search/view_doc.asp?symbol=A/55/1000 (accessed 13 June 2017).

United Nations (2003), *Monterrey Consensus on Financing for Development*, International Conference on Financing for Development, Monterrey (Mexico), 18–22 March 2002, New York: United Nations, http://www.un.org/esa/ffd/monterrey/MonterreyConsensus.pdf (accessed 13 June 2017).

United Nations (2009), Report of the Commission of Experts of the President of the United Nations General Assembly on Reforms of the International Monetary and Financial System (Stiglitz Report), New York: United Nations General Assembly (21 September), http://www.un.org/ga/econ-crisissummit/docs/FinalReport_CoE.pdf (accessed 13 June 2017).

United Nations (2010), Report of the High-level Advisory Group on Climate Change Financing, New York: United Nations https://www.iatp.org/files/451_2_107756.pdf (accessed 22 June 2017).

United Nations (2011), *World Economic and Social Survey 2011: The Great Green Technological Transformation*, New York: United Nations, http://www.un.org/en/development/desa/policy/wess/wess_current/2011wess.pdf (accessed 22 June 2017).

United Nations (2012), *World Economic and Social Survey 2012: In Search for New International Development Finance*, New York: United Nations, http://www.un.org/en/development/desa/policy/wess/wess_current/2012wess.pdf (accessed 13 June 2017).

United Nations (2015), *Addis Ababa Action Agenda of the Third International Conference of Financing for Development*, UN General Assembly Resolution A/RES/69/313, New York: United Nations (27 July 2015), http://www.un.org/ga/search/view_doc.asp?symbol=A/RES/69/313 (accessed 13 June 2017).

Vos, Rob (2015), 'Thought for food: strengthening global governance for food security', in José Antonio Alonso and José Antonio Ocampo (eds), *Global Governance and Rules for the Post-2015 Era*, London: Bloomsbury Academic, pp. 249–282.

Vos, Rob and Manuel F. Montes (eds) (2013a), *Retooling Global Development and Governance*, London: Bloomsbury Academic.

Vos, Rob and Manuel F. Montes (2013b), 'Rethinking global development', in Rob Vos and Manuel F. Montes (eds), *Retooling Global Development and Governance*, London: Bloomsbury Academic, pp. 1–18.

5. Global inequality and global poverty since the Cold War: how robust is the optimistic narrative?

Peter Edward and Andy Sumner[1]

INTRODUCTION

What has happened to global inequality and global poverty since the 'end of history', meaning the end of Cold War? Based on how the headlines of reports from international agencies are reproduced and re-presented in the media, a dominant narrative can be identified as percolating into received wisdom on development policy discourse. This is an optimist's narrative which can be summed up as suggesting that global inequality and global poverty have fallen substantially since the end of the Cold War in the late 1980s. Central to this narrative is the argument that the globalized spread of prosperity in the post-Cold War era has led to rapidly falling poverty, an evolution towards a more equal world and the emergence of a new global middle class. In this chapter it is argued that this narrative on the contemporary era of globalization is considerably more methodologically fragile than it at first seems. This is significant because this dominant and optimistic narrative suggests that falling global poverty and inequality, and the rise of a global middle secure from poverty and willing and able to consume more, are a direct consequence of liberal market-oriented policies and therefore that governments need primarily to focus on economic growth and integration into the global economy and not be too much concerned with redistribution. The purpose of this chapter is to test how robust that narrative is. Of course in reality, many in international agencies have taken a more nuanced view of progress. We would thus note at the very outset that our characterization of the dominant narrative is stylized and should not be taken as absolute. We note that many others, including authors of numerous international reports such as the annual MDG monitoring reports, have recognized both that China explains much of the global progress on poverty and that the distribution of the benefits of global growth has been very uneven both between and within countries. Of course, notwithstanding this unequal distribution, any progress in raising the consumption of the poorest is to be welcomed, however modest it may be. But, there is a danger that developing a narrative predominantly around what is happening to the poorest of the poor in global society risks marginalizing, and even losing sight of, what may be a much less optimistic story if one considers what is happening when one looks at the global distribution in its entirety, and particularly among those who while not the very poorest are still very poor. The new SDG agenda also motivates such concerns by placing issues of inequality much more centrally on the global agenda.

In this chapter we consider the robustness of the dominant narrative by presenting new, alternative estimates of the evolution of global inequality and global poverty. By exploring who have been the relative winners and losers from global growth since the end of the Cold War, we argue that global inequality and global poverty have changed rather less than the dominant narrative would suggest. The impression, that because global inequality is falling it is not necessary to be unduly concerned about redistribution, is misleading. This is because most of the global fall is due solely to the impact of the rise in average per-capita consumption in China on global between-country inequality. Beyond this effect, remarkably little improvement has been made to global inequality despite global consumption increasing by over 85 per cent (in PPP terms)[2] from 1990 to 2012. One implication of this is that, notwithstanding, there has been a substantial (1.1 billion) rise in the number of people living at consumption levels where they might be considered to form a global 'middle' not at risk of sliding back into poverty. The largest rise (1.6 billion people) has occurred in the group of people who whilst not below the extreme poverty line are nevertheless either very poor or still precariously at risk of sliding back into poverty.

The chapter is structured as follows: The next two sections discuss respectively, trends in global inequality and global poverty since the Cold War. The final section concludes.

METHODOLOGY

This chapter makes use of a custom-built model of growth, inequality and poverty. Henceforth this model is referred to as the GrIP ('Gr'owth, 'I'nequality and 'P'overty) model (version 2.0, 2015). For an earlier version of the model (GrIP model v1.0) see Edward and Sumner (2014). The GrIP model includes extensive functionality to test the sensitivity of results to different datasets and different assumptions about how to handle the data. The descriptions provided in this chapter relate only to the model as configured for the analysis presented in this chapter and should not be assumed to apply to the way the model is configured in other published analyses based on the GrIP model. For this chapter we have configured GrIP to align with the overall approach used by the World Bank when producing poverty estimates through PovcalNet. This means that our approach here is to combine survey distributions with survey (rather than national account) means and to rely wherever possible on data in Povcal in preference to other sources, on the basis that data in Povcal has already been selected for reliability and robustness through scrutiny of available competing survey datasets. This does not mean that GrIP replicates Povcal calculations because there are a number of additional adjustments in GrIP, rather that they are included to develop a truly global distribution that can allow reasonable comparison across time periods. Principal among these are: the use of other sources and methods to add in estimates for countries where data is not available in Povcal; the way that underlying survey data is interpolated between surveys; and the use of changes in national account data to inform scaling of survey means (mean per capita consumption) between surveys. We would refer the reading to earlier discussions (such as Edward and Sumner, 2014) where much more detail can be found. In this chapter we also introduce two new additional measures namely the adjustment of income-based surveys to align more consistently with consumption-based surveys, and an adjustment to estimate the possible impact of top income earners who are often missed from surveys. These further issues are discussed in depth in Edward and Sumner (2015, pp. 8–19).

The core approach in the GrIP model is to take for each country the distribution (quintile and decile) data and, by combining this with data on national population and on the mean consumption per capita in internationally comparable PPP \$, develop for each country an estimate of how many people live at any specific consumption (\$-a-day) level. Having identified for each country the number of people living at each consumption level, the GrIP model then aggregates these to build a global distribution of how many people live, and how much those people consume, at every consumption level from the poorest to the richest in the world and a wide variety of sub-global aggregations are also readily produced. These aggregations are then interrogated to investigate issues such as poverty levels, trends in inequality and who are the absolute or relative winners and losers from global growth.

The data sources for the GrIP v2.0 are the World Bank's PovcalNet, World Development Indicators, UNU WIDER's WIID3b and UNPD World Population Prospects. Throughout this chapter we use the new

PPP rates (for 2011). While we acknowledge that significant uncertainties remain concerning this data (for a discussion of these issues see Edward and Sumner, 2015), nevertheless we use them because we recognize that they are generally thought to be the best available data and superior to previous PPP data (Deaton and Aten, 2014).

GLOBAL INEQUALITY

To illustrate what is happening with global consumption inequality we provide here both Gini and Theil index estimates for the period from 1990 to 2012. In each case, we calculate the inequality between individuals (as per Milanovic, 2012), both with and without the top incomes adjustment described above. We also calculate separately inequality between countries and inequality within countries (population-weighted in both cases). The Gini index is the more widely used measure of inequality largely because of its close and relatively intuitive association with the Lorenz curve; however it is not readily decomposable (that is, there is an interaction term between the within-country and between-country effects so that two estimates are not fully independent of each other).[3] The less commonly used Theil index is fully decomposable and so may be more relevant when comparing within-country and between-country effects. Furthermore, whereas the Gini index is more sensitive to changes in the middle of the distribution the Theil index is more sensitive to changes at the extremes (see for full discussion, Cowell, 2000).

Figure 5.1 shows the global Gini indices. In view of the widely recognized dominance of China in the changing global growth, inequality and poverty situation, Figure 5.2 shows the Gini indices for the world excluding China. Figures 5.3 and 5.4 present the relevant Theil indices.

Between 1990 and 2000, global consumption inequality between individuals hardly changed, but from 2000 to 2012 it did start to fall. The effect is most pronounced in the Theil indices where inequality between individuals was 77 per cent of its 2000 value. These falls are, however, solely due to changes in between-country inequality. Within-country inequality stayed effectively the same in 2012 as it was in 2000,[4] and perhaps even slightly higher than in 1990, whilst the between-country Theil index fell to 67 per cent of its 2000 value. As a result, and based on the Theil indices, whereas in 1990 between-country inequality accounted for 64 per cent of global inequality, by 2012 this figure had fallen to 55 per cent.

The dominance of China here is clearly illustrated. Inequality between individuals has fallen since 2000 across the rest of the world but the effect is

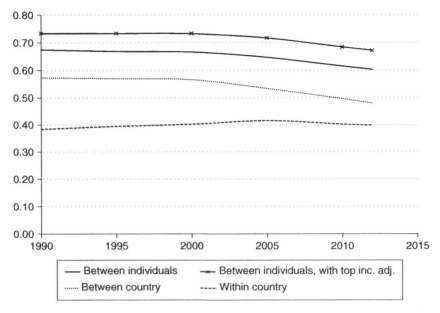

Source: GrIP v2.0.

Figure 5.1   Global Gini coefficient (with and without top income adjustment), 1990–2012

more modest. In 2012 the between-individuals Theil, excluding China, was 86 per cent of its 2000 value. However, rising between-country inequality (excluding China) from 1990 to 2000 meant that this was only slightly lower than (93 per cent of) 1990 values. Again, most of the fall since 2000 was due to changes in between-country inequality. Within-country inequality was little changed in 2012 being just slightly lower (94 per cent) than it was in 2000. So, while in 1990 between-country inequality accounted for 60 per cent of global inequality, when China is excluded, by 2012 this share had probably fallen, but only very slightly to 58 per cent.

GLOBAL POVERTY

It was much heralded in the run up to the 2015 end-date for the Millennium Development Goals that substantial progress had been made in reducing global extreme poverty. The GrIP ('Gr'owth, 'I'nequality and 'P'overty model version 2.0) analysis confirms that this is indeed the case with

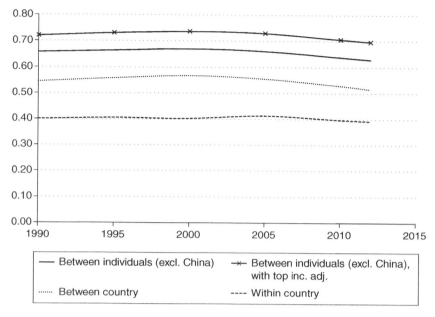

Source: GrIP v2.0.

Figure 5.2 *Global Gini coefficient excluding China (with and without top income adjustment), 1990–2012*

headcounts below the new $1.90-a-day extreme poverty line falling by more than half, from 1.8 billion in 1990 to 860 million in 2012. Yet again though the rapid rise of China has been a dominant effect. In the rest of the world extreme poverty fell by just 28 per cent, from 1.1 billion to 790 million, meaning that over 90 per cent of global extreme poverty is now outside China.

Recalling that the $1.90 poverty line is measured in Purchasing Power Parity dollars, it is worth observing that this represents a level of consumption that most people would consider to be closer to destitution than a reasonable subsistence consumption level. For most people living at this level the difference between living just 10 cents below or 10 cents above this level could hardly be considered to represent a substantively different quality of life. Nevertheless it is by crossing this threshold that people are no longer deemed to be in extreme poverty.

Figure 5.5 demonstrates just how sensitive global poverty headcounts are to the choice of poverty line. The $1.90 a day line is set at a level

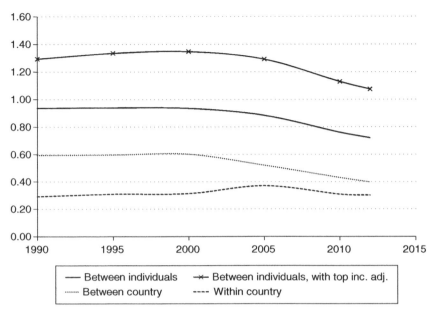

Source: GrIP v2.0.

Figure 5.3   Global Theil coefficient (with and without top income adjustment), 1990–2012

where the greatest density of the world's population live. In this region a difference of just 10 cents in the poverty line can add or subtract almost 100 million people to global poverty headcounts. With poverty lines in this region, very modest changes in the poverty line, or in the survey and consumption data on which analyses of poverty headcounts are built, can make very substantial differences to calculated poverty headcounts. It is only when poverty lines increase to around $5 that this sensitivity to measurement and assumption differences starts to reduce significantly.

This is not merely an intriguing statistical issue. The poverty line one adopts makes a substantial difference not only to the level and trend of global poverty observed but also influences policy makers' and activists' understanding of both where the world's 'deserving' poor actually live and the scale of the challenge (in terms of the value of the poverty gap) of ending poverty.[5]

What then would be a reasonable global poverty line? The 'official' global poverty line has recently been rebased to $1.90 in 2011 PPP from $1.25 in 2005 PPP (Ferreira et al., 2015; Jolliffe and Prydz, 2015). While the

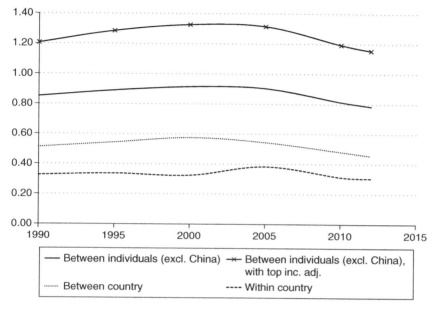

Source: GrIP v2.0.

Figure 5.4 Global Theil coefficient excluding China (with and without top income adjustment), 1990–2012

logic of this is open to contention, as in previous adjustments (see Lahoti and Reddy, 2015 and the historic, Ravallion, 2002, 2008; Reddy and Pogge, 2002, 2005), the new line does have one underlying rationale in that it is the median of the national poverty lines in the world's low income countries (rather than merely the 15 countries that were used to estimate the earlier $1.25 line). There is though still an arbitrary element here, because the group of LICs is still arbitrary to some extent although not totally without logic (see Sumner, 2016 for discussion). Jolliffe and Prydz (2016) provide an interesting discussion of the critiques of the international poverty line and propose a new dataset of estimates for national poverty lines in 2011 PPP by inferring national poverty lines from the poverty rate to estimate national poverty lines. They note (p. 4) that the average poverty line produced from the set of 15 national poverty lines of the poorest countries is very sensitive to quality of inflation data. Mali, for example, requires 22 years of CPI data to estimate its poverty line in 2011 and in three of the 15 countries (Ghana, Malawi and Tajikistan), the CPI data was thought to be so questionable that household survey data was used to construct a temporal deflator. If CPI in World Development Indicators had been used for those three countries it would have added 20 cents to the international poverty line and 200 million poor to global poverty counts.

An alternative to the $1.90 poverty line would be a set of lines (as Jolliffe and Prydz, 2016 propose). Candidates for higher lines would be $2.50, $5 and $10. The first of these, $2.50 is approximately 50 per cent of global median consumption in 2012 and generates a comparable headcount to estimates of multidimensional poverty (1.6 billion in 2010, see Alkire et al., 2014), although we note that the multidimensional poor and the monetary poor are not necessarily the same 1.6 billion people. Alkire et al. (2014) review numerous studies and argue that the monetary poor and the multidimensional poor are not synonymous. A further limitation of the $2.50 line is that it is still in the region where poverty headcounts show maximum sensitivity to assumptions and measurement errors (cf. Figure 5.5). A $2.50 line is an approximation of the average poverty lines of all developing countries (see discussion in Hoy and Sumner, 2016). The median poverty line of *all* developing countries in the Jolliffe and Prydz (2016) dataset is $2.79 and population weighted mean is $2.46. Raising the $1.90 line to $2.50 or even $2.80 would add 600 million to 900 million people. In short it could double the global poverty headcount.

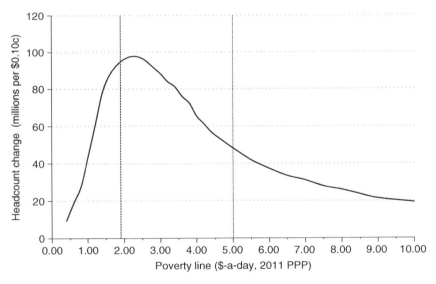

Source: GrIP v2.0.

Figure 5.5   Sensitivity of global poverty headcount, 2012, $0–$10 per day

Another possibility would be to take a poverty line of $5 on the basis that it is both the average value of national poverty lines in all countries (see Jolliffe and Prydz, 2016) and close to global median consumption in 2012 (that is, the level below which the poorer half of the world's population live). This would move the poverty line to a region much less sensitive to assumptions and measurement errors thereby making it a more reliable indicator of real progress in global well-being. Both this line and the $2.5 line also open the possibility that rather than measuring poverty in terms of headcounts it might be better to measure changes in median consumption because these are more 'distribution aware' indicators of development progress (see for discussion, Birdsall and Meyer, 2014).

A further possibility might be the substantially higher line of $10-a-day that is associated with a permanent escape from poverty in longitudinal studies of Brazil, Mexico and Chile (López-Calva and Ortiz-Juarez, 2014) and Indonesia (Sumner, Yusuf and Suara, 2014). The $10 poverty line is a proposal for a 'security from poverty' consumption line developed and used by López-Calva and Ortiz-Juarez (2014) based on the 10 per cent probability of falling back below national poverty lines (which are $4–$5/ day in 2005 PPP) in the near future in Mexico, Brazil and Chile.[6] To put some additional context on this, just 11 per cent of OECD population and 8 per cent of G7 population live below this $10 a day level.

Global poverty levels at each of these four poverty lines ($1.90, $2.50, $5 and $10) are presented as percentages of global population in Figures 5.6 and 5.7 (with and without China respectively) and as absolute numbers (millions) in Figures 5.8 and 5.9.

How robust and significant one considers the fall in global poverty to be depends on what line one uses, whether it includes China or not, and whether one considers proportion of population or total number of poor people. Figures 5.6 and 5.7 show that the falls in poverty tend to be more substantial as the poverty line falls. For example, at $10 per day the fall in global poverty is just 10 per cent over the period, falling from about 80 per cent of the world's population to about 70 per cent. If one excludes China, $10 poverty is about the same proportion of population in 2012 as it was in 1990. However, at $1.90 or $2.50 the fall is more substantial, respectively from 35 per cent and 45 per cent of world population in 1990 to just over 10 and 20 per cent in 2012. Again, without China the falls are much less impressive.

When one considers actual absolute numbers of people by each line, the record on poverty reduction further weakens drastically. Figures 5.8 and 5.9 show that even including China, $10 poverty has risen from 4 billion people to close to 5 billion people while $5 poverty is about the same as it was in 1990 (3.4 billion in 1990, 3.2 billion in 2012). Poverty at the two lowest lines has fallen more convincingly if one includes China. However,

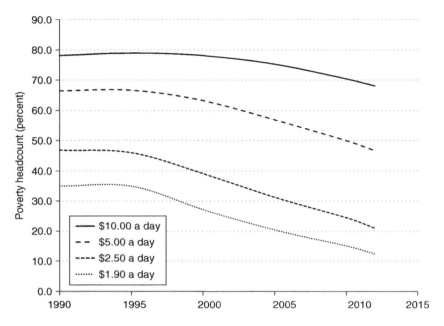

Source: GrIP v2.0.

Figure 5.6   Global poverty headcount (% of population), 1990–2012

once again the exclusion of China reveals patterns counter to the dominant narrative. For example, at the new global poverty line of $1.90 poverty has fallen from just over 1 billion people to just under one billion but at a slightly higher line which is the median for all developing countries, $2.5 per day poverty only fell below 1990 levels in 2010 and is now only slightly below those levels.

If one were to consider that the definition of being 'middle class' is to be sufficiently well off that you are secure from the risk of sliding into poverty (and assume that that is achieved at consumption levels above $10 a day) then since 1990 an additional 1.1 billion people have been added to this group, so there certainly has been a significant increase in the size of the global 'middle class'. However, in the same time the number living above the extreme ($1.9) poverty line but below the ($10) secure-from-poverty line has increased by 1.6 billion. This group would include many people one might consider to still be very poor (living only a little above the extreme poverty line) plus those living precariously at risk of sliding back into poverty. Arguably, this represents a significant challenge to the dominant narrative.

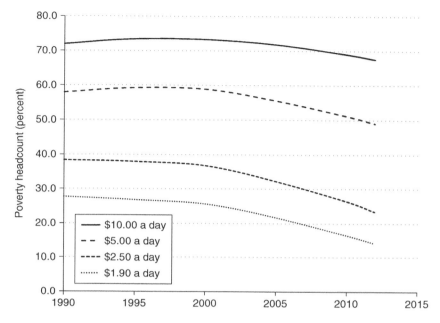

Source: GrIP v2.0.

Figure 5.7   *Global poverty headcount (% of population) excluding China, 1990–2012*

The total poverty gap gives a consistent picture to the above discussion (see Figures 5.10 and 5.11). The global poverty gap at $10 rose over the last two decades but is now back to the point it was in 1990. At $5 per day the total poverty gap fell by approximately a third in value. The fall in the value of the total poverty gap at the lower lines is more substantial: at $1.90 and $2.50 per day the total poverty gap fell in 2012 respectively to 38 per cent and 47 per cent of its value in 1990 ($424bn to $164bn at $1.90 and $888bn to $417bn at $2.50). However, when China is excluded the $10 poverty gap has risen from $7150bn in 1990 to $8383bn in 2012. And the total poverty gap excluding China at the $5 poverty line is about the same level as 1990 but the total poverty gap excluding China at $1.90 and $2.50 has fallen from $258bn to $155bn and from $549bn to $385bn respectively.

By focusing rather narrowly on the global success at reducing poverty against the very low extreme poverty line and on the success at lifting many people into a condition where they are newly secure from poverty, the dominant narrative rather obscures that in terms of absolute numbers the

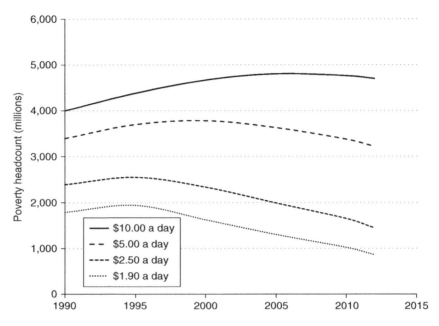

Source: GrIP v2.0.

Figure 5.8   Global poverty headcount (millions), 1990–2012

biggest change globally has been the increase in the size of the global poor and 'precariat' living between $1.90 and $10 a day.[7]

We should make clear that we are not dismissive of the progress that evidently has been made in terms of lowering poverty at the extreme, as well as at the $2.50 poverty lines (including when excluding China). Rather we are noting that the decline is of course welcome but really rather modest. The real contention is of course whether anyone can live on $1.90 and if that does provide the capacity to purchase minimum food requirements. Because the global population is very dense at around that level, the fact that the use of official inflation data would raise this minimum poverty line only slightly but would add 200 million people to the poor count is in itself sobering. In short, we are not saying the world should not care about the poorest. We are saying the world is not even counting some of the poorest.

In sum, we have argued thus far that changes in global inequality are modest and largely due to between, not within, country effects, and that the between-country changes are so dominated by China's rise that the

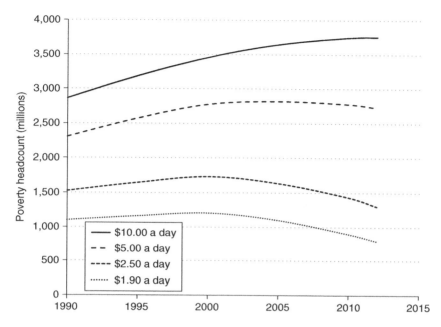

Source: GrIP v2.0.

Figure 5.9 *Global poverty headcount (millions) excluding China, 1990–2012*

fall in global inequality largely evaporates once China is excluded from analysis. We also find that very low poverty lines (such as $1.90 a day) are so hypersensitive to small differences in the data that they create the impression that progress in the global battle against poverty has been more significant than it appears when poverty lines that are both more globally representative and less sensitive to measurement errors (such as $5 a day) are applied. And we suggest that, far from witnessing the simplistic emergence of a new 'middle class', most of the world's burgeoning middle is highly precarious in the sense that they live a considerable distance away from the consumption levels associated with permanent escape from poverty in longitudinal surveys in developing countries.

The Global Distribution Curve

This implies that, rather than focusing on overall economic growth and extreme poverty headcounts, closer attention needs to be paid to the

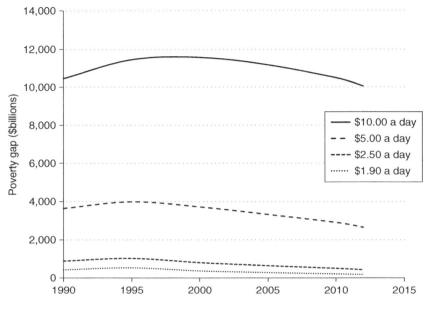

Source: GrIP v2.0.

Figure 5.10   Global poverty gap, 1990–2012 (US$bn, 2011 PPP)

distribution of the benefits of growth. Figures 5.10 to 5.12 present global density curves that illustrate the distribution of population (plotted positively on the y-axis) and consumption (plotted negatively on the y-axis) across the full range of global consumption. Areas beneath curves are standardized relative to the 2012 population and consumption totals, respectively. This means that the change in area (between each curve and the x-axis) between 1990 and 2012 (say) is proportional to the change in the number of people living at any particular consumption level (above the x-axis) or to the change aggregate consumption of the people living at a particular consumption level (below the x-axis). Figure 5.12 presents the figures without the top incomes adjustment. Figure 5.13 includes the top incomes adjustment.

What can be clearly seen is the growth in the global middle, evidenced by the filling out of the concavity in the population curve above $2.5 a day since 1990. This concavity, which was even deeper in the 1980s, led Quah (1996) to describe us as living in a 'twin-peak' world. It remains to be seen, however, whether the current situation represents a permanent end to that twin-peak rich-poor divide or whether it indicates merely a

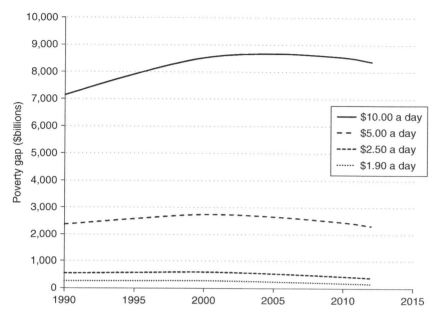

Source: GrIP v2.0.

Figure 5.11 *Global poverty gap, excluding China, 1990–2012 (US$bn,*
2011 PPP)

transition to the emergence of a new divide. For example, the incipient
return of the concavity between $5 and $10 a day when top incomes are
added in might be a precursor of the return of such a divide. It is notable
also that when China is removed (Figure 5.14) the concavity persists still
in 2012, indicating that its current absence at the global level may merely
be evidence of China's progression from the lower under-developed peak
to a higher-developed location rather than an indicator of any more
fundamental changes in the fairness of the global economy.

The curves also clearly illustrate who benefitted most from global consumption growth. Between 1990 and 2012 global consumption increased
by 90 per cent, with most of that growth occurring after 2000; reminding us
that despite the financial crisis of the late 2000s the world is still consuming
a lot more now than it was at the end of the Cold War. Of that growth,
four-fifths went to those who in 2012 were consuming more than $10 a day.
The remaining one-fifth (the figure falls to 15 per cent if top incomes are
included) went to the more than two-thirds of the world's population who
exist precariously on less than $10 a day.

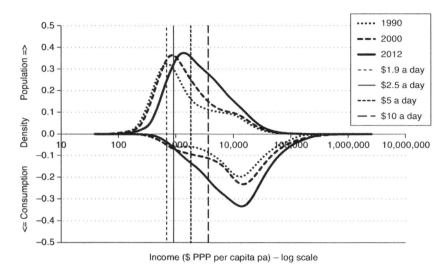

Source: GrIP v2.0.

*Figure 5.12   Global density curves, 1990, 2000 and 2012 without top
income adjustment*

Growth incidence curves provide further insight into the winners and
losers from global growth since 1990. Figure 5.15 shows how people across
the global consumption spectrum (from the poorest to the richest fractiles)
have benefitted in relative terms (that is, percentage change in consumption
from 1990 levels). Again the dominance of China is starkly revealed. With
China included, people living in 2012 on between $2.5 and $10 a day had
typically seen their per capita consumption levels rise, in percentage terms,
by twice the global average or more. However, once China is removed the
picture becomes very different with those living on less than $5 a day seeing
their relative consumption rise much less, albeit nevertheless broadly in line
with the global average (in percentage terms). Typically, most of those on
higher consumption levels have seen their relative consumption rise more
slowly than the global average so that *in relative terms* it is both the global
precariat (those between $1.90 and $10 a day) and most of what might be
called the 'securiat' (those above $10 a day with the possible exclusion of
the very richest fractile) who have seen their consumption rise more slowly
than global averages.

   In this (relative) sense the distribution of global growth since 1990 could
be seen as having been generally pro-poor, even when China is excluded.
However it must be remembered that these relative consumption rises rep-

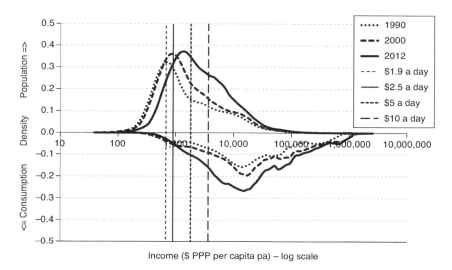

Income ($ PPP per capita pa) – log scale

Source: GrIP v2.0.

Figure 5.13   Global density curves, 1990, 2000 and 2012 with top income adjustment

resent percentage changes on already very low consumption levels. When absolute consumption levels are considered the picture is, of course, very different (Figure 5.16). Here it is the richest 40 per cent who have seen their per capita consumption rise, in $-value, by more than the global average. And if China is removed it is only the richest 10 per cent who have benefitted by more than the global average.

Overall then, analysis of the distribution of the absolute benefits of global growth hardly seems to point to the emergence, within developing economies, of a burgeoning 'middle class'. Certainly, there has been a significant growth (1.1 billion) in the number living secure from sliding back into poverty. There are now 2.2 billion people in this 'global securiat' living above the $10 a day level. The 400 million of them who live in China have benefitted enormously, as have the 700 million who constitute the world's richest decile. But the remaining 1.1 billion of them have seen their consumption grow in absolute terms by less than the global average and in relative terms by much less than (around 50 per cent of) the global average since 1990.

In sum, contrary to the dominant narrative, therefore, far from witnessing a simplistic end to poverty and the rise of a global 'middle class' we may well be witnessing something much more complex. A key dynamic is,

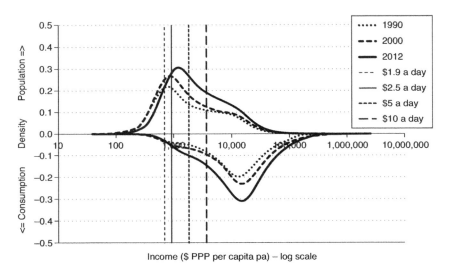

Source: GrIP v2.0.

Figure 5.14   *Global density curves (excluding China), 1990, 2000 and*
                2012 without top income adjustment

unsurprisingly, the rapid transition of China on a trajectory to becoming a
highly developed economy. This 'success story' however can mask the fact
that since 1990 the largest change in headcounts has been in the number
of people globally living either in poverty, albeit not extreme poverty, or
at risk of sliding back into poverty. Almost 80 per cent of people in this
group live outside China but the precarious nature of their existence is
largely absent from the dominant narrative. And at higher consumption
levels, among those secure from poverty, there is evidence that, other than
for the world's top decile and for the 400 million people in China who are
newly above the $10 a day consumption level, the distribution of global
growth since 1990 has seen them benefit by less than global averages in
both absolute and relative terms.

   Overall then, once the 'China effect' is carefully disaggregated from the
analysis, what emerges is a picture of a world in which remarkably little
has changed in terms of global inequality. Meanwhile, much heralded
falls in extreme poverty seem both to overstate the world's success in
addressing global poverty, broadly defined, and to be rather unreliable due
to their sensitivity to measurement and assumption differences. This risks
obscuring the very significant increase in the number of people in the world
who, while above the extreme poverty line, are either still poor or at risk

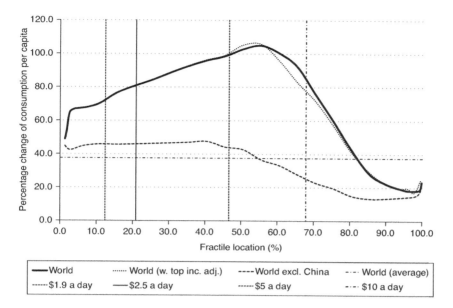

Note: Fractile locations of $-a-day lines are based on world without top income adjustment.

Source: GrIP v2.0.

Figure 5.15   *Growth incidence curve (relative benefits), with and without top incomes adjustment, 1990–2012*

of sliding back into poverty. At higher consumption levels, among those living more securely (the 'global securiat' above $10 a day) around half of them, those in the global top decile and those now living in China on more than $10 a day, have seen their consumption rise, in absolute terms, well above global averages. But for the rest of the 'global securiat', on average they have seen their share of global consumption eroded both in absolute and relative terms. The dominant narrative therefore risks obscuring a far less promising picture, of a burgeoning global middle where well-being and financial security seem precarious or increasingly insecure.

CONCLUSIONS

In conclusion, we can make three observations on how global inequality and global poverty have changed since the end of the Cold War. First, a

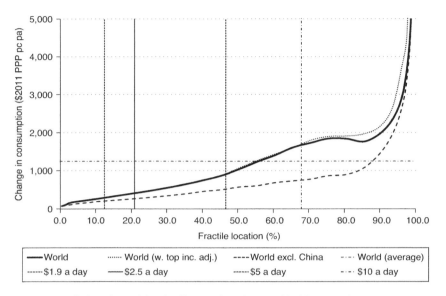

Note: Fractile locations of $-a-day lines are based on world without top income
adjustment.

Source: GrIP v2.0.

Figure 5.16   *Growth incidence curve (absolute benefits), with and without
               top incomes adjustment, 1990–2012*

much heralded fall in global inequality is largely explicable with reference
to the impact of China's rise on between-country inequality. When China
is excluded, changes in aggregate inequality across the world are much
more modest with inequality levels in 2012 being marginally lower than in
1990. Throughout this entire period within-country inequality has, overall,
been remarkably constant – as some countries have become less equal,
others have become more so. In short, in the last 25 years, falls in total
global inequality, and in global between-country inequality are almost all
attributable to rising prosperity in China.

    Second, while it is the case that falls in global poverty look impressive at
$1.90 or $2.50 those falls look less convincing at $5 and $10. And even the
falls at the lower poverty lines start to look unimpressive if one looks at the
rest of the world outside China and considers absolute numbers of people
under each line. In any event, the fact that global poverty counts are so
hypersensitive at the lower poverty lines ought to be reason enough to use
higher lines that are less sensitive to measurement errors and differences

in analysis assumptions. To reiterate we are not dismissing the raising of the consumption of the very poorest. Rather we are noting that progress is rather modest and that the lowest poverty lines actually cut off some of the poorest whose consumption may be just a few cents higher than these extreme levels. We note also that the global poverty line ought to be 20 cents higher if national CPI data were used, or even 60 cents or 90 cents higher if one took the estimated value of the average poverty line of all developing countries. We would thus argue that multiple poverty lines are more useful than fixating excessively on the $1.90, and especially so given that recent reductions in the number of extreme poor arise because a large number of people have merely moved from just below that line to just above it. Whether they are still 'poor' depends on whether one accepts that someone can live on the average poverty line of the world's 15 poorest countries in 2005, with those national poverty lines adjusted by national inflation, minus 20 cents (due to the three countries where CPI data is too poor to use). Higher lines would be better in the sense of generating poverty counts that are less hyper-sensitive to small variations in the value of the line, although only when those poverty lines have the logic of being the average for all countries (a truly global poverty line) or the consumption needed to permanently escape poverty. We are not saying higher poverty lines are better for the sake of it but rather that higher poverty lines that have a conceptual logic would seem to be stronger proxies for global poverty.

Finally, certainly the twin peak world of the 1980s has softened and a new middle has emerged. However, this does not seem to herald the arrival of a global middle class safe from poverty. Global growth has increased the numbers of people living above a consumption line associated with permanent escape from poverty, but the largest increase in numbers has been in the burgeoning precariat who live above the lower poverty lines of $1.90 or $2.50 per day but still a long distance from a consumption line associated with security from falling back in to poverty in the future of $10 per day. And among those at higher consumption levels, other than for the newly rich in China and the world's richest decile, most of these people have seen their financial security eroded.

In sum, we would argue that the narrative that economic growth since the Cold War has led to a new age of falling global inequality and poverty is considerably more fragile than it at first seems. We suggest instead that the dominant narrative, of falling poverty and an emerging 'middle class' largely free from the threat of poverty, disguises both considerable growth in the size of the 'global precariat' living in conditions that most in the developed world would consider to be well below 'middle class', and an erosion of the financial security of a significant proportion of those living at higher consumption levels. Both the exclusion of China and the adoption of less extreme (and less hypersensitive) poverty lines reveal how the way that global poverty and global inequality are measured can distort our understanding of the complex changes in inequality between and within nations at a global level. Recognizing and exposing the impact of these issues gives a rather less optimistic view of the impact of economic growth since the end of the Cold War on global inequality and poverty.

NOTES

1. We would like to thank the anonymous reviewers for comments.
2. The analysis rebases national account data (as used in World Development Indicators, for example) to make it compatible with survey data (as used in World Bank, 2015, for example).
3. Methods to approximately decompose the Gini into additively separable components do exist but it is not a simple procedure and they are not widely used (see Pyatt, 1976; Araar, 2006).
4. This does not mean that there have been no changes in inequality within individual countries, merely that as some countries have become more unequal others have become less so with the result that at the aggregate level little has changed.
5. Edward and Sumner (2015) discuss these matters originally raised in Deaton (2010), in more depth. In short, lower poverty lines 'push' global poverty into sub-Saharan Africa and slightly higher lines 'Asianize' global poverty.
6. The 10 per cent probability line is actually $8.50–$9.70 depending on whether Brazil, Mexico or Chile are used (and comparable estimates for Indonesia are $8.37 for a $4 national poverty line and $13.03 at $5, in 2005 PPP – see Sumner, Yusuf and Suara, 2014). Thus, the mean is $9.27 and if the mean is inflated to 2011 prices it is $10.47.
7. We take the term 'precariat' here from Standing (2011).

REFERENCES

Alkire, S., J. Foster, S. Seth, M. Santos, J. Roche and P. Ballon (2014). 'Multidimensional poverty measurement and analysis: chapter 1: introduction'. Oxford Poverty and Human Development Initiative (OPHI) Working Paper. Oxford: OPHI.

Araar, A. (2006). 'On the decomposition of the Gini coefficient: an exact approach, with illustration using Cameroonian data'. SSRN Electronic Journal. February 2006.

Birdsall, N. and C. Meyer (2014). 'The median is the message: a good enough measure of material well-being and shared development progress'. Centre for Global Development Working Paper 351. Washington, DC: CGD.

Cowell, F. (2000). 'Measurement of inequality'. In A. Atkinson and F. Bourguignon (eds), *Handbook of Income Distribution*, Amsterdam: North Holland, pp. 87–166.

Deaton, A. (2010). 'Price indexes, inequality, and the measurement of world poverty'. *American Economic Review*, **100**(1), 5–34.

Deaton, A. and B. Aten (2014). 'Trying to understand the PPPs in ICP2011: why are the results so different?'. NBER Working Paper. NBER: Massachusetts MA.

Edward, P. and A. Sumner (2014). 'Estimating the scale and geography of global poverty now and in the future: how much difference do method and assumptions make?'. *World Development*, **58**, 67–82.

Edward, P. and A. Sumner (2015). 'New estimates of global poverty and inequality: how much difference do price data really make?'. Centre for Global Development (CGD) Working Paper. Washington, DC: CGD.

Ferreira, F., S. Chen, A.L. Dabalen et al. (2015). 'A global count of the extreme poor in 2012: data issues, methodology, and initial results'. World Bank Working Paper. Washington, DC: World Bank.

Hoy, C. and A. Sumner (2016). 'Gasoline, guns and giveaways: is there new capacity for redistribution?'. CGD Working Paper. Washington, DC: CGD.

Jolliffe, D. and E. Prydz (2015). 'Global poverty goals and prices: how purchasing power parity matters'. World Bank Policy Research Working Paper. Washington, DC: World Bank.

Jolliffe, D. and E. Prydz (2016). 'Estimating international poverty lines from comparable national thresholds'. World Bank Policy Research Working Paper 7606. Washington, DC: World Bank.

Lahoti, R. and S. Reddy (2015). '$1.90: what does it say?'. Paper downloaded 1 July 2016 at: reddytoread.files.wordpress.com/2015/10/wbpovblogoct6final1.pdf.

López-Calva, L.F. and E. Ortiz-Juarez (2014). 'A vulnerability approach to the definition of the middle class'. *The Journal of Economic Inequality*, **12**(1), 23–47.

Milanovic, B. (2012). 'Global income inequality by the numbers: in history and now – an overview'. World Bank Policy Research Working Paper. Washington, DC: World Bank.

Pyatt, G. (1976). 'On the interpretation and disaggregation of Gini coefficient'. *The Economic Journal*, **86**(342), 243–255.

Quah, D. (1996). 'Twin peaks: growth and convergence in models of distribution dynamics'. *The Economic Journal*, **106**(437), 1045–1055.

Ravallion, M. (2002). 'How not to count the poor? A reply to Reddy and Pogge'. Mimeo. World Bank.

Ravallion, M. (2008). 'How not to count the poor? A reply to Reddy and Pogge'. In Sudhir Anand, Paul Segal and Joseph Stiglitz (eds), *Debates on the Measurement of Poverty*. Oxford: Oxford University Press, pp. 937–980.

Reddy, S. and T. Pogge (2002). 'How not to count the poor (version 3.0)'. Mimeo. Barnard College, New York.

Reddy, S. and T. Pogge (2005). 'How not to count the poor. (version 6.2)'. Mimeo. Barnard College, New York.

Standing, G. (2011). *The Precariat*. London and New York: Bloomsbury Academic.

Sumner, A. (2016). 'The world's two new middles'. UNU WIDER Working Paper. UNU-WIDER, Helsinki.

Sumner, A., A. Yusuf and Y. Suara (2014). 'The prospects of the poor: a set of poverty measures based on the probability of remaining poor (or not) in Indonesia'. Working Papers in Economics and Development Studies (WoPEDS). Bandung: Department of Economics, Padjadjaran University, Indonesia.

World Bank (2015). PovcalNet. Washington DC: World Bank.

6. Is Latin America's recent inequality decline permanent or temporary?

Giovanni Andrea Cornia[1]

ORIGINS OF THE LATIN AMERICAN INCOME INEQUALITY

Engerman and Sokoloff (2005) have analyzed the colonial origins of the high income inequality that has afflicted Latin America for centuries. In their view, the high land, assets, human capital and power concentration inherited from the colonial era led to the development of institutions that perpetuated well after the Second World War the privileges of a small agrarian and commercial oligarchy. In principle, such path-dependent inequality should have been eroded by the withering away of the share of agriculture in GDP. Yet, high inequality persisted due to imperfect financial markets that lent only to wealthy households, the mapping of the initial assets inequality into a low and unequally distributed human capital accumulation, and the late democratization of most of the region. For Prados de la Escosura (2005) the colonial inequality was exacerbated by the boom in commodity exports and prices that took place during the globalization of 1870–1914. Indeed, better export prices raised land rents and the land rental/wage ratio, to the benefit of large landowners. This trend was interrupted during the inter-war years but resurfaced after the Second World War (Prados de la Escosura, 2005).

THE RISE OF INCOME INEQUALITY DURING THE 1980s AND 1990s

Since the mid-late 1970s, most Latin American countries abandoned the Import Substituting Industrialization paradigm followed during the first three decades after the Second World War and adopted liberal policies in the fields of macroeconomic stabilization, domestic liberalization, and privatization. These measures paved the way to the liberalization of international trade, FDI and portfolio flows. The supporters of such an approach claimed that such policies would have created the conditions for rapid growth and that, in line with the predictions of the Stolper-Samuelson corollary of the Hercksher-Ohlin theorem, trade and capital account liberalization would have raised investments and reduced domestic inequality in nations endowed with an abundant supply of unskilled labor.

Yet, during the turbulent 1980s, inequality fell only in Colombia, Costa Rica, Honduras and Peru (Altimir, 1996). Despite the return to moderate growth and extensive internal and external liberalization, during the 1990s income concentration worsened further in two-thirds of the countries of the region, albeit at a slower pace than in the 1980s (Gasparini et al., 2009; Figure 6.1). As a result, the average regional Gini index rose by 2.2 points from the early 1980s to 1990, by another 1.7 points between 1990 and 2000, and 1.2 points during the recession of 2001–2002, that is 5.1 points for the two neo-liberal decades taken together. A key feature of this trend was a decline of the labor share in total income and a parallel rise in the capital share (Sainz and Calcagno, 1992). Five structural changes explained this shift. First, with the economic stagnation of the 1980s, the regional unem-

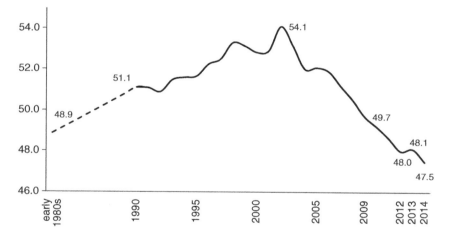

Note: The trend for 1990–2006 covers 18 countries. That for 2006–2014 covers 15 countries, as it excludes Venezuela and Guatemala and Nicaragua for which there are only few data for this period. Over these years in Guatemala and Nicaragua the drop was respectively 6.4 and 4.1 Gini points. If interpolated data for these two countries were included, the Gini decline over 2006–2014 would be slightly more pronounced.

Source: Author's elaboration on Cornia (2014) and SEDLAC data (http://sedlac.econo.unlp.edu.ar/esp/estadisticas.php, accessed 10 June 2016).

Figure 6.1   Regional Gini index of the distribution of household income per capita, early 2000s–2014

ployment rate rose sharply. Second, there was a substantial expansion of the low-wage informal sector. Third, formal sector wages rose more slowly than GDP per capita while the minimum/average wage ratio fell, and wage differentials by skill level widened (Sainz and Calcagno, 1992).

What were the underlying causes of the inequality increase of the 1980s and 1990s? The literature focuses on two complementary explanations: the skill-biased technical change (SBTC) and the impact of neoliberal policies. The SBTC was the result of the liberalization of imports of capital- and skill-intensive investment goods that raised the demand for skilled workers capable of operating imported equipment. At the same time, the supply of skilled workers rose slowly because of limited public spending on education and the inability of most households to finance the secondary education of their children. As a result, the relative wage of skilled workers rose in the 1990s (Cornia, 2014) though it is not obvious that this was due solely to the SBTC. Indeed, institutional changes, such as the abandonment of collective bargaining and falling real minimum wages, contributed to the rise of the skill premium. As for the second explanation, there is consistent evidence that the neo-liberal policies affected income inequality. In a study covering the years 1980–1998, Behrman, Birdsall and Székely (2000) found that such policies caused an overshooting of inequality that was particularly marked on occasion of domestic financial reforms, capital account liberalization and tax reforms. Similar results were found by Taylor (2004), Koujianou-Goldberg and Pavcnik (2007), and Cornia (2004). Though with different emphasis, these studies conclude that trade and financial liberalization generated adverse growth and distributive effects due to the intensified competition by low-cost Asian exporters and the limited inter-sectoral mobility of production factors that scarcely moved from the declining import-competing sector to new sectors. The informalization of employment caused by the appreciation of the real exchange rate following the liberalization of the capital account, the regressive effects of devastating financial crises[2] and regressive tax reforms were also key in pushing inequality upward (Figure 6.1).

THE INEQUALITY DECLINE OF 2002–2012

Things changed significantly in the 2000s. Since the end of the Argentinean crisis of 2001–2002, the region enhanced its growth performance, improved macroeconomic stability and did not experience any financial crisis. The most striking gain was a 6.1 points decline of the Gini index (Figure 6.1) over 2002–2012, that more than offset in only ten years the 5.1 Gini increase recorded during the two prior decades. Such decline was recorded under various types of center-left regimes.[3] The fastest decline (a drop of 0.54 points for each year in power) was recorded by the social-democratic regimes, followed by the radical left (0.42), centrist (0.20) and center-right regimes (0.08). It is important to underscore that the Latin America inequality decline stands out, as during the same period most OECD and Asian countries and the mining economies of sub-Saharan Africa experienced widespread inequality rises (Cornia and Martorano, 2012).

Drivers of the Recent Inequality Decline

What explains the inequality decline observed between 2002 and 2012? A micro-econometric decomposition by income source of the drop of the Gini index over 2002–2009/10 for Chile, Ecuador, El Salvador, Honduras, Mexico and Uruguay (Cornia, 2014) shows that such fall was due (in order of importance) to a drop of the skill premium, an increase in social transfers, and lower concentration of capital incomes. In rural economies such as Honduras, a fall in the urban–rural wage gap, and in countries of emigration (such as El Salvador and Mexico) increasingly better distributed migrant remittances contributed to reducing inequality. In addition, the faster relative decline of the fertility rate among the poor over 2002–2012 generated a moderately equalizing effect (Baradacco, Gasparini, and Marchionni, 2016).

The key research question concerns, however, the identification of the underlying causes of the changes in income shares and concentration coefficients of the above sources of income. Were these changes due to the favorable global economic conditions that lasted until 2008, or were they due to the adoption of new policies? The relevance of these two explanations is discussed hereafter.

Impact of global economic conditions
Some observers have argued that the inequality decline of 2002–2008 was due to 'luck', that is, an improvement in global economic conditions. For sure, the rise of the world prices of commodities exported by the region (Figure 6.2), the enhancement of its international terms of trade, and an increase in migrant remittances produced beneficial effects on growth. Furthermore, between 2002 and 2008 and again in 2010 the region experienced portfolio inflows amounting to 2.4 percent of the region's GDP (Cornia, 2014). Yet, given the high concentration of assets in the export sector, the polarized access to credit prevailing in the region, and the high land-, capital- and skill-intensity of production in the export sector, the partial equilibrium effect of the improvements in external conditions generated, *ceteris paribus*, an un-equalizing effect. Yet, these

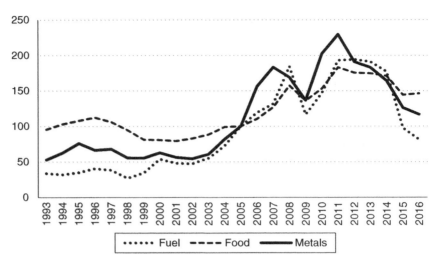

Source: IMF, World Economic Outlook database (accessed in March 2017).

*Figure 6.2   Trend in the indexes of commodity prices (2005=100),
            1993–2016*

improvements also generated a positive income effect, contributed to the growth of tax revenue and a broadening of the fiscal space. They also relaxed the balance of payments constraint to growth and so facilitated the imports of capital goods, easing in this way an acceleration of GDP growth. Yet, faster growth per se is no guarantee of falling inequality, as shown by Latin America in the nineteenth century and the recent growth spurt of China and India, where very fast GDP growth went hand in hand with an equally rapid rise of income polarization. The point made here is that the beneficial effects of better external conditions on inequality would not have materialized without the introduction of the policy changes discussed below.

Indeed, the relation between inequality and external conditions is ambiguous and depends on the existence of appropriate taxation, public expenditure, redistributive and macroeconomic policies. For instance, until 2002 in all three groups of countries considered (oil/mineral exporters, agricultural exporters and 'other countries' that are mostly dependent on remittances), the Gini coefficient and the international terms of trade were not related to each other. Indeed, except for the 1980s, for the Latin American countries taken together and for the agricultural exporters, inequality rose between 1980 and 2002 while the terms of trade stagnated or slightly improved. It is only since 2002 that inequality fell in parallel with gains in terms of trade, as most Latin American governments introduced policies to redistribute the benefits generated by terms of trade gains.

Likewise, Figure 6.4 shows that until 2002 an increase in the volume of exports correlated positively with the Gini coefficient, while such relation became negative for all groups of countries since 2002. Obviously, the inequality decline over 2002–2012 was influenced also from other factors discussed below, but Figures 6.3 and 6.4 suggest that there was a clear break in the 'external conditions – inequality relation' after 2002 (see next sub-section).

To validate these conclusions, we tested econometrically the relation between the Gini coefficient and the international terms of trade and export volumes on the basis of a panel of the 18 Latin American countries over the years 1980–2013. We do not include in the regression – as done in multivariate analyses (see for instance Cornia, 2014) – all the determinants of inequality, as this test aims only at assessing the bivariate relation between the Gini coefficient and its two determinants mentioned above.[4] Given the panel structure of our dataset, the test was conducted with a fixed effect estimator that takes the form

$$Gini_{i,t} = \beta_0 + \beta_1 T.O.T_{i,t} + \beta_2 Export\ Volume_{i,t} + \alpha_i + \epsilon_{i,t} \qquad (6.1)$$

where the term a_i is the country fixed effect, $e_{i,t}$ the random error and b_1 and b_2 parameters to be estimated. A bold parameter in Table 6.1 indicates that an increase in the international terms of trade and export volume reduced income inequality, while an italic parameter suggests it raised it. The non-bold/non-italics parameters are not significantly different from zero. We estimate the above model for the 1980–2002 years of Washington Consensus policies, the years 2003–2008 of center-left policies and stable global conditions, and for 2009–2013. The latter period is highly heterogeneous as in 2009 exports, terms of trade and growth collapsed, while they rebounded in 2010 and 2011, to stagnate again since 2012–2013 (Figures 6.3 and 6.4). During this period growth slowed down and in 2013 there was a slight inequality uptick.

The parameters estimates in the last column are less robust due to the smaller number of observations and – especially – the instability of terms of trade and export volumes during this period. They should therefore be interpreted with caution, and be recomputed when additional yearly data become available. Overall, the results of Table 6.1 suggest a break in the statistical association between international economic conditions and income inequality, as discussed above. Such statistical association should not be understood as causation, as the trend in the Gini index depends also

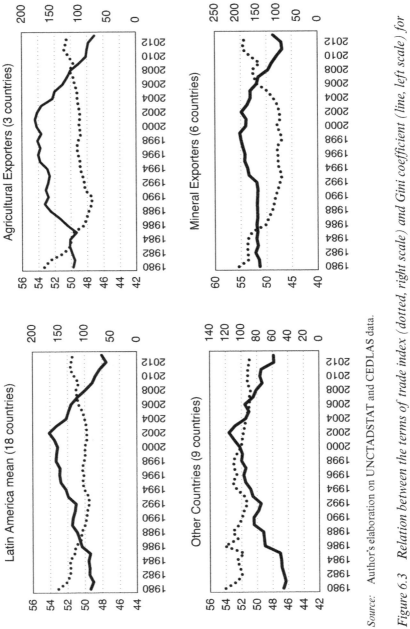

Source: Author's elaboration on UNCTADSTAT and CEDLAS data.

Figure 6.3   Relation between the terms of trade index (dotted, right scale) and Gini coefficient (line, left scale) for Latin America as a whole and three country subgroups, 1980–2012

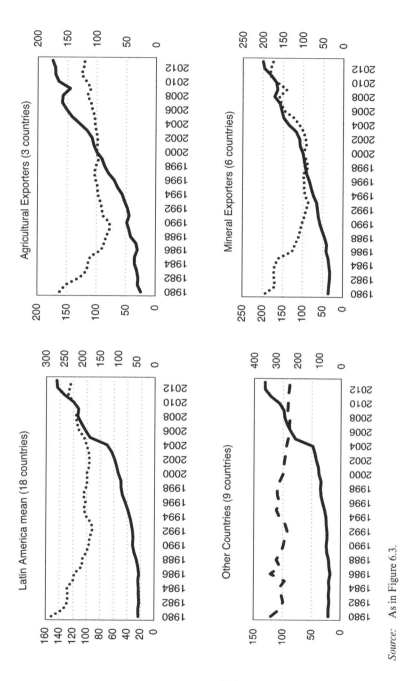

Figure 6.4 Relation between the export volume index (dotted, right scale) and Gini coefficient (line, left scale) for Latin America as a whole and three country subgroups, 1980–2012

Source: As in Figure 6.3.

x

105

Table 6.1   Regression of international terms of trade and export volumes on the Gini coefficient, 1980–2013

		1980–2002	2003–2008	2009–2013
Mineral	Terms of Trade	0.0048	−0.0319***	−0.0228*
exporters	Export Volume	*0.0428****	−0.0341***	−0.0130
(6)	n. of observations	131	36	29
	R-squared	0.17	0.59	0.32
Agricultural	Terms of Trade	0.0055	−0.0936**	−0.0124
exporters	Export Volume	*0.0531****	−0.0498***	−0.0324
(3)	N. of observations	69	18	14
	R-squared	0.31	0.80	0.24
Other	Terms of Trade	−0.0257***	0.0787	0.0604
countries (9)	Export Volume	*0.0235****	−0.0023	−0.0020
	N. of observations	163	54	39
	R-squared	0.13	0.11	0.03
All countries	Terms of Trade	−0.0022	−0.0434***	−0.0253*
(18)	Export Volume	*0.0353****	−0.0043***	−0.0040
	N. of observations	363	108	82
	R-squared	0.16	0.28	0.08

Source: Author's elaboration. Notes: Mineral/oli exporters include Bolivia, Chile, Colombia, Ecuador, Peru, Venezuela. Agricultural exporters include Argentina, Brazil, Mexico. Other countries include Costa Rica, Dominican Republic, El Salvador, Guatemala, Honduras, Nicaragua, Panama, Paraguay, Uruguay. *, ** and***denote that the estimated parameters are significantly different from zero at the 90%, 95% and 99% probability levels.

on other explanatory variables such as taxation, social transfers and so on. Yet, Table 6.1 shows that during the years of the Washington Consensus a rise of terms of trade had – with the exception of the 'other countries' – a statistically non-significant effect on inequality. In contrast, an increase in the export volume was significantly un-equalizing, as export rents accrued only to the owners of land and mines. In contrast, during the years of the center-left regimes improvements in terms of trade and export volumes had (again, with the exception of the 'other countries') a clear equalizing effect due to the creation of redistributive institutions financed – inter alia – with the revenue generated by higher export proceeds and faster commodity-driven growth. Finally, the last column shows that the statistically significant equalizing effects of changes in global conditions registered over 2003–2008 continued in part over 2009–2013. While only a few parameters of this period are statistically significant, their signs (except in part for the 'other countries') are negative and only a little smaller than those for the prior period. The standard errors however increased due to large variations in terms of trade and export volumes between 2009 and 2013, reducing in this way the significance of the parameters estimated for this period.

Overall, Figures 6.3 and 6.4, and the results of Table 6.1 suggest that, until the early 2000s, the terms of trade were unrelated to inequality while a surge in export volumes increased it. Since 2002, improvements in these variables have helped in reducing inequality via the pathways discussed below. This was particularly true in the nine countries exporting mineral and agricultural commodities. These conclusions are highly relevant as they indicate that future redistribution may depend also on the trend in terms of trade and export volumes. Indeed, distributive tensions and electoral reversals increased since the sharp and steady decline in world metal prices of 2011 and of oil and agricultural commodities in 2014 (Figure 6.3).

The Left Turn and the new policy approaches of the 2000s

A second, more comprehensive and econometrically verified explanation of the inequality decline of the 2000s focuses on the changes in governments' political orientation and the progressive policies they introduced (Cornia, 2014). In this regard, it must be recalled that since the early 1990s the region experienced a gradual return to and consolidation of democracy and from the late 1990s a Left Turn in the political orientation of most incumbent governments. As a result, the number of countries run by a center-left regime rose from 2 to 13 between 1998 and 2009, and remained almost unchanged until 2013, while the number of center and center-right regimes fell from 16 to 5 (Figure 6.5). As suggested by various issues of the Latino Barometro (http://www.latinobarometro. org/lat.jsp), a major factor behind this political turnaround was growing frustration with the disappointing results of the Washington Consensus policies implemented in the 1980s and 1990s. These policies, as well as the world recession and debt crisis of the 1980s triggered by the massive US interest rate increase of 1979, led to a sharp GDP contraction and sluggish growth for all the 1980s, a shrinkage of manufacturing and public services, rising unemployment, an enlargement of the informal sector and increasing inequality. Growth recovered moderately in the 1990s while the Washington Consensus package evolved into its 'Augmented' version. Yet, inequality kept rising. Thus, more than an ideological realignment of the electorate, the Left Turn of the 2000s was the result of a retrospective economic voting and of a demand for a more active role of the state in the provision of public goods.

Such political shift was also the result of a reorganization of the left movements. As noted by Panizza (2005), the political coalitions supporting the new center-left regimes included organizations of the urban and

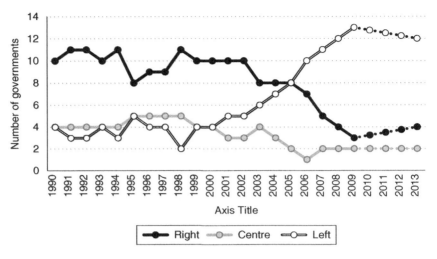

Source: Cornia (2014) updated by the author to 2013.

Figure 6.5 *Trends in the number of incumbent governments according to*
their political orientations, Latin America, 1990–2013

rural poor, unemployed and informal sector workers, indigenous groups and community organizations that replaced the official trade union and traditional left parties at the forefront of social mobilization. Key to our analysis, the new coalitions included also part of the business community and professional middle class that had traditionally voted for conservative parties but that switched their political allegiance after experiencing a decline in their level of income and income share during the two prior decades (Table 6.2, left panel). This shift of political preferences was important for the sustainability of the policy model illustrated below. Indeed, as underscored by the recent debate, the middle class often plays a significant role in promoting capital accumulation, entrepreneurship, human capital formation, political stability and redistributive policies (OECD, 2011). In this chapter, we define the middle class as the social groups belonging to the 6th to 9th income deciles, and we proxy its incentives to support governments with the changes over time in its income share. In this regard, it must be underlined again that slow growth and rising inequality of 1990–2002 affected not only the low-income groups (deciles 1 to 5), who suffered the largest income share losses, but also the middle class (Table 6.2, left panel). Symmetrically, in most countries the distributive gains recorded over 2002–2009 benefited not only the low-

Table 6.2 *Changes in the income shares of the low income group (deciles 1–5), middle class (deciles 6–9) and upper class (top decile), 1990–2002, 2002–2009 and 2009–2013*

Deciles	1990–2002				2002–2009				2009–2013				
	1–5	6–9	10	Δ Gini	1–5	6–9	10	Δ Gini	1–5	6–9	10	Δ Gini	Δ Gini 2013
Argentina	−4.68	+ 0.94	+3.74	+7.7	+5.01	+ 2.81	−7.82	−9.0	+1.8	0.2	−1.9	−2.5	−0.3
Brazil	+1.32	+ 0.07	−1.39	−2.1	+2.49	+1.63	−4.12	−4.6	+0.9	−0.1	−0.7	−1.0	+0.3
Dom. Rep.	−1.61	−0.74	+2.35	+2.8	+0.97	−0.86	−0.05	−1.1	+1.0	+0.3	−1.3	+0.1	+1.4
El Salvador	−0.45	+2.78	−2.33	−0.5	+3.76	−0.98	−2.78	−5.6	+1.4	0.1	−1.8	−1.8	+1.9
Mexico	+0.42	+0.85	−1.27	−1.1	+0.25	+044	−0.68	−0.5	+0.7[b]	−0.3[b]	+0.4[b]	−0.6	+1.8[a]
Paraguay	+ 0.86	+1.54	−2.40	−1.8	+3.20	+2.11	−5.41	−5.9	+0.8	−0.1	−0.6	−0.6	+0.3
Venezuela	−2.97	−0.62	+3.68	+5.0	+2.45	+0.45	−2.90	−4.0	...	.....	...	...	...
Bolivia	−1.24	− 0.66	+1.90	+2.1	+1.87	+0.04	−1.91	−2.9	+0.7	+0.8	−1.5	−3.0	+1.3
Ecuador	+1.82	−1.49	−0.33	−2.3	+2.87	+2.65	−5.51	−5.6	+0.8	+0.5	−1.7	+0.1	+0.8
Chile	+0.51	−0.28	+0.23	−0.5	+1.44	+0.79	−2.23	−2.7	+0.8	+0.5	−1.3	−1.9	−0.4
Colombia	+0.36	+ 0.84	−1.24	−0.9	−1.89	−1.21	+3.11	+3.4	+1.1	+1.5	−2.6	−3.0	−0.2
Peru	− 0.67	−2.12	+2.79	+2.9	+2.99	+4.17	−7.18	−6.5	+1.8	+0.8	−2.7	−3.9	−0.5
Uruguay	−2.15	+0.16	+1.99	+3.0	+0.87	− 0.85	−0.01	−1.0	+2.3	+1.9	−4.4	−5.9	+0.7
Costa Rica	−2.82	−3.23	+6.05	+5.8	−0.18	−0.53	+ 0.71	+0.4	+0.5	+1.8	−2.1	−0.6	+0.8
Guatemala	+1.53	− 2.92	+1.40	−4.0	−0.47	+1.16	−0.70	−3.6	...	...	...	...	...
Honduras	−2.66	+ 0.89	+ 1.78	+5.3	−0.82	+2.46	−1.78	−1.4	−0.8	−1.5	+2.3	+3.2	−4.1
Nicaragua	+3.63	+ 1.00	−4.63	−4.1	−0.78	−2.05	+2.82	+2.1	...	...	...	...	...
Panama	−0.33	− 2.46	+2.79	+1.4	+2.52	+ 0.88	−3.40	−4.3	+0.1	+0.5	−0.6	0.0	−0.3
Average	−0.63	−0.30	+0.93		+1.40	+0.73	−2.13		+0.93	+0.50	−1.43		

Notes: The first seven countries in Table 6.2 are those where the share of the middle class declined over 2009–2013 and Gini rose in 2013. a refers to 2012, b refers to 2010–2012.

Source: Author's elaboration on CEDLAS data accessed in late 2015.

income groups (Table 6.2, middle panel) but also the middle class. Indeed, during these years the latter experienced a rise of its income share in 12 of the 15 countries that recorded a fall in inequality. The changes over 2009–2013 are discussed in the next section.

Policies Adopted in the 2000s by the Center-left Regimes

Social justice and redistribution were at the core of the policy model adopted by the center-left governments. In a way, their policy approach was inspired (especially in the Southern Cone) by the European social-democratic model and is broadly consistent with the 'redistribution with growth' paradigm discussed in Chenery et al. (1974). In contrast, the policies adopted by Bolivia, Nicaragua, and Venezuela shared some elements with the 'redistribution before growth' paradigm that sees assets redistribution as an essential prerequisite for growth and equity. Both approaches, however, paid little attention to the deep-seated problems facing the region in terms of evolution of the production structure and dependence of foreign exports and finance, as discussed later. The main components of the social-democratic policy package are discussed below in a decreasing order of their impact on the decline of inequality:

(i) A key role was played by an increase of social spending, in particular public expenditure on education. While its absolute value rose on average by 50 percent in the 1990s, it almost doubled in the 2000s (Gasparini, Cruces and Tornarolli, 2016). In addition, better targeting on the poor led to an increase in net enrolments and secondary completion rates among the children of low-middle income families. In this regard, Table 6.3 shows that net secondary enrolments rates rose faster between 2000 and 2013 than between 1990 and 2000, while the ratio between the enrolment rate of the children of the first quintile (Q1) and top quintile (Q5) rose much more rapidly during the second than the first period. This entailed a gradual decline in human capital concentration among workers. Furthermore, the increased supply of semi-skilled and skilled workers reduced the skill premium and wage inequality (Cruces, Domench and Gasparini, 2014). The drop in the skill premium was also due to a rise in the demand of unskilled workers, changes in labor policies (see later) and a decline in the supply of unskilled workers due to the prior slowdown of population growth. In this regard, the decline of fertility rates recorded over the 1990s among the bottom deciles continued unabated until 2012 and so raised the per capita income and labor force participation of women in poor households (Baradacco, Gasparini and Marchionni, 2016). A microsimulation exercise suggests that such a pattern of fertility decline reduced the Gini coefficient over 1990–2012 by between 0.7 points (in

Table 6.3   Trend in net secondary enrolment rate and inter-quintile enrolment ratio (Q1/Q5) for 1990, 2000 and 2013 (or closest year) for 16 Latin American countries

	Net secondary enrolment rate (NSER)			Inter-quintile ratio (Q1/Q5)		
	1990	2000	2013	1990	2000	2013
Bolivia	...	56.6	86.5	...	0.29	0.86
Brazil	17.0	41.6	63.3	0.04	0.18	0.52
Colombia	...	75.0	79.9	...	0.60	0.76
Costa Rica	39.8	48.0	79.8	0.34	0.40	0.69
Dominican Republic	...	40.3	67.4	...	0.26	0.54
Ecuador	...	61.9	82.8	...	0.59	0.83
El Salvador	17.5	26.4	40.3	0.14	0.15	0.36
Honduras	27.3	43.2	46.3	0.26	0.33	0.36
Mexico	52.5	67.9	77.8	0.34	0.53	0.77
Nicaragua	26.9	39.0	42.5	0.19	0.21	0.36
Panama	60.7	70.9	77.7	0.34	0.53	0.62
Paraguay	...	59.0	79.0	...	0.43	0.70
Peru	...	62.4	86.7	...	0.38	0.79
Argentina	63.7	81.3	88.1	0.53	0.71	0.87
Chile	65.7	74.1	84.3	0.61	0.67	0.85
Uruguay	65.0	75.7	82.0	0.45	0.58	0.73

Note: No recent secondary enrolment data are available for Guatemala and Venezuela.

Source: Author's elaboration on http://sedlac.econo.unlp.edu.ar/eng/statistics-detalle. php?idE=37 accessed on June 30, 2016.

Chile) and 2.0 points (in Peru), with half of the decline taking place in the 2000s.

(ii) During the 2000s tax policy placed more emphasis than during the prior 20 years on revenue collection, reduced exemptions, and direct taxation. It also extended the scope of presumptive taxation, reduced excises, raised indirect taxes on luxuries, and, in some countries, imposed a surrogate tax on financial transactions and a selective export tax. As a result, the regional tax/GDP ratio rose by 3.5 points over 2002–2012 and fell by only half a point during the 2009 recession (Figure 6.6). These are average values, and cross-country variations in taxation remain large, especially between Mexico and Central America on the one side and the Southern Cone on the other. The increase in world prices contributed to the revenue rise in six commodity exporters, but revenue had begun rising

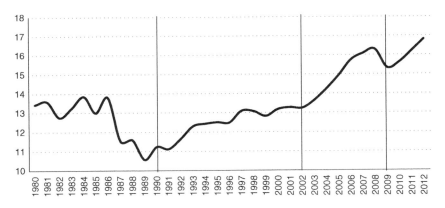

Source: Martorano (2016).

*Figure 6.6   Average regional tax/GDP ratio (excluding social security
contributions), 1980–2012*

well before the commodity price boom and involved also non-commodity
exporters. Studies of tax incidence for 11 countries of the region suggest
that improvements in tax progressivity between the 1990s and the 2000s
reduced on average by two points the Gini index of post-tax income. In
addition, greater revenue generation allowed to finance equalizing social
assistance and educational programs without putting pressure on inflation
and indebtedness.

(iii) As noted, public social expenditure started rising in the 1990s
but accelerated its upward trend since the early 2000s. Part of this
increase was allocated to social security/assistance and housing. Such
policy switch generated positive redistributive effects that appear to have
become gradually more progressive over time. Practically all governments
introduced, if to different extents, progressive social assistance programs to
complement the fragmentary coverage of social insurance. These programs
were funded domestically, absorbed between 0.2 and 1 percent of GDP,
covered an important share of the population at risk, and were directed
to new political constituencies such as the urban and rural poor. Such
programs included: conditional cash transfers aiming at reducing child
poverty by ensuring that poor children remain in school and have access
to health services and proper nutrition, as in the case of Brazil's famous
Bolsa Familia; temporary employment schemes; subsidized formal sector
employment for the youth; and the promotion of Small and Medium
Enterprises. In addition, Argentina, Bolivia, Brazil, Chile and Costa Rica
introduced non-contributory social pensions entailing a public expend-

iture of between 0.18 and 1.30 percent of GDP (Cornia, 2014). Several studies document the favorable distributional impact of services in kind and cash transfers (Lustig, Pessino and Scott, 2013).

(iv) In the 2000s labor policy explicitly addressed the problems inherited from the 1980s and 1990s, that is, high unemployment, job informalization, falling unskilled and minimum wages, declining social security coverage, and weakening of institutions for wage negotiations and dispute settlements. Most center-left governments and a few conservative ones decreed hikes in real minimum wages that reduced the minimum/average wage ratio and improved the wage distribution (Cornia, 2014). Average wages grew moderately, due to the recognition that, unless backed by increases in productivity, nominal wage raises may fuel inflation.

(v) The above policies helped reducing inequality but could not have been sustained in the absence of prudent and progressive macroeconomic policies that helped averting the un-equalizing macroeconomic and financial crises experienced in the past. Such measures included:

- A prudent external policy aiming at reducing the exposure to un-equalizing external shocks such as sudden stops in capital inflows and contagion. To do so, the Latin American governments avoided the large deficits and foreign debt accumulation recorded in the past by raising tax/GDP ratios, attempting to reduce the dependence on foreign finance, and cutting the region's gross foreign debt.
- With the exception of Brazil, Venezuela and Ecuador, most countries abandoned the free floats and fixed pegs of the past, and opted for managed regimes aiming at preserving a competitive real effective exchange rate (REER) and limiting its appreciation in periods of *bonanza*. Consistent with this approach, central banks raised the international reserves from US$150 to 639 billion over 2002–2010 for the region as a whole (ECLAC, 2014), while Argentina and Venezuela introduced in 2009 capital controls, followed later on by other countries. In spite of this, the REER came under pressure in countries experiencing large inflows of export receipts, foreign capital, or remittances. Such appreciation eroded in part the competitiveness achieved with the large real devaluations of 2001–2002. Yet, without capital controls, accumulation of reserves, and central bank interventions, the REER appreciation, and related un-equalizing asset price inflation, would have been greater.
- The fiscal and monetary stance of most countries avoided the traditional pro-cyclical biases of the past. With few exceptions, budget deficits were reduced below 1 percent of GDP (ECLAC, 2014) by raising taxation from generally low levels. Governments

also created stabilization funds to draw upon in times of revenue shortfalls. There was also a drive to expand money supply, reduce interest rates and expand lending by public banks in periods of crisis. Finally, the financial sector was regulated to avoid a repeat of the banking crises of the 1980s and 1990s. As a result, the region did not experience any financial crisis even during the recession of 2009.

THE DECLINE OF INEQUALITY OVER THE TURBULENT 2009–2012 AND ITS STAGNATION OVER 2013–2014

The US subprime and EU sovereign debt crises, and the growth slowdown of the East Asian economies caused a fall, rebound and then collapse of export volumes and commodity prices (Figures 6.2 and 6.3). As noted, in 2009 GDP fell by 2 percent while the average regional growth rate fell from 5 percent over 2002–2008 to 3 percent over 2009–2013 and to 1.2 percent in 2014. Such slowdown would have been more pronounced in the absence of the expansionary fiscal and monetary policies introduced to sustain public and private consumption.

During 2009–2010, labor markets were little affected by the recession. While unemployment rose in eight of the 11 countries analyzed in a study by the World Bank (2010), the average increase in joblessness was only 0.9 percent. In turn, real wages remained relatively strong except in hard-hit oil exporters (World Bank, 2010). Informality rose on average by only 0.4 points, but increased substantially in the subsequent five years (ECLAC, 2015). In addition, the skilled/unskilled, formal/informal and male/female wage gaps continued to fall because of the adoption of vigorous labor market policies and the steady supply of educated workers. Finally, as noted, the countercyclical fiscal policy implemented over 2009–2013 permitted to sustain domestic consumption and investments and equalizing social assistance programs that had gained a large political support in the region. Thus, despite the 2009 recession and subsequent growth slowdown, inequality continued falling until 2012 (Figure 6.1).

In contrast, over 2013–2014 the Gini coefficient fell, if at times marginally, in nine countries (including all the Central American ones that had recorded smaller declines in the past), stagnated in two and rose in five. On average the Gini coefficient declined by 0.4 points for the entire biennium, that is, less than half as fast as over 2002–2012. However, if the exceptional 6.9 Gini points decline recorded in Honduras over 2013–2014 is excluded, the regional Gini fell by only 0.07 points. This quasi-stagnation in inequality is not surprising given six years of slow GDP growth, unstable terms of trade, mounting uncertainty and domestic policy mistakes in some countries. Thus, the declining Gini trend seems to have a strong structural component. Yet, its stagnation of 2013–2014 may signal a trend slowdown that may be exacerbated by policy changes in countries (such as Argentina, Brazil and Paraguay) where the center-left regimes suffered in 2015 electoral reversals and mounting political opposition for the reasons discussed below. What then explains the 2013–2014 quasi-flattening of the Gini trend? Three complementary explanations are presented hereafter.

The first is that the social-democratic policies that drove the inequality decline of 2002–2012 exhausted their redistributive potential in a good part of the region, particularly in South America (Gasparini, Cruces and Tornarolli, 2016). For instance, a further expansion of the successful cash transfer programs implemented during the prior ten years faced a natural limit, as by the early 2010s most of the target population had already been covered. Likewise, the large and steady increases in real minimum wages could not continue forever, and their level broadly stabilized around 2010. In addition, by the early 2010s the male and female unemployment rate had already fallen to 3.5 and 5.5 percent on average (Gasparini, Cruces and Tornarolli, 2016). Finally, the decline of the fertility rate in poor families (that reached on average 1.9–2.0 in the 2000s) slowed down in the 2010s, implying a deceleration of its equalizing impact. The suggestion that the redistributive potential of the social democratic policies has been exhausted is true only in most South America. Indeed, in Central America, Mexico and a few other countries inequality can be further reduced by intensifying the reforms in the fields of education, taxation, public expenditure, labor market, fertility control and the macroeconomy.

A second explanation emphasizes that almost nowhere in the region structural, if politically difficult, reforms were introduced to tackle the region's historical inequality in the access to land, assets, credit and tertiary education. Land redistribution was a key element on the electoral manifesto of Brazil, Bolivia and Paraguay but was not implemented anywhere due to the strong opposition of the agrarian elites. Meanwhile, while the access to secondary education became more egalitarian, this was not generally the case for tertiary education (Cornia, 2014). In addition, the 2008 crisis exposed once more the dependent nature of the region's development strategy. The foreign-financed, export-led growth strategy promoted by the neoliberal reformers of the 1980s and 1990s was not abandoned during the center-left decade. Even during years of rapid growth, the region experienced a large-scale deindustrialization that sacrificed middle-class jobs, led to the re-primarization of exports and output (Ocampo, 2012), and exposed once more the region's dependence on the export of primary commodities and foreign finance.

A final explanation focuses on falling terms of trade, policy mistakes in key countries, and loss of middle class support to center-left governments in the aftermath of the world crisis of 2008 and subsequent sluggish world growth. Until 2013, the center-left regimes continued dominating the political scene in the region and their number fell only marginally (Figure 6.5). However, the longevity of the social-democratic policy model started to be threatened by the difficulty of sustaining a broad-based redistribution benefitting both low income groups and the middle class in a period of slow growth, unstable or falling terms of trade and stagnant revenue. Policy mistakes (discussed below for Brazil and Argentina) made things worse. It is plausible that under such circumstances, state redistribution favored the poor and neglected the middle class, part of which had supported the new center-left coalitions since the early 2000s. This conjecture is supported by SEDLAC data in Table 6.2 that show that, in Brazil, Argentina, Venezuela, Mexico, El Salvador and Paraguay, the inequality decline of 2010–13 benefited mainly deciles 1-5, while the income share of the middle class (deciles 6–9) stagnated or fell modestly. These are precisely the countries that experienced a slight increase in the Gini index already in 2013 and suffered electoral reversals in 2015–2016.[5]

The Latino Barometro 2013 captures well the dissatisfaction surfacing in 2013 in several countries run in 2013 by center-left regimes. In about half of these countries (including Brazil, Argentina, Paraguay, Peru and Venezuela that later on suffered electoral reversals) the majority of the people interviewed that year had a perception that the country had recorded a worsening in economic conditions in relation to 2011. Yet, in almost as many center-left countries (where the income share of the middle class rose, see Table 6.2, and where center-left regimes are still in power), the general perception was one of overall progress.

The cases of Argentina and Brazil offer a good illustration of the relation between worsening global economic conditions, domestic policy mistakes, erosion of distributive policies and loss of middle class support. As noted by Saad-Filho (2015), on March 2015 hundreds of thousands of middle class people took to the streets of Brazil to protest against the center-left government. For over a decade the latter delivered growth, formal jobs, minimum wages, and social transfers that – altogether – helped reducing inequality by a remarkable 7.1 Gini points between 1998 and 2012. The global commodity boom sustained redistribution, a modest expansion of infrastructure, industrial restructuring towards agriculture, mining, and oil extraction, and the creation of 21 million low-wage and low-productivity service jobs. Continuation of such a trend was however hampered by the recent global stagnation and a conservative macro policy (pivoting around inflation targeting, free capital movements, a floating exchange rate, and a tight fiscal stance) that precluded fiscal expansion, industrial restructuring and a devaluation of a vastly overvalued *reais*. Because of such overvaluation, the country de-industrialized and 4.5 million middle class manufacturing jobs disappeared in the 2000s while urban services and infrastructure deteriorated (Saad-Filho, 2015). The Roussef government found increasingly more difficult to fund its redistributive policies in a situation of zero growth and falling commodity prices. Inadequate investment in infrastructure during the boom years led to a worsening in the quality of transport, water and health services that affected the middle class that had been paying high taxes during the golden years. As shown by the Latino Barometro (2013) already in 2013 Brazil showed the higher rate of perceived regression in relation to 2011. Such policy mistakes and a corruption scandal led in 2016 to the impeachment of the head of state.

Argentina represents another case of policy mistakes that led to growing middle class disaffection and electoral reversal in 2015. In this case, the loss of political support derived from both internal and external factors. The slow growth of the world economy reduced the demand for and prices of Argentinean exports while the exhaustion of the domestic oil fields raised oil imports and further worsened the balance of payments. In addition, the continuation of an expansionary fiscal policy (that fueled a steady decline in inequality) during a period of deteriorating external environment pushed upward the rate of inflation to around 25 percent starting from 2010 to 2011. Yet, the government continued posting an inflation rate of 10 percent. Such policy of 'repressed inflation' led to a large real appreciation of the exchange rate and the emergence of a parallel peso market, and an incentive erosion of exporters and professional groups, including part of the middle class working in the traded sector, which in this way lost employment opportunities and income share (Table 6.2, right panel).

CONCLUSIONS: POLICIES FOR A CONTINUED INEQUALITY DECLINE IN THE YEARS AHEAD

Despite the unparalleled inequality improvements recorded over 2002–2012, Latin America remains together with Southern Africa the region with the highest inequality in the world. The struggle for a more egalitarian society needs therefore to go on. In much of the region – and particularly in Central America and the Andean countries – the distributive gains of 2002–2012 can be furthered by intensifying the timid educational, taxation, public expenditure, labor and macroeconomic reforms introduced during the 2000s. In most countries, additional if politically costly reforms should aim at tackling the region's historical biases in the field of unequal access to land, credit and tertiary education, excessive dependence on foreign capital and low domestic savings. Inability to deal, if in part, with these problems may hamper the future decline of inequality and a shift to a sustainable long-term equitable growth path once the social-democratic reforms will have fully exhausted their redistributive potential. In the countries of the region that made important policy mistakes and lost the support of the middle class, such Argentina, Brazil and Venezuela, it is essential to correct these mistakes while avoiding a return to neoliberal policies that may deepen – once more – the dependence on foreign finance and commodity exports, and weaken redistributive institutions. It is also clear that pursuit of redistribution in the future will have to focus not only on the poor but also on that part of the middle class whose political support is essential for the implementation of progressive policies.

Finally, the 2008 crisis brought to the fore the limitation of the region's export-led, foreign-financed and dependent-economy approach that was not modified during the recent social-democratic policy experiment. While the latter produced remarkable results in terms of inequality reduction, human capital formation, and avoidance of financial crises, it did not try to tackled the structural problems of the Latin American economy. As noted, the region experienced a large-scale deindustrialization that sacrificed middle class jobs, and increased dependence on the export of primary commodities. As shown by history and the instability of the international commodity prices over the last several years, such strategy is exposing again the region to the risk of terms of trade shocks, sudden stops in capital inflows, and a further contraction of the industrial sector that is a key source of long-term efficiency gains, economies of scale, learning by doing and technological upgrading.

Reversing the deindustrialization and reducing the new commodity dependence experienced over the last three decades is a key policy challenge with important implications in terms of middle class support for progressive regimes aiming at lowering a still high income inequality. A continuation of a rapid integration in the world economy with no changes in structural policies is unlikely to help. Such problem could be tackled by adopting an open-economy industrial policy or soft industrial policies that supports the re-development of labor-intensive but high-value added manufacturing and services. This could be achieved by attracting FDI in manufacturing, introducing competitive exchange rates, supporting the technological upgrading of domestic firms, promoting public–private partnership to enter in new sectors, furthering regional integration, and correcting trade asymmetries with China and other emerging economies.

NOTES

1. I would like to thank Antonio Scognamillo for his help in data collection and for carrying out the regression analysis in Table 6.1, and an anonymous referee for useful comments on a prior version of this chapter. The usual caveats apply.
2. Between the early 1980s and 2002 the region experienced 26 major banking crises involving 15 countries.
3. The social democratic regimes include Chile, Uruguay and Brazil. A second group, which includes Argentina and Ecuador, developed left-nationalist platforms, while Venezuela, Bolivia and Nicaragua since 2007 followed a radical populist approach that entailed some redistribution of assets.
4. For a detailed regression analysis of the determinants of income inequality over 1990–2009 see Cornia (2014).
5. The initial SEDLAC data for 2013 and 2014 reported in Table 6.5 are likely to be revised in the future, and the new revised data may alter the empirical evidence presented in Table 6.5 for the period 2009–2013. The hypothesis about the weakening of the middle-class support to center-left regimes is however supported by other data and arguments.

BIBLIOGRAPHY

Altimir, O. (1996). 'Economic development and social equity', *Journal of Interamerican Studies and World Affairs*, 38(2/3): 47–71.

Baradacco, N., L. Gasparini, and M. Marchionni (2016). 'Distributive implications of fertility changes in Latin America', *International Journal of Population Research*, volume 2016, Article ID 8717265, 11 pages.

Behrman, J., N. Birdsall, and M. Székely (2000). 'Economic reform, and wage differentials in Latin America', RES Working Paper 4235, Washington, DC: Inter-American Development Bank.

Chenery, H., M. Ahluwalia, C. Bell, J. Duloy, and R. Jolly (1974). *Redistribution with Growth*, Oxford: Oxford University Press.

Cornia, G.A. (ed.) (2004). *Inequality, Growth and Poverty in an Era of Liberalization and Globalization*, Oxford: Oxford University Press.

Cornia, G.A. (ed.) (2014). *Falling Inequality in Latin America: Policy Changes and Lessons*, Oxford: Oxford University Press.

Cornia, G.A., and B. Martorano (2012). 'Development policies and income inequality in selected developing regions, 1980–2010', UNCTAD Discussion Paper 210, November 2012.

Cruces, G., C.G. Domench, and L. Gasparini (2014). *Inequality in Education: Evidence for Latin America*, in G.A. Cornia (ed.), *Falling Inequality in Latin America: Policy Changes and Lessons*, Oxford: Oxford University Press, pp. 318–339.

ECLAC (2014). *Preliminary Balance of the Latin American Economy*, Santiago de Chile: ECLAC.

ECLAC (2015). *Preliminary Balance of the Latin American Economy*, Santiago de Chile: ECLAC.

Engerman, S.L., and K.L. Sokoloff (2005). 'Colonialism, inequality and long run paths of development', NBER Working Paper 11057, Cambridge, MA: NBER.

Gasparini, L., G. Cruces, and L. Tornarolli (2016). 'Chronicle of a declaration foretold: income inequality in Latin America in the 2010s', Documento de Trabajo Nro. 198, May 2016, Universidad Nacional de La Plata.

Gasparini, L., G. Cruces, L. Tornarolli, and M. Marchionni (2009). 'A turning point? Recent developments on inequality in Latin America and the Caribbean', Documento de Trabajo 81. De la Plata: CEDLAS Universidad Nacional de La Plata.

Koujianou-Goldberg, P., and N. Pavcnik (2007). 'Distributional effects of globalization in developing countries', NBER Working Paper 12885, Cambridge, MA: NBER.

Latino Barometro (2013). Annual Report, http://www.latinobarometro.org/docu mentos/LATBD_INFORME_LB_2013.pdf (accessed June 13, 2017).

Lustig, N., C. Pessino, and J. Scott (2013). 'The impact of taxes and social spending on inequality and poverty in Argentina, Bolivia, Brazil, Mexico, Peru and Uruguay: an overview', Working Papers 1313, Tulane University, Department of Economics.

Martorano, B. (2016). 'Taxation and inequality in developing countries: lessons from the recent experience of Latin America', WIDER Working Paper Series 098, World Institute for Development Economic Research (UNU-WIDER), Helsinki: UNU/WIDER.

Ocampo, J.A. (2012). 'The development implications of external integration in Latin America', UNU/WIDER Working Papers 48/2012, Helsinki: UNU/ WIDER.

OECD (2011). 'Latin American economic outlook 2011: how middle class is Latin America?', Paris: OECD Development Centre.

Panizza, F.E. (2005). 'Unarmed utopia revisited: the resurgence of left-of-centre politics in Latin America', *Political Studies*, 53(4): 716–734.

Prados de la Escosura, L. (2005). 'Growth, inequality, and poverty in Latin America: historical evidence, controlled conjectures', Working Paper 05-41 (04). Madrid: Department of Economic History and Institutions, Universidad Carlos III de Madrid.

Saad-Filho, Alfredo (2015). 'A critical review of Brazil's recent economic policies', Development Viewpoint, Number 84, Centre for Development Policy Research, School of Oriental and African Studies, London.

Sainz, P., and A. Calcagno (1992). 'En busca de Otra Modalidad de Desarrollo', *CEPAL Review*, 48(December).

Taylor, L. (2004). 'External liberalization, economic performance and distribution in Latin America and elsewhere'. In G.A. Cornia (ed.), *Inequality, Growth and Poverty in an Era of Liberalization and Globalization*, Oxford: Oxford University Press, pp. 166–196.

World Bank (2010). 'Did Latin America learn to shield its poor from economic shocks?', World Bank Brief 61273, Washington, DC: World Bank.

7. Thirty years in Africa's development: from structural adjustment to structural transformation?

Tony Addison

INTRODUCTION[1]

Africa has come a long way since the economic turmoil of the 1980s, the decade of 'structural adjustment'. The term was first coined by the World Bank to describe its programme lending, made in support of economic reform (Please, 1984; World Bank, 1981).[2] At the time most of Africa's economies were in deep distress. Subsequently, the African lions roared again (until the slowdown starting in 2014 as the prices of many export commodities fell). GDP growth has averaged more than 4 per cent over the last decade (peaking at 6.4 per cent during 2002–2008), with per capita growth just under 2 per cent (World Bank, 2015a: 4) (Figure 7.1). And a number of countries have moved from low-income to middle-income status, notably Ghana (which in the 1980s was the epitome of a once-promising country turned economic disaster). Human development indicators have also improved, with child and maternal mortality down, and school enrolment significantly up.

Yet poverty measured by household income and expenditures presents a mixed picture. The incidence of poverty is down, from about half of all Africans in 1990 to about one-third today (World Bank, 2015b).[3] But the number of Africans in poverty is expected to remain high; 392–416 million in 2011 to 317–344 million in 2030 – which are higher absolute numbers than in 1990 (Jolliffe and Prydz, 2015: 37).[4] Millions are grouped just above and below national poverty lines; their employment is insecure and highly vulnerable to shocks. On current World Bank estimates, poverty will be concentrated in the sub-Saharan Africa region by 2030, when more than 85 per cent of the global poor will be Africans (Jolliffe and Prydz, 2015: 26). Progress in the reduction of poverty incidence and in better human

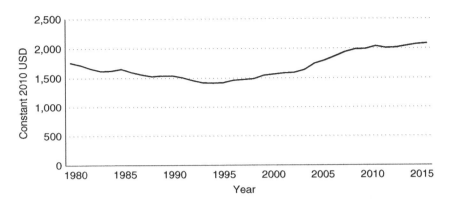

Note: Real GDP is calculated with country level real GDP and population data by dividing the aggregate real GDP of African countries in each year by their respective population. As data coverage increases, countries in the sample increase from 43 to 52 over the period.

Source: World Bank World Development Indicators.

Figure 7.1   Africa, real GDP

development indicators should be celebrated, but not make us blind to the big tasks still ahead.

The economies of the region have yet to show the diversification that underpinned Asia's success stories (on the latter see: Nayyar, 2013; Rodrik, 2007). This is why East Asia accounted for half of the world's poor in 1990, and SSA 15 per cent, while today the numbers are reversed: SSA now accounts for half the world's poor, and East Asia's share has dropped to 12 per cent (Cruz et al., 2015). Lack of diversification makes the economies as vulnerable to global shocks as in the 1970s and 1980s. Africa's continued dependence on unprocessed commodity exports has been exposed by the price downturn of 2014–2015. The terms of trade deterioration was 18 per cent and more up to early 2015, with declines of over 40 per cent for oil producers (World Bank, 2015a: 5). Labour productivity remains below other developing regions, especially in agriculture. Africa's yields are low and mostly stagnant or improving only slowly – resulting in low earnings and deep rural poverty. The good news on Africa's human development is not matched by good news on livelihoods and income.

At the root of the poverty problem is disappointing progress in transforming Africa's economies. The central argument of this chapter is that while Africa has shown sustained growth, structural transformation has not, by and large, taken place on the required scale. In consequence, the creation of 'good' jobs – remunerative employment in decent working conditions – is failing to match the growth-rate of new labour-force entrants. While Africa's middle-class has expanded, and top income-earners are doing very well, social inequality is widening given the lack of opportunity for those at the bottom. If unchecked this trend will threaten social stability. Structural transformation, which is intimately linked to the goal of inclusive growth, remains on the policy table – as it did 30 or more years ago in the era of structural adjustment.

This chapter is organized as follows. The next section revisits the 1980s and early 1990s, to assess the rationale as well as the successes and failures of structural adjustment. Economic reform was far from being the only significant event at the time. Many countries became mired in war. Accordingly, the chapter then turns to the structural changes brought about by war, which were often of the worst kind. It is argued that war's impact interacted with the economic liberalization, often producing worse social inequality. The chapter then assesses today's agenda of structural transformation, and where the region now stands. The chapter concludes that today's policy agenda is subtle, and one in which the challenges have no easy answers.

STRUCTURAL ADJUSTMENT

Back in the early 1980s, the IMF and the World Bank (the 'Bretton Woods Institutions') had a relatively clear idea of what economic reform should consist of. The message to governments was straightforward: devalue currencies when overvalued; strip out rent-seeking in the way external trade was organized; undertake sector reforms (to restore agricultural price incentives, in particular); reduce the fiscal deficit to eliminate the crowding-out of private-sector investment (and reduce the inflationary finance of deficits); and generally reduce public-spending relative to GDP, via the privatization of loss-making state enterprises. Underlying the policy detail was the aim of rebalancing economies towards the export sectors, and shifting the mix of public-sector and private-sector activity to the advantage of the latter.

Devaluation was intended to shift incentives towards the production of tradables (exportables and import-substitutes). Trade liberalization – the shift from quantitative import restrictions to (simplified and lower) tariffs – was intended to raise further the incentive to produce exportables, and to displace (inefficiently) produced domestic-goods by imports. It was hoped to thereby improve the overall efficiency of economies, by better deploying scarce capital, in particular. Such comprehensive change upturned the dominant post-independence strategy of import-substitution. It also had profound implications for the politics of Africa, as reforms implied major distributional changes, both via the rise and decline of economic opportunities, as well as the functions of the state (and who it employed and on what terms).

The package was intended to adjust African economies towards a structure that was more open to the world economy and its opportunities, and more focused on the private sector as a development driver. Structural adjustment was expected to impose losses on capital and labour in activities losing protection; but their reduced profits and wages were expected to be relatively short-lived and offset by new opportunities once growth picked up (World Bank, 1990). Adjustment's social costs were accordingly thought to be limited; unemployment would be temporary until new jobs were found (or wage workers became self-employed in activities boosted by liberalization). Accordingly, little mitigation via public works programmes was undertaken until the later 1980s when it became evident that adjustment would be a more protracted affair than initially thought (Jolly, 1991; van der Hoeven, 1991). These assumptions prevailed in structural adjustment programmes outside Africa as well, but Africa's economies were generally the weakest (especially on the economy's supply-side), and were therefore the slowest to recover.

For economies that were already in deep recession, structural adjustment programmes (SAPs) eventually led to growth. In part this was due to the removal of disincentives to the production of traditional exports (Ghana's cocoa producers had been locked into an ineffective state-marketing system prior to liberalization, for example). As important to growth was the injection of foreign-exchange (via supporting concessionary loans) into economies where capacity utilization had been curtailed by lack of essential imports. To take one example, in Ghana prior to the start of reform, per capita output had fallen by one-third over 1974–1983 as the foreign-exchange constraint dug deeper into output; Ghana then registered a positive and stable rate of per capita growth every year after the mid-1980s (Fosu, 2009: 2).

Yet there were major problems with structural adjustment too. Fixed exchange rates were maintained far too long, thereby depressing output and investment as deflation (via fiscal contraction) shouldered the burden of the adjustment process. This was very evident in the CFA Franc Zone, which maintained a fixed peg to the (then) French Franc, at the insistence of the French Treasury. This hindered the ability of the region to respond to external shocks and induced severe recession, including in Côte d'Ivoire, once a star West African performer (Devarajan and de Mello, 1987; Tchatchouang, 2015). Devaluation, when it eventually came, imposed a large and sudden adjustment to these economies.

Africa's aid donors were over-optimistic about the supply-side response that could be expected from devaluation, import liberalization, and sector reform. They were unrealistic about the ability of low-income economies to respond to the size and suddenness of the external shocks that hit them in the late 1970s and early 1980s (notably, the second oil price shock of 1979–1980). At the time, economists of a 'structuralist' persuasion warned that large relative price changes would do little to improve economies that were characterized by the kinds of structural rigidities that define 'underdevelopment'.[5] In agriculture, smallholders switched between crops in response to changing incentives, but were often unable to raise their *total* output (and hence income), as structural constraints (of low farm-productivity, little input use, and the time burdens of women farmers) held back the supply-side.

By the early 1980s much of Africa's (very small) manufacturing sector was in deep trouble. It was highly import dependent for its intermediate inputs, and industrial capacity utilization fell as foreign-exchange rationing (in response to external shocks) became increasingly severe. The woes of domestic manufacturers increased further as World Bank conditionality required import liberalization – and much domestic manufacturing was uncompetitive at world prices, never having moved out of the infant-industry stage. IMF conditionality also required the end of fiscal subsidies to state-owned industries. Many manufacturers shut down in the 1980s and, without a compensating rise of new firms, manufacturing as a sector contracted across much of the region.

There was a mismatch between the structural reform and stabilization agendas, advanced respectively by the World Bank and the IMF. Problems in reform sequencing were not confined to Africa, but the region was especially vulnerable to policy mismatch, given its inherent economic weakness. Zimbabwe is an illustrative case. Premature financial liberalization led to a jump in interest rates that contributed to a surge in the cost of servicing public debt. This compounded the problem of restoring fiscal sustainability, and crowded out development spending (Addison and Laakso, 2003: 461). Rising interest rates combined with rapid import liberalization then hammered Zimbabwean industry: the once thriving clothing and textiles industry contracted in the early 1990s to a point from which it has never recovered. The IMF's own Independent Evaluation Office later concluded that the overall adjustment had been badly designed (IMF, 1998).

Did SAPs achieve their objective of transforming the structures of Africa's economies in ways that were positive for economic development? By and large, the answer is no. As discussed in more detail later, by the 1990s manufacturing had less of a role in African economies than it did in the 1970s. In agriculture, in which two-thirds of Africans work, the region has not achieved a large-scale transformation towards higher labour productivity and yields, thereby raising farm income and off-farm employment (via rising rural demand for rural goods and services) (de Janvry and Sadoulet, 2012).

Meanwhile, East Asian economies such as Vietnam – which had also been in dire straits in the 1980s – recovered and then grew spectacularly via a careful phasing of liberalization that enabled the national economy to integrate successfully with the global economy. This stimulated new investments and activities in sectors of increasing value-added. Such structural transformation in East Asia enabled rapid poverty reduction via a sustained growth in agricultural productivity; this released labour for jobs (and higher earnings) in new industrial (export) clusters (Thoburn, 2009). In turn such dynamism helped contain social inequality. Paradoxically, donors who backed rapid market liberalization for Africa – which largely failed to transform economies – financed more sequenced reform in Vietnam, which did yield structural transformation. In reforming the Vietnamese economy from the 1980s onwards, Vietnam's planners had a well-articulated idea of how they wanted to use foreign aid to reduce the constraints, particularly in infrastructure, that held back the productive economy.

There are parallels between what happened in Africa and events in the former Soviet Union (FSU) and Eastern-Europe (EE) as they went through transition from the late 1980s onward. When the existing political order is under question – either in periods of political transition from autocracy to 'democracy' and/or during violent conflict – those with access to capital and political connections (or as members of the ruling elite themselves) are able to drive the liberalization process in ways that shift assets and opportunities into their own hands. This is evident in, for example, the restructuring of financial systems: state banks in default are often recapitalized with private money, including international investment, and then frequently left to operate in weak regulatory environments (Addison et al., 2005). While policy economists (such as myself) typically work with a conceptual separation between the state and the private sector, with the former supposedly regulating the latter in the 'public interest', economic reform shows the 'straddling' that can occur as state and private sector actors work together for mutual gain – especially in wartime and post-war economies when politics is 'fluid' and a new political settlement is yet to be worked out (see discussion later). One consequence is the embedding into economies of structures that subsequently place societies such as Angola (and much of the FSU) onto pathways characterized by high asset inequality (and hence rising income inequality) (Addison, 2003).

As in the FSU-EE, aid donors took a naïve view of what market-liberalization could accomplish for Africa. And they recognized too late how its outcomes can be manipulated when regulatory institutions are broken or still under construction. While liberalization can be done at the 'stroke of a pen', institutional construction is slow and resource-intensive (Noman and Stiglitz, 2015). The dynamics of wealth accumulation by elite insiders favour halting reform after the first stage of privatization – once the assets (banks, utilities, mineral rights and so on) are in their hands – and before regulatory mechanisms are in place (Hoff and Stiglitz, 2001: 419) The resulting 'partial reform equilibrium' (a term used in the transition-economics literature) will then favour private interests over the public interest, thus blocking subsequent institutional improvement (including increased transparency around ownership), which is necessary to protect the public interest against misuse of private economic power (Hellman, 1998; Frye, 2010).

There is a tension at the heart of rapid economic reform when the political settlement is itself changing in unpredictable ways. Nervous investors need to be enticed so that private investment delivers on reform's promise of structural change. Offering 'low-hanging fruit' via privatization with 'light' (or non-existent regulation) is tempting for hard-pressed governments. It may well consolidate support for reform among society's powerful, thereby making reform irreversible (an argument heard in donor circles during the privatizations in EE-FSU, Africa and elsewhere in the 1980s and 1990s). Yet as well-connected groups gather the fruit for themselves, leading to more investment, so society finds itself on a political and economic path that promises trouble for the future (social tensions around rising and uncontainable inequality leading to a tightening control of the 'democratic' process by the powerful, in particular).

Africa's national efforts at adjustment began in the context of a global economic system that was far from supportive. This was pointed out at the time (see Helleiner, 1983). Supplying more exportables meant supplying more primary commodities (mostly unprocessed), the traditional means of foreign-exchange generation. But this was during the years in which world commodity prices were weak and declining. Accordingly, the budgetary 'space' to allow a more careful reorganization of the state's role in economic life was largely absent, limiting its ability to further the public interest.

Moreover, the small scale of the domestic market in most African countries has made import substitution much less viable than in Asia's more populous countries. Import substitution in Africa requires levels of protection that are a gift to rent-seekers, with little prospect of achieving international competitiveness. At independence, pan-Africanists recognized these limitations and pressed for regional cooperation. This agenda is still to be realized. To take one example, the collapse of the East African trade area added to Tanzania's woes in the 1980s, as industries that had been established on the assumption of a larger regional market were reduced to supplying (declining) domestic markets. This is still a problem: the share of intra-African exports in total merchandise exports in Africa stands at 11 per cent, way below the 50 per cent of developing Asia (UNCTAD, 2013: 2).

With weak export earnings, and concessional loans rather than grants making up the bulk of official finance provided to support SAPs, Africa's debt-to-GDP and debt-to-export ratios went skyward (Addison, 2006). Africa found itself trying to service debts using a very narrow (traditional) export base. A transactions-heavy process that constituted the various HIPC (Heavily Indebted Poor Countries) initiatives, lasting over a decade, then resulted (Addison, Hansen and Tarp, 2004). Underlying Africa's debt problem were over-optimistic assumptions about its ability to raise export earnings given supply constraints and depressed commodity prices.

Structural adjustment's legacy was stronger macro-economic policy, and more robust fiscal and monetary institutions. Much improved management of the public finances, better tax policy, and stronger central banks were real achievements (though achieved with unnecessary pain). This has helped avoid a repeat of the catastrophic policy mistakes that led to the growth collapses of the 1970s and 1980s. But structural transformation – the movement of economies into activities with higher value-added – was the disappointing part of the legacy. Countries adjusted in the 1980s, but without big changes in structure. When growth returned it was mostly on a narrow and traditional economic base, and this narrow pathway was indeed reinforced by the commencement of the global commodity 'supercycle' in the late 1990s.

The era of structural adjustment showed that price incentives alone are insufficient to accelerate growth in ways that really reduce poverty and inequality (Cornia, van der Hoeven and Mkandawire, 1992). Towards the end of the 1980s there was some attempt to take into the World Bank the lessons of UNICEF's 'Adjustment with a Human Face' initiative (World Bank, 1990). Nevertheless, during structural adjustment, poverty reduction was at best an 'add-on' to the growth agenda rather than the central goal it was starting to become with the launch of the 'Basic Needs' approach in the late 1970s, which had some take-up in the World Bank (Hopkins and van der Hoeven, 1983; Streeten et al., 1981).

Growth returned to Africa in the 1990s, but growth is, by and large, delivering a disappointing amount of poverty reduction (Arndt et al., 2015). To take one example, Tanzania saw per capita income rise by 30 per cent over 2000–2010; but per capita consumption in poor households barely improved over the same period, and the poverty rate in 2010 was the same as at the start of the Millennium (and the MDGs) (Atkinson and Lugo, 2010).

STRUCTURAL DAMAGE

It is not just deliberate policy change that causes structural change in economies: social conflict and political breakdown (with violence) has profound effects too. Structural adjustment overlapped and interacted with rising conflict. Structural adjustment and violent conflict cannot be treated as independent. But neither is conflict simply the outcome of economic crisis (nor peace simply the outcome of economic recovery).

The Cold War was winding down by the mid-1980s, but the decade saw the continuation and intensification of fighting that began at independence in the 1970s in Angola (the war ending in 2002) and Mozambique (ending in 1992) (Addison, 2003; Westad, 2005). Ethiopia's Derg was overthrown by 1991, Ethiopia and newly independent Eritrea began reconstruction, but then went to war with each other over 1998–2000. After backing dictators for years, the West suddenly awoke to the virtues of democratization as competition with the Soviet Union ended. The client sates of both superpowers slid into chaos and conflict as state power fragmented and then collapsed. Long-standing grievances and histories of political instability resulted in conflict in Sierra Leone, Uganda, and Sudan as well as genocide in Rwanda. Geopolitical shifts, which destabilized authoritarians, together with the factors of identity, culture, and ideology – that mobilized groups against each other – were as important to generating violent social breakdown as the continent's deepening economic malaise.

Mass violence creates changes in economic structure, but of a perverse and regressive kind. Uncertainty and conflict work against long-term investment by communities and entrepreneurs, unless they are protected from predation (Addison and Murshed, 2005). Rural communities retreat into subsistence and away from market production. Traditional exports contract, although extractive industries in protected enclaves may continue unhindered and may indeed expand, and wartime economies can register high growth (but of a very distorted kind, including the export of conflict commodities).

These processes of accumulation continue to this day in economies such as South Sudan and Somalia, undergoing periodic outbursts of conflict, interspersed with periods without much large-scale fighting ('peace') (De

Waal, 2015). The commodity 'super-cycle', which lifted world prices over the last decade (until their recent slump) raised the stakes in the control of the revenue streams around natural resource wealth. Such control is one of the principal drivers of Africa's social inequality, given the fortunes to be made, both legitimately and illegitimately. The straddling of private and public sectors reaches its pinnacle in the petro states of West Africa (Soares de Oliveira, 2007: 129). The nexus between conflict, resource dependence and poverty is evident in the statistic that 37 per cent of the world's poor live in countries that have economies dominated by natural resource activities, and at least 12 per cent live in countries that the World Bank classifies as fragile and conflict-affected – most of which are natural-resource based economies, many in Africa (Cruz et al., 2015: 9).

One outcome of war is higher inequality. The assets of the rural poor, few as they are, are more vulnerable to predation and loss. High-income groups have more opportunity to protect their living standards, and indeed can profit from wartime parallel-markets in scarce commodities, leading to much greater social differentiation, especially in the rural economy (Wuyts, 2003: 147). Conflict leads to unplanned liberalization as the state simply loses control over territory, as well as 'spontaneous' privatization of state assets by powerful private actors (Castel-Branco, Cramer and Hailu, 2003). This can be reinforced when, as discussed earlier, the wartime economy is also going through a process of economic reform: examples include Angola, Ethiopia, and Mozambique (Addison, 2003).

War-to-peace transition also provides ample opportunity to profit from new commercial opportunities. Peace raises the returns from access to land, mineral rights and other valuable resources, as do reforms in sector policy, especially in agriculture, investment laws and so on. The period in which societies move from war to peace can be times of chaos when property rights are ill-defined, offering powerful actors an ability to gain control over assets and to mould the political settlement in ways that benefit their wealth accumulation. Using resources accumulated in war to buy influence, warlords can convert themselves into highly successful peacetime politicians and businessmen (the creation of banks is an ideal vehicle for this). Of course, such actors also have the means to ensure that economic reform goes down a path that secures their private interest, by means of the 'partial reform equilibrium' discussed earlier. Again, there are parallels between Africa and those countries of Central Asia and the Balkans where economic transition was accompanied by civil war in many cases.

STRUCTURAL TRANSFORMATION

Africa has not diversified its economies to the extent expected. Overall, the region is more dependent on primary commodity exports than it was 30 years ago (AfDB/OECD/UNDP/UN-ECA, 2013). Manufacturing development is disappointing. There are some bright spots, notably Ethiopia's new light-manufacturing cluster. However, on average manufacturing accounts for around 10 per cent of GDP in Africa, which is where it stood in the 1970s; Africa's share of global manufacturing is only 2 per cent which is less than in 1970 (Page, 2011 using UNIDO data). Manufacturing output per person is one third of the developing country average and manufactured exports are about 10 per cent of the average for low-income countries (Newman et al., 2016: 6).

Causation runs both ways: from structural change to growth, and from growth to structural change. The robust economic growth of the last decade has been associated with the less than expected structural change. Thus many of the region's 'success stories' for growth (Ghana, Kenya, Uganda and so on) still have smaller manufacturing sectors than their GDP per capita would predict (Page, 2015: 258). Structural change cannot simply be subsumed into the creation of formal manufacturing (the classic development model). It must include high-value services (those linked to tourism, for example) as well as agriculture at the higher end of the value-chain (Page, 2015). While manufacturing employment growth has not met expectations, more people are finding employment outside agriculture. This is often in rural non-farm enterprises, and a small-subset of informal enterprises (both rural and urban) have high productivity – which is positive for transformation (McMillan and Harttgen, 2015). Despite this, and despite the return to growth after the era of structural adjustment, Africa's economic transformation is still awaited.

SSA's population will grow from 900 million today to 2.1 billion by 2050 (UN-DESA, 2013). This is a potential demographic dividend, as some 10 million young people enter SSA's workforce annually (World Bank, 2012a). Yet this flow far exceeds the availability of good jobs. One comparison is illustrative: the annual *flow* of new labour is about equal to the total *stock* of manufacturing employment across the region (Lin, 2011: 29).

Africa's demographic dividend is only realizable if young people can be productively employed at ever-rising levels of skill so that incomes grow. More young people and little in the way of good jobs is a dangerous combination, often leading to social conflict. Not surprisingly, issues around wages and working conditions were the two top drivers of public protests in Africa in 2014 and 2015 (AfDB/OECD/UNDP/UN-ECA, 2015: xv).

In Africa, overall social inequality is closely associated with high spatial inequality. Infrastructure investment can partly overcome this, if the presently disconnected area has good economic potential (in cash crops, for example). But low-income countries (LICs) in SSA lag at least 20 percentage points behind the LIC average on nearly all measures of infrastructure investment (Page and Söderbom, 2012: 16). Reducing the indirect costs of business can stimulate internationally competitive manufacturing and services in Africa, since low wages as a competitive 'advantage' are at present more than offset by the very high costs of power, water, and transport in the cost structure of firms (Eifert, Gelb and Ramachandran, 2008). Africa's exports are 16 per cent lower than what we would expect given the standard determinants of trade (Freund and Rocha, 2011: 361). In the 1980s, export taxes and import protection were top constraints on Africa's international trade: now it is often transport infrastructure and cumbersome border processes.

Funding large-scale infrastructure requires a level of finance that exceeds domestic revenues (the main funding source at present) and official development assistance (ODA). Infrastructure has shown a strong relative decline in aid allocations over the last 30 years. To meet the gap, infrastructure requires co-financing with private investors, and the Africa50 fund of the African Development Bank (AfDB) shows one way ahead. Equally important is sound project preparation, including environmental and social assessment.[6] Many countries lack a well-defined pipeline of projects, ready to start once finance becomes available.

ODA's contribution to growth has been larger than many critics allow (see UNU-WIDER, 2014 for a comprehensive picture). Moreover, private finance (foreign direct investment, portfolio flows and remittances, which are all on the rise) cannot entirely substitute for official flows. Sovereign borrowing can be risky (and is discussed later). Aid donors focus mostly on human development these days – especially since the start of the MDGs era in 2000 and its transition into the SDGs. Accordingly, donors have cut back on their support to the productive sectors (remaining assistance is small-scale and fragmented). The rise in school enrolment rates (if not always school quality and outcomes), and reduced child and maternal mortality are a tribute to national efforts supported by aid (official and philanthropic). Yet more educated and healthy young people need good livelihoods, either informal or formal, if poverty is to be reduced further.

Donor understanding of what creates new and better livelihoods is quite shallow. There is a fixation on the 'Doing Business' index of the World Bank, which emphasizes ad hoc regulatory reform. But the evidence shows that infrastructure and enterprise finance are far more important as constraints on starting and growing a business in Africa (UNU-WIDER, 2014). Over-regulation of the labour market is not a constraint cited as in the top ten of problems by surveys of Africa's businessmen. And cheapening further the cost of labour by moving yet more people into jobs with poor working conditions is not a viable solution to Africa's employment challenge.

Donors also favour small- and medium-scale enterprises for their labour-intensity, but there is no evidence that these are any better at *net* job creation than larger enterprises (Page and Söderbom, 2012). East Asia's spectacular success was driven by establishing and nourishing enterprises that eventually grew large, each creating thousands of good jobs not just tens or hundreds. Wages rose, and poverty fell in East Asia, as firms linked themselves into the value-chains of the global economy. It is not surprising that African governments seek collaboration with Asia's donors – Japan, South Korea, and China – with their ideas of industrial policy, and their own track record of national success (Addison and Tarp, 2015).

Employment as a goal had a shaky relationship with the process around the MDGs (van der Hoeven, 2014). It received more attention in the process around the Sustainable Development Goals (SDGs) but this is true about almost *every* dimension of development; hence the number of SDG goals and targets (van der Hoeven, 2015). The distribution of aid reveals the preferences of donors: and shows that helping create more livelihoods is way down their priority list. The rhetoric of the SDG process – which called for a 'quantum leap' in livelihoods (UN, 2013: 8) – is not matched by the level and distribution of aid (Addison, Singhal and Tarp, 2015).

This is seen in the relative neglect of aid to agriculture over the last 30 years. Donor support to agriculture fell precipitously in the era of structural adjustment, and well into the 1990s, before a small upturn in recent years. Agriculture's share in total aid fell from 23 per cent in the mid-1980s to 6 per cent in the late 1990s and then rose to 9 per cent by 2010 (OECD, 2012: 117). World Bank assistance fell as it took the view that agricultural price liberalization could do most of the heavy lifting to get African farming out of its low-productivity trap.

For sure, by the 1980s many countries were over-taxing agriculture, which was bad for output and bad for the rural poor (although the scale of agricultural taxation was overestimated at the time of reform: see Jensen, Robinson and Tarp, 2010). Reducing taxation via reform of agricultural marketing helped to move agriculture back towards its production-possibility frontier. But that frontier was, and still is, at a level so low that it keeps many people trapped in rural poverty. This is caused by low farm-productivity linked to the structural constraints of low input-use and weak infrastructure and marketing. Indeed, some of the 'distortions' that the donors sought to remove in the past benefitted rural food-security and poverty reduction, notably Malawi's fertilizer subsidy. Although expensive, the subsidy has helped to raise productivity and income among Malawi's rural poor (Arndt, Pauw and Thurlow, 2014).

In this era of 'evidence-led policy', it is a paradox that many of Africa's governments, as well as its donors, have failed to absorb the plentiful and long-standing evidence that strong agricultural growth contributes to strong overall poverty reduction. This is especially so when agricultural research and project interventions help break the constraints on poorer small farms. Across the developing world as a whole a 1 per cent (annual) increase in agricultural growth delivers between 2 and 3 per cent of income growth for the poor (de Janvry and Sadoulet 2009: 6; World Bank 2007: 30). Agricultural growth is more difficult in Africa given the rain-fed nature of much of its farming, and the technical challenges of raising yields (in the face of increased weather severity under climate change). Yet despite the occasional high-profile initiative, agricultural research remains the Cinderella that it has always been, especially in the creation of strong national research facilities for crops and technologies benefitting poor people.

If higher and sustained agricultural productivity growth cannot be achieved then non-farm employment must take up the burden of ending Africa's poverty (McArthur, 2015: 176). While some increase in off-farm livelihoods is possible, the demand for products and services will remain limited until farm-incomes grow (taking Africa down East Asia's successful path). This leaves migration to the cities, a route many young people are already taking, adding to the natural population growth of urban centres. Africa's cities have buoyant economies, but their infrastructure is underdeveloped, and coastal cities are vulnerable to flooding as sea levels rise with climate change. Managing the process of structural transformation and all its attendant spatial dimensions requires careful planning and financing, and is an urgent task.

Africa's natural resource wealth is immense, a development driver, and a big revenue generator. But the sharp fall in global commodity prices since 2014 has revealed the vulnerability of the African Lions story. For sure, some net oil importers like Rwanda are benefiting from a lower oil import bill and their growth projections are rising. But the fiscal impact is quite urgent for the region's resource-rich economies, such as Angola, Nigeria and Zambia, which did not build sufficiently large fiscal buffers in boom times. Many are trying to patch up their financing gap with sovereign bond issues but this can lead to future debt problems.

Less recognized, but fundamentally more important, is the consequence of international agreement on measures to contain the rise in the average global temperature to below 2°C. Large amounts of fossil fuels (oil, gas, and coal) will become unusable: only 20 per cent of fossil fuels available to exploit globally can be utilized if carbon emissions are to remain at target levels (McGlade and Elkins, 2015). The investment slowdown in the sector – which has already started with the halving of world oil prices over 2014–2015 – will increase as international oil companies absorb the implications of climate change agreements for their business models. African countries may well feel that international climate action denies them a driver of growth. Climate finance must amply compensate the region, and accelerate the growth of renewables in its energy supply, as well as innovate in the provision of energy to remote and poor communities.

CONCLUSIONS

A common thread runs through this chapter: the importance of 'structure'. The era of structural adjustment advanced a very simple theory of structural change: the main driver was relative price incentives guiding the market to efficient outcomes. The role of the state was to stand back, lightly regulate (if at all), protect private property rights, and provide public goods including infrastructure. In this model, inequality might show a modest rise in the early stage of development but was ultimately contained as economies moved from low-income to middle-income status, thereby providing more opportunity for all. Inclusive growth would follow almost automatically, and poverty reduction with it.

But we have arrived at a point, with the commencement of the SDGs, where it is clear that Africa has yet to achieve the level and speed of structural transformation it requires. The last decade's super-cycle in commodities seems to be over, dangerously exposing the weakness of undiversified economies. Moreover, African policy makers have yet to absorb the implications for investment in their extractive industries of what real progress on international climate change agreements will mean for the demand for exports of fossil fuels.

In the 1980s achieving structural change appeared to be a straightforward process, and one to be largely driven by market mechanisms. That structural change has not occurred as expected illustrates the weakness of relying on market mechanisms alone (despite their importance), and the need for better models of state and enterprise cooperation suitable for Africa's economies. Such cooperation is inherently political: to be effective, as well as transparent, it must mesh with the democratic politics of each country.

The old forms of state and enterprise cooperation that characterized the one-party systems of post-independence Africa, and which degraded into unproductive rent-seeking (and which sometimes fed into violent conflict), are not viable for today's democracies. Nor are they capable of delivering integration with the global economy in ways that facilitate national structural transformation. Today's policy agenda is a more subtle one. Raising farm productivity; creating clusters of high value-added manufacturing and services; managing natural resource wealth in the public interest; making the right infrastructure choices; constructing financial systems that facilitate diversified economies; achieving inclusive urbanization; and adapting to climate change are challenges with no easy answers. The development states that Africa needs to create must have a deep knowledge of what the private sector is capable of achieving (and what it cannot without help). Then high-value synergies of private and state action can be identified and acted upon – while ensuring that business operates within a framework of supporting regulation that protects the public interest.

NOTES

1. For comments, the author thanks conference participants, especially S. Mansoob Murshed, an anonymous reviewer of an earlier draft, and Margaret McMillan.
2. Unless otherwise stated, 'Africa' refers to sub-Saharan Africa (SSA) in this chapter.
3. On the basis of the World Bank's new poverty line of USD1.90 per day. The Bank's new poverty estimates are controversial in the extent to which they show a drop in poverty incidence over the last two decades.
4. Poverty estimates vary depending on the poverty line chosen, and assumptions regarding Purchasing Power Parity (PPP) (Jolliffe and Prydz, 2015).
5. For structuralist perspectives on macro-economic adjustment see in particular Helleiner (2002); Taylor (1988, 1993) and Stiglitz et al. (2006).
6. Some of this infrastructure can be built using labour-intensive methods, and one of Africa's largest social protection programmes, Ethiopia's Productive Safety Net Programme (PSNP), which reaches nearly 10 per cent of the population, is doing just that (World Bank, 2012b).

REFERENCES

Addison, T. (ed.) (2003) *From Conflict to Recovery in Africa*. Oxford: Oxford University Press for UNU-WIDER.

Addison, T. (2006) 'Debt Relief: the Development and Poverty Impact', *Swedish Economic Policy Review* 13: 205–230.

Addison, T. and L. Laakso (2003) 'The Political Economy of Zimbabwe's Descent into Conflict', *Journal of International Development* 15: 457–470.

Addison, T. and S.M. Murshed (2005) 'Post-Conflict Reconstruction in Africa: Some Analytical Issues', in A.K. Fosu and P. Collier (eds) *Post-Conflict Economies in Africa*. Palgrave Macmillan: 3–17.

Addison, T. and F. Tarp (2015) 'Lessons for Japanese Foreign Aid from Research on Aid's Impact', WIDER Working Paper 2015/058. Helsinki: UNU-WIDER.

Addison, T., H. Hansen and F. Tarp (eds) (2004) *Debt Relief for Poor Countries*. Basingstoke: Palgrave Macmillan for UNU-WIDER.

Addison, T., A. Geda, P. Le Billon and S. Murshed (2005) 'Reconstructing and Reforming the Financial System in Conflict and "Post-Conflict" Economies', *Journal of Development Studies* 41(4): 703–718.

Addison, T., S. Singhal and F. Tarp (2015) 'Aid to Africa: The Changing Context', in J.Y. Lin and C. Monga (eds) *The Oxford Handbook of Africa and Economics: Volume 2 – Policies and Practices*. Oxford: Oxford University Press: 698–710.

AfDB/OECD/UNDP/UN-ECA (2013) *African Economic Outlook 2013: Structural Transformation and Natural Resources*. Tunis: African Development Bank, Organisation for Economic Co-operation and Development, United Nations Development Programme, UN Economic Commission for Africa.

AfDB/OECD/UNDP/UN-ECA (2015) *Africa Economic Outlook 2015; Regional Development & Spatial Inclusion*. Abidjan: African Development Bank, Organisation for Economic Co-operation and Development, United Nations Development Programme, UN Economic Commission for Africa.

Arndt, C., K. Pauw and J. Thurlow (2014) 'The Economywide Impacts and Risks of Malawi's Farm Input Subsidy Programme', WIDER Working Paper 2014/099. Helsinki: UNU-WIDER.

Arndt, C., L. Demery, A. McKay and F. Tarp (2015) 'Growth and Poverty Reduction in Tanzania', WIDER Working Paper 2015/051. Helsinki: UNU-WIDER.

Atkinson, A.B. and M. Lugo (2010) 'Growth, Poverty and Distribution in Tanzania', IGC Working Paper 10/0831. London: International Growth Centre.

Castel-Branco, C., C. Cramer and D. Hailu (2003) 'Privatization in Economic Strategy', in T. Addison (ed.) *From Conflict to Recovery in Africa*. Oxford: Oxford University Press for UNU-WIDER: 155–170.

Cornia, A., R. van der Hoeven and T. Mkandawire (eds) (1992) *Africa's Recovery in the 1990s: From Stagnation and Adjustment to Human Development: Policy Conflicts and Alternatives*. London: Macmillan.

Cruz, M., J. Foster, B. Quillin, and P. Schellekens (2015) 'Ending Extreme Poverty and Sharing Prosperity: Progress and Policies', Policy Research Note 15/03. Washington DC: World Bank, Development Economics Group.

de Janvry, A. and E. Sadoulet (2009) 'Agricultural Growth and Poverty Reduction: Additional Evidence', *The World Research Observer* 25(1): 1–20.

de Janvry, A. and E. Sadoulet (2012) 'Why Agriculture Remains the Key to Sub-Saharan African Development', in E. Aryeetey, S. Devarajan, R. Kanbur, and L. Kasekende (eds) *The Oxford Companion to the Economics of Africa*. Oxford: Oxford University Press: 70–78.

De Waal, A. (2015) *The Real Politics of the Horn of Africa*. Cambridge: Polity Press.

Devarajan, S. and J. de Mello (1987) 'Evaluating Participation in African Monetary Union: A Statistical Analysis of the CFA Zones', *World Development* 15(4): 483–496.

Eifert, B., A. Gelb and V. Ramachandran (2008) 'The Cost of Doing Business in Africa: Evidence from Enterprise Survey Data', *World Development* 36(9): 1531–1546.

Fosu, A. (2009) 'Country Role Models for Development Success: the Ghana Case', WIDER Working Paper 2009/42. Helsinki: UNU-WIDER.

Freund, C. and N. Rocha (2011) 'What Constrains Africa's Exports?', *World Bank Economic Review* 25(3): 361–386.

Frye, T. (2010) *Building States and Markets After Communism: The Perils of Polarized Democracy*. Cambridge: Cambridge University Press.

Helleiner, G.K. (1983) 'Africa and the IMF in the 1980s', *Essays in International Finance* 152. Princeton, NJ: Department of Economics Princeton University.

Helleiner, G.K. (ed.) (2002) *Non-Traditional Export Promotion in Africa: Experience and Issues*. Basingstoke: Palgrave for UNU-WIDER.

Hellman, J. (1998) 'Winners Take All: The Politics of Partial Reform in Post-Communist Transitions'. *World Politics* 50(2): 203–234.

Hoff, K. and J.E. Stiglitz (2001) 'Modern Economic Theory and Development', in G.M. Meier and J.E. Stiglitz (eds) *Frontiers of Development Economics: The Future in Perspective*. New York: Oxford University Press for the World Bank: 389–459.

Hopkins, M. and R. van der Hoeven (1983) *Basic Needs in Development Planning*. Aldershot: Gower Publishing, for the International Labour Office, World Employment Programme.

IMF (1998) *External Evaluation of the Zimbabwe ESAF: Report by a Group of Independent Experts*. Washington, DC: International Monetary Fund.

Jensen, H.T., S. Robinson and F. Tarp (2010) 'Measuring Agricultural Policy Bias: General Equilibrium Analysis of Fifteen Developing Countries', *American Journal of Agricultural Economics* 92(4): 1136–1148.

Jolliffe, D. and E.B. Prydz (2015) 'Global Poverty Goals and Prices: How Purchasing Power Parity Matters', Policy Research Working Paper 7256. Washington, DC: World Bank, Development Research Group.

Jolly, R. (1991) 'Adjustment with a Human Face: A UNICEF Record and Perspective on the 1980s', *World Development* 19(12): 1807–1821.

Lin, J.Y. (2011) 'From Flying Geese to Leading Dragons: New Opportunities and Strategies for Structural Transformation in Developing Countries'. *WIDER Annual Lecture* 15, Helsinki: UNU-WIDER.

McArthur, J.W. (2015) 'Agriculture's Role in Ending Extreme Poverty', in L. Chandy, H. Kato and H. Kharas (eds) *The Last Mile in Ending Extreme Poverty*. Washington, DC: Brookings Institution Press: 175–218.

McGlade, C. and P. Elkins (2015) 'The Geographical Distribution of Fossil Fuels Unused When Limiting Global Warming to 2°C', *Nature* 157: 187–190.

McMillan, M. and K. Harttgen (2015) 'Africa's Quiet Revolution', in J.Y. Lin and C. Monga (eds) *The Oxford Handbook of Africa and Economics: Volume 2 – Policies and Practices*. Oxford: Oxford University Press: 39–61.

Nayyar, D. (2013) *Catch Up, Developing Countries in the World Economy*. Oxford, Oxford University Press.

Newman, C., J. Page, J. Rand, A. Shimeles, M. Söderbom and F. Tarp (2016) *Made in Africa: Learning to Compete in Industry*. Washington, DC: Brookings Institution.

Noman, A. and J. Stiglitz (2015) 'Economics and Policy: Some Lessons from Africa's Experience', in J.Y. Lin and C. Monga (eds) *The Oxford Handbook of Africa and Economics: Volume 2 – Policies and Practices*. Oxford: Oxford University Press: 830–848.

OECD (2012) 'Statistics on Resource Flows to Developing Countries'. Paris: OECD.

Page, J. (2011) 'Should Africa Industrialize?', *WIDER Working Paper* 2011/47. Helsinki: UNU-WIDER.

Page, J. (2015) 'Rediscovering Structural Change: Manufacturing, Natural Resources and Industrialization', in J.Y. Lin and C. Monga (eds) *The Oxford Handbook of Africa and Economics: Volume 2 – Policies and Practices*. Oxford: Oxford University Press: 257–271.

Page, J. and M. Söderbom (2012) 'Is Small Beautiful? Small Enterprise, Aid and Employment in Africa', Working Paper 2012/94. Helsinki: UNU-WIDER.

Please, S. (1984) *The Hobbled Giant: Essays on the World Bank.* Boulder, CO: Westview Press.

Rodrik, D. (2007) *One Economics, Many Recipes: Globalization, Institutions and Economic Growth.* Princeton, NJ: Princeton University Press.

Soares de Oliveira, R. (2007) *Oil and Politics in the Gulf of Guinea.* London: Hurst.

Stiglitz, J.E., J.A. Ocampo, S. Spiegal, R. French-Davis and D. Nayyar (2006) *Stability with Growth: Macroeconomics, Liberalization and Development.* New York: Oxford University Press.

Streeten, P., S.J. Burki, M. ul Haq, N. Hicks and F. Stewart (1981). *First Things First: Meeting Basic Human Needs in the Developing Countries.* New York: Oxford University Press for the World Bank.

Taylor, L. (1988) *Varieties of Stabilization Experience: Towards Sensible Macroeconomics in the Third World.* Oxford: Oxford University Press for UNU-WIDER.

Taylor, L. (ed.) (1993) *The Rocky Road to Reform: Adjustment, Income Distribution and Growth in the Developing World.* Cambridge MA: MIT Press for UNU-WIDER.

Tchatchouang, J-C. (2015) 'The CFA Franc Zone: A Biography', in J.Y. Lin and C. Monga (eds) *The Oxford Handbook of Africa and Economics: Volume 2 – Policies and Practices.* Oxford: Oxford University Press: 114–129.

Thoburn, J. (2009) 'Vietnam as a Role Model for Development', WIDER Working Paper 2009/30. Helsinki: UNU-WIDER.

UN (2013) *A New Global Partnership: Eradicate Poverty and Transform Economies Through Sustainable Development.* New York: United Nations.

UNCTAD (2013) *Economic Development in Africa Report 2013: Intra-African Trade – Unlocking Private Sector Dynamism.* Geneva: United Nations Conference on Trade and Development.

UN-DESA (2013) *World Population 2012.* New York: United Nations Department of Economic and Social Affairs (Population Division).

UNU-WIDER (2014) 'Aid, Growth and Employment', *ReCom Position Paper.* Helsinki: UNU-WIDER. http://www.recom.wider.unu.edu.

van der Hoeven, R. (1991) 'Adjustment with a Human Face: Still Relevant or Overtaken by Events?' *World Development* 19(12): 1835–1845.

van der Hoeven, R.E. (2014) 'Full Employment Target: What Lessons for a Post-2015 Development Agenda?' *Journal of Human Development and Capabilities* 15(1–2): 161–175.

van der Hoeven, R.E. (2015) 'Can the Sustainable Development Goals Stem Rising Income Inequality in the World?' Valedictory Lecture 8 October 2015. International Institute of Social Studies, Erasmus University Rotterdam, The Hague.

Westad, O.A. (2005) *The Global Cold War.* Cambridge: Cambridge University Press.

World Bank (1981) *Accelerated Development in Sub-Saharan Africa.* Washington, DC: World Bank.

World Bank (1990) *Making Adjustment Work for the Poor: A Framework for Policy Reform in Africa.* Washington, DC: World Bank.

World Bank (2007) *World Bank Assistance to Agriculture in Africa: An IEG Review.* Washington, DC: World Bank Independent Evaluation Group.

World Bank (2012a) *World Development Report 2013: Jobs.* Washington, DC: World Bank.

World Bank (2012b) *Ethiopia: Additional Financing for the Third Productive Safety Nets Program (APLIII) Project.* Washington, DC: World Bank.

World Bank (2015a) *Africa Pulse* 11. Washington, DC: World Bank.

World Bank (2015b) 'World Bank Forecasts Global Poverty to Fall Below 10% for First Time; Major Hurdles Remain in Goal to End Poverty by 2030', *Press Release* 4 October. Washington, DC: World Bank.

Wuyts, M. (2003) 'The Agrarian Question in Mozambique's Transition and Reconstruction', in T. Addison (ed.) *From Conflict to Recovery in Africa.* Oxford: Oxford University Press for UNU-WIDER: 141–154.

8. Poverty, employment and inequality in the SDGs: heterodox discourse, orthodox policies?

Malte Luebker[1]

INTRODUCTION

Launched with the ambition to build the 'most inclusive development agenda the world has ever seen' (in the words of Ban Ki-moon; United Nations, 2014), one of the most visible innovations of the SDGs is the prominence they give to inequality, labour and employment. While the issue was entirely absent from the original version of the MDGs in 2000, references to decent work are plentiful in their successor. To achieve 'Sustained, inclusive and sustainable economic growth', SDG goal 8 contains targets on productivity-enhancing policies, employment and decent work, and makes reference to three out of the four fundamental labour rights. While these are necessary ingredients for a sustained increase in living standards and important elements of heterodox accounts of development, they are compatible with orthodox policy prescriptions. Their underlying logic emphasizes that productivity growth, if combined with employment and labour rights, drives inclusive and sustainable economic development. This is an unproblematic preposition from an orthodox standpoint, but it need not hold when approached from a heterodox perspective.

This chapter places the treatment of labour in the SDGs in the larger discourse around employment, inequality and poverty to assess how fundamental the shift from the MDGs is. How far do the SDGs reflect the heterodox discourse, and do they signal a breach with orthodox policies? Section 1 lays the ground by sketching two conflicting narratives of growth and poverty, and how they conceptualize the role of labour markets and inequality in the fight against poverty. Section 2 then places the trajectory from the MDGs to the SDGs within these two narratives. Section 3 provides some empirical illustrations from emerging Asia – the 'most likely case' for the predictions of the orthodox frame to hold. Motivated by this,

141

Section 4 argues that the SDGs will only be transformative in the presence of equity-enhancing labour market institutions and collective labour rights. Section 5 concludes.

TWO ACCOUNTS OF POVERTY, PRODUCTIVITY AND GROWTH

Before going into analysis of the SDGs, it is useful to consider how the two dominant narratives in the development discourse understand central concepts and infuse them with meaning – in other words, how they frame them. In an often cited definition, to frame means 'to select some aspects of a perceived reality and make them more salient in a communicating text, in such a way as to promote a particular problem definition, causal interpretation, moral evaluation and/or treatment recommendation for the item described' (Entman, 1993: 52). Frames are ideal-typical, internally consistent accounts of reality (and not necessarily the positions held by any one individual); they can be used as a heuristic tool to differentiate between conflicting interpretations of the world around us.

Frames have repercussions for reality because they define problems, diagnose causes, make moral judgements and suggest remedies (Entman, 1993). How we conceptualize poverty and relate it to growth and economic development, how we link it to labour and inequality, can therefore shape our understanding of the causes of poverty, and hence policy recommendations. Faced with the same reality (in as far as one objective reality exists), different frames can lead to polar opposite interpretations and suggest conflicting solutions. The discourse around poverty, employment and inequality is a good example how orthodox and heterodox accounts of development differ in terms of problem analysis, causal interpretations and ultimately policy recommendations. Placing the MDGs and the SDGs – arguably the two single-most important pieces of text for the development discourse of the past two decades – within these two frames can therefore help understanding how decisive the shift between them is.

Economic Orthodoxy and the Magic of Growth

From the orthodox perspective, poverty is essentially a problem of insufficient income. The solution then is to raise incomes, which – to be sustainable – is required to increase production (which gives rise to incomes). This is why rich countries have escaped absolute poverty and poor countries have not. In other words, growth holds the key to poverty reduction. Accelerating development by removing obstacles that hinder the efficient use of resources and adopting other growth-enhancing policies is then the natural strategy to combat poverty. Labour and distributional issues are not central to this narrative since, if growth is allowed to take hold, the incomes of the poor rise just like those of everyone else (Dollar and Kraay, 2002). Labour markets are best treated with 'benign neglect' so that, like in any other market, the invisible hand can balance supply and demand. In this world, labour is a normal good and wages are simply the price of labour that reflects the marginal productivity of labour. If they did not, employers could reap extra profits by hiring more workers – and would do so until they drive up wages so that this source of arbitrage is closed.

If workers become more productive over time, the same logic applies and employers bid up wages until they match productivity, closing this source of arbitrage. This implies that, at the micro-level, wages grow in line with productivity and, by extension, average wages will grow in line with average productivity and the benefits of growth are widely shared. It follows that, at the macro-level, the share of wages in national output will stay constant: simply multiply average wages and average productivity by the number of workers, and the numerical identity is apparent. If labour shares nonetheless change over time, this reflects a change in the mix of factors of production (or, in fact, artefacts of national accounting).[2] Falling labour shares are therefore nothing alarming, but simply a consequence of greater capital-intensity of production. These two axioms – stability of labour shares and wage growth in line with productivity – are central to link growth to rising incomes and poverty alleviation.

A third cornerstone of the orthodox narrative concerns the role of labour market institutions and their potentially adverse impact on allocative efficiency. If wages reflect the productivity of an individual worker, setting their level is a micro-economic problem best solved by the worker and her employer. Wage inequality reflects the relative scarcity of different skill levels; investment in education and training is the preferred response to contain pay differentials. Any state intervention that tries to force the invisible hand is likely to be self-defeating. Minimum wages are a prime exhibit in this narrative: set them below the market-clearing level and they are redundant. Set them above the market-clearing wage, and they price workers with the lowest productivity out of the market and hence hurt the poorest. Even where minimum wages are not enforced, they still cause harm by deterring law-abiding would-be employers from investing. Minimum wages are, in other words, portrayed as a classic case of the 'big trade-off' between equality and efficiency (Okun, 1975).

From the orthodox viewpoint, another set of perceived inefficiencies is introduced by trade unions and collective agreements. By setting working conditions above the level that would emerge from the market, they serve the interest of a narrow group of privileged insiders, at the expense of outsiders and society at large. Collective labour rights such as freedom of association, the right to collective bargaining and most notably the right to strike therefore sit uneasily within the orthodox frame. If at all, they derive their justification from external sources (such as human rights). Less problematic than rights that affect the relationship between labour and capital are the abolition of child labour and forced labour and an endorsement of non-discrimination principles (albeit this often comes with the reservation that well-meaning anti-discrimination legislation can have adverse side effects). In sum, the orthodox frame puts its emphasis on the self-regulating principles of the market and remains lukewarm and partial in its endorsement of labour rights.

Heterodox Counter-narratives of Inequality, Institutions and Rights

The heterodox frame turns most of these conjectures on their head. Poverty is primarily seen as a function of distributive processes, which explains why relative deprivation is found in rich and poor countries alike. Growth is a biased metric of social progress since it weights the income growth of the top deciles more heavily than growth at the bottom. If the goal is to fight poverty, growth is therefore not a sufficient condition: what matters more is the relative incidence of growth across different strata. To explain distributional outcomes, the heterodox account emphasizes the central role of labour markets which are unlike other markets and characterized by persistent power asymmetries between workers and employers. Moreover, labour is not a normal good. Cut wages, and workers may increase (not decrease) their supply of labour, given that they have to feed a family. This gives rise to rents and multiple equilibria; the invisible hand remains, alas, invisible.

While productivity gains are welcome, from a heterodox standpoint it is an open question how they are shared between workers and employers. Measuring productivity at the level of an individual worker is seen as elusive, given that labour and capital – and workers of different skill levels – are complements. Whether productivity gains feed into higher wages or boost profits is essentially determined by the relative power of the two sides. Hence, labour shares need not be stable: shift the power in favour of capital, and labour shares will fall; strengthen workers' rights, and they will stabilize or rise (see also Krämer, 2010). From this perspective, vertical redistribution between labour and capital is a central problem. Rising labour costs need not cause unemployment, but they force firms to find productivity gains and allow the most efficient firms to grow at the expense of the laggards (the so-called 'cleansing effect'; see Mayneris, Poncet and Zhang, 2014).

Heterodox interpretations of labour market institutions stress such dynamic efficiencies and distributional impacts, sometimes dubbed 'equity efficiency' (van der Hoeven and Saget, 2004; see also Freeman, 2008). Outcome equity and long-term growth are seen as macro-economic challenges that require institutional solutions to solve coordination problems. Proponents of this view give prominence to the equity-enhancing impact of trade unions and collective bargaining (see Hayter, 2015) and minimum wages (Belser and Rani, 2015). While these affect the primary distribution of incomes, the heterodox frame also stresses the redistributive function of institutions closely intertwined with labour markets, namely social insurance and social assistance mechanisms (see Behrendt and Woodall, 2015).

Labour rights play a prominent role in this frame. Discrimination, child labour and forced labour are not only seen as a violation of individual rights, but as having broader repercussions by undermining fair competition and the prospects of other workers. The right to organize, the right to bargain collectively and the right to strike become central for workers to counter the inherent power imbalances of labour markets.[3] These collective labour rights help them to appropriate some of the gains from productivity growth, but also to safeguard other labour rights. Without these process rights, all other labour rights become hollow and vulnerable. Labour rights are therefore not only derived as human rights, but find an additional justification that is internal to labour markets.

Though necessarily incomplete and sketchy, the description of these two frames – doubtlessly familiar to most readers – provides a good backdrop to analyse how the MDGs and the SDGs conceptualize poverty, employment and inequality. How radical has the shift been? One way to assess this shift is to draw on the three central conjectures of the orthodox paradigm: that productivity gains translate into wage gains and benefit everyone; that hence labour shares are broadly stable (and if not, that they change for good reasons); and that even well-meaning interventions such as minimum wage legislation ultimately do more harm than good. All of these are disputed by the heterodox account, which – unlike the orthodox frame – also puts emphasis on collective labour rights.

FROM THE MDGs TO THE SDGs: EQUITY LOST AND FOUND?

The MDGs: Counting the Poor

One undisputable achievement of the Millennium Development Goals (MDGs) is that they focused minds on eradicating extreme poverty. Half a century after Harold Wilson (1953) had appealed to the 'conscience of mankind' to launch a 'war on world poverty', this battle had still not been won: At the eve of the new millennium, 1.75 billion people were living in adjacent poverty (defined as living on less than $1.25 per day at purchasing power parities).[4] The Millennium Declaration brought this embarrassment back into public awareness, combining it with other goals such as achieving universal primary education, reducing child mortality and improving maternal health. Looking forward in a spirit of optimism, the General Assembly did not dwell on the most puzzling question of all: How was it possible that, despite unprecedented global prosperity, millions of people were still subsiding in poverty?

In many respects, goal 1 to 'Eradicate extreme poverty and hunger' was the corner piece of the MDGs that dominated public and academic attention alike. While reminiscent of Harold Wilson's writing in the 1950s, the basic conceptual framework behind the poverty goal had been developed much earlier: by Charles Booth (1902–1903) and Seebohm Rowntree (1901) in their path-breaking work on poverty in London and York. Both used the poverty line and the poverty headcount ratio (the proportion of the population below that line) in the same way as done in MDG target 1A to '[h]alve, between 1990 and 2015, the proportion of people whose income is less than $1.25 a day'. Described by Sen (1976: 219) as 'obviously a very crude index', the poverty headcount ratio became the defining metric of the MDGs.

While specific on the objective, the Millennium Declaration remained silent on the causes of poverty, and vague in the analysis of the concrete actions needed to achieve its goals. The text includes a commitment to 'create an environment – at the national and global levels alike – which is conducive to development and to the elimination of poverty' and mentions good governance, resource mobilization, trade and debt (United Nations, 2000: para. 12ff.). Neither income inequality nor the labour market received particular attention. Apart from a reference to youth employment, the Millennium Declaration neither mentions 'employment', 'labour' or 'jobs' (see United Nations, 2000). By divorcing the objective of poverty alleviation from the social processes that generate poverty, the text fell short of the standards set by Rowntree (1901) a century earlier. He had studied poverty in the context of an inquiry into the 'social and economic condition of the wage-earning classes in York' and concluded that a central cause of poverty was the 'lowness of [the] wage' (Rowntree, 1901: 12, 120). This insight later led Rowntree (1918) to investigate 'the human needs of labour' and to demand that the additional wealth created by productivity gains should be devoted to 'the payment of a living wage'. To this end, trade boards should set 'minimum wages which would enable [workers] to marry, live in a decent house, and bring up a family of normal size' (Rowntree, 1918: 138).

The omission of labour became so glaring that, at the 2005 World Summit, leaders pledged to support decent work in the further implementation of the MDGs.[5] The new target 1B to 'Achieve full and productive employment and decent work for all, including women and young people' partly filled the gap in the original list of MDGs (United Nations, 2008). Necessitated by the requirement that data be widely available, the indicators to monitor progress were largely proxies for the underlying concepts: labour productivity, the employment-to-population ratio, the proportion of own-account and contributing family workers in total employment (so-called 'vulnerable employment'), and working poverty. The rationale for including these elements was simple: increasing labour productivity and wage employment[6] should lead to a reduction of working poverty (that is, those who subside below the poverty threshold despite having a job).

From Poverty to Inequality: Shifts in the Discourse of the 2000s

By stating poverty reduction as an objective but remaining vague on the specifics, the MDGs left space for both orthodox and heterodox interpretations. On the orthodox side, the idea that 'growth is good for the poor' was a central paradigm (Dollar and Kraay, 2002). This rested on the finding that average incomes of the poorest quintile, across a large panel of countries, tend to rise in line with average incomes.[7] This relationship was said to hold irrespective of 'policies and institutions that explain growth rates of average incomes' (Dollar and Kraay, 2002: 195). Accelerating growth through market-friendly reforms, it was argued, was the best poverty-reduction strategy. This narrative allowed institutions such as the World Bank to re-cast Washington Consensus policies under the banner of 'pro-poor growth'. The strategy had some success. With a fine sense of irony, Martin Ravallion (2004: 1) concluded that '[t]hese days it seems that almost everyone in the development community is talking about "pro-poor growth"', and continued by asking what exactly pro-poor growth is. To some in the orthodox camp, the answer was simple: 'Growth is pro-poor if the poverty measure of interest falls' (Kraay, 2006: 198). Applied to the MDGs, this was setting a low bar: As long as growth led to an increase in average incomes, it is likely that some fraction of the gains, however small, reaches the poorest in society, bringing down the poverty headcount ratio.

This account avoided posing a question central to the heterodox narrative: How are the gains from development distributed? Academics and institutions[8] that stressed the distributional impacts of growth shaped the debate in two important ways: First, they produced a wealth of data that showed the importance of different distributional paths for poverty reduction, that growth has a lower impact on poverty at higher levels of inequality, and that rising inequality over the past decades had undermined much of the poverty-reducing potential of growth (see, for example, Shorrocks and van der Hoeven, 2004; Dagdeviren, van der Hoeven and Weeks, 2002; Addison and Cornia, 2001). Second, the heterodox literature brought back into focus how institutions and policy choices shape the distribution of incomes. This leads the poverty debate into more controversial, more political questions – such as how trade liberalization, financial markets or the labour market institutions shape outcomes (see, for example, Ocampo and Jomo, 2007).

Unlike 15 years ago, inequality and increasingly labour are now topics of the mainstream development debate. A good illustration for this shift is the World Bank's choice of themes for its World Development Report: *Attacking Poverty* (2000–2001), *Equity and Development* (2006) and *Jobs* (2013). The change in emphasis – towards distributional outcomes and the mechanisms that generate them – was an important backdrop to the 'post-2015' development agenda (to which several authors in this volume contributed).[9] Jan Vandemoortele, one of the architects of the MDGs, was among those who argued most forcefully that inequality should become a centrepiece of the SDGs: 'A focus on extreme poverty and hunger is obviously more convenient, but even if the post-2015 agenda were universal, neither poverty nor climate change should be the centre of attention, but inequality' (Vandemoortele, 2015).

The SDGs: How Radical a Departure from Orthodoxy?

How far have the SDGs heeded these calls? For those with enough patience, reading through the 35 pages of the resolution adopted at the 2015 World Summit holds some surprises. World leaders 'resolve, between now and 2030, to end poverty and hunger everywhere; to combat inequalities within and among countries' (United Nations, 2015: para. 3) and that '[a]s we embark on this great collective journey, we pledge that no one will be left behind' (United Nations, 2015: para. 4). They commit to 'combating inequality within and among countries' (United Nations, 2015: para. 13) and recognize that '[t]here are rising inequalities within and among countries. There are enormous disparities of opportunity, wealth and power' (United Nations, 2015: para. 14). Moreover, world leaders go into what they omitted in 2000, labour markets. They talk about 'shared prosperity and decent work for all' (United Nations, 2015: para. 3) and that they 'envisage a world in which every country enjoys sustained, inclusive and sustainable economic growth and decent work for all' (United Nations, 2015: para. 9).

So have inequality and labour – two central elements of the heterodox frame – moved to the centre of a new development consensus, or are the SDGs still firmly grounded in orthodox policy prescriptions? There is, of course, the easy criticism that an agenda that ranges from pastoralist and fisheries development to desertification and dust storms, and has targets on modern energy systems and waste generation, has in fact very little focus at all. With 17 sustainable development goals and 169 targets, the world might have gotten more than it had bargained for. But then, the world is complex. So it is worth asking what the SDGs have to say about inequality and labour markets. Is there anything new that goes beyond the wisdom of the MDGs?

SDG 8: Productivity, Employment and Labour Rights

The promise of goal 8 is to 'Promote sustained, inclusive and sustainable economic growth, full and productive employment and decent work for all'. With 12 targets that run for almost a full page, it is one of the longer SDGs. However, it arguably boils down to a narrative that relies on three ideas: productivity, employment and labour rights.

Productivity is the starting point of SDG 8 (and an element familiar from the MDG Indicator 1.4). However, there is now much more detail on how to achieve this: The first four targets are concerned with increasing output, diversification to achieve higher productivity, and policies that support entrepreneurship, innovation and formalization of small enterprises. Added to the mix is resource efficiency to decouple economic growth from environmental degradation, and access to banking in target 8.10. Next are full and productive employment and decent work for all (in target 8.5), expanding slightly on the familiar language by making reference to persons with disabilities. Other points concern youth employment (8.6), the reference to decent job creation in target 8.3 and job creation in tourism (8.9).

The genuinely new element is the recognition of labour rights. Goal 8 makes explicit reference to three of the four fundamental principles and rights at work, namely the right to equal pay for work of equal value (target 8.5), the eradication of forced labour and the abolition of child labour, in particular in its worst forms (both under target 8.7). While there is a general reference to 'labour rights' (target 8.8), a notable absence from the list of rights enumerated in goal 8 is the right to freedom of association and the right to collective bargaining – and hence precisely those human rights that many UN member States systematically violate.[10] So we are left with a three-quarter set of the fundamental labour rights that sidesteps those aspects that make them most threatening to authoritarian governments.

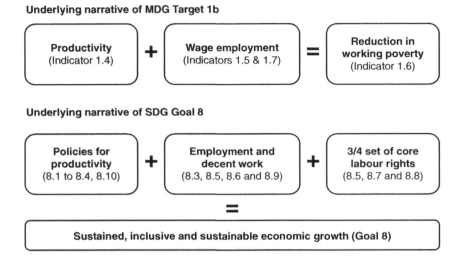

Source: Author's interpretation of United Nations (2008 and 2015).

Figure 8.1   Underlying narratives of MDG target 1b and SDG goal 8

The narrative of SDG 8 is therefore broadly familiar (see Figure 8.1). It recognizes that economic growth and higher productivity are a precondition for sustained welfare gains, and then turns to employment as a transmission mechanism through which growth reaches people. The main innovation is the (albeit incomplete) recognition of labour rights. Hence, goal 8 uses many of the key concepts of the heterodox frame. However, it mainly reflects 'agreed language' of UN fora and ILO declarations[11] and contains nothing that is directly offensive from an orthodox viewpoint. In fact, the underlying narrative of SDG 8 is broadly compatible with an orthodox account of productivity as the driver behind social progress. By contrast, the question that motivates heterodox inquiries – how and under what conditions productivity gains translate into higher incomes – is given less prominence in goal 8.

SDG 10: Reducing Inequality and the Role of Institutions

More radical departures from the orthodox account come in SDG 10 'Reduce inequality within and among countries'. Target 10.1 aims to 'achieve and sustain income growth of the bottom 40 per cent of the population at a rate higher than the national average'. While it omits a reference to the worsening of inequality due to ever-larger income shares at the very top of the distribution, it breaks with the idea that growth is pro-poor as long as it (even to the slightest degree) benefits the poor. Instead, it endorses a growth path that Chenery et al. (1974) had called 'redistribution with growth'. Target 10.3 goes beyond the conventional promise to ensure equal opportunity, and calls for a reduction in inequalities of outcome.

Rather than seeing these inequalities as unavoidable, the text alludes to institutions that shape distributive outcomes and refers (albeit some-what vaguely) to 'legislation, policies and action in this regard'. Target 10.4 singles out the role of fiscal, wage and social protection policies to 'progressively achieve greater equality'. These are, in fact, some of the main levers for domestic redistribution (see Luebker, 2015). And it does not end here. Target 10.5 goes into the need to '[i]mprove the regulation and monitoring of global financial markets and institutions and strengthen the implementation of such regulations' (for a critical appraisal, see Rixen, 2013). In the aftermath of the global financial crisis, this might no longer raise any eye-brows, but was controversial a decade ago when some argued that uncontrolled financial liberalization has little direct benefits for developing countries but can have devastating outcomes for their labour markets (van der Hoeven and Luebker, 2007).

The SDGs and Labour: What is New?

In sum, when judged by their content, the SDGs present a significant departure from the MDGs on two fronts: First, they incorporate a labour market perspective – largely by elaborating on the themes of productivity and employment that entered the MDGs a decade ago, but adding the perspective of labour rights (though shying away from naming the rights to freedom of association and collective bargaining, not to mention the right to strike). Second, they reject the post-MDG discourse that equated poverty reduction with orthodox 'growth policies'. Instead, they advocate a redistributive growth path and policies that promote equality of oppor-tunity and outcome.

In what follows, this chapter argues that action on SDG 8 will only be transformative for development policies if the messages of SDG 10 are taken seriously – and that labour market institutions can play an import-ant role to achieve more equitable growth. In other words, it wants to make the heterodox case that optimism implied by Figure 8.1 cannot be taken for granted: productivity growth, even when combined with full and decent employment and some labour rights, does not necessarily lead to equitable development. For this to happen, one needs to focus on institu-tions and policies that shape the distribution of growth (see Berg and

Kucera, 2008). In other words, labour markets need governance and not 'benign neglect'.

PRODUCTIVITY AND WAGES: LESSONS FROM EMERGING ASIA

Most empirical research on the role of growth and labour markets in the development process is carried out (especially on the orthodox side) in the form of quantitative studies that 'test' relationships across a large panel of countries. By contrast, many heterodox researchers have invested into the in-depth case studies and sought to derive concrete, practical knowledge from them (see Cornia, van der Hoeven and Mkandawire, 1992; van der Geest and van der Hoeven, 1999). This section is inspired by this tradition and turns to three cases from emerging countries in Asia to assess the three orthodox conjectures mentioned earlier: (1) that productivity growth leads to wage growth, (2) that labour shares are stable and (3) that, where minimum wages succeed in pushing up wages, they also destroy employment.

The case selection is heavily biased in favour of confirming orthodox views: they are Thailand and China, two countries that experienced substantial productivity growth and operated under conditions nearing full employment (a critical, if rarely met assumption of the orthodox model). The third is Cambodia, which more than doubled its minimum wage within a few years – a move that, according to orthodox accounts, should have devastated its garment sector. In other words, the sample contains only cases that present favourable conditions for orthodox predictions to hold. Flyvbjerg (2006: 230) refers to them as 'critical cases' that permit logical deductions of the type 'If this is not valid for this case, then it applies to no cases'.

In the orthodox discourse, the emerging economies of Asia are frequently cited for their record in terms of growth and poverty reduction (and, in many countries, light-touch regulation). Moreover, East and South-East Asian economies are often portrayed as an example of equitable growth (Birdsall, Ross and Sabot, 1995). In a context of rising global inequality and slowing growth, Asia's economic transformation and its record in terms of poverty reduction has indeed been unprecedented – despite the Asian financial crisis in the late 1990s and the recent slow-down in China. In the 25 years to 2015, labour productivity doubled in South-East Asia, almost tripled in South Asia and, propelled by China, rose six-fold in East Asia (see ILO, 2015). At the same time, the continent almost single-handedly achieved MDG 1 as the number of people in extreme poverty fell by 1.2 billion in Asia (see World Bank, 2015: 35).

But it is easy to forget that many parts of today's Asia still resemble the conditions Rowntree found a century ago in Britain when he concluded that 'the wages paid for unskilled labour in York are insufficient to provide food, shelter, and clothing adequate to maintain a family of moderate size at a state of bare physical efficiency' (Rowntree, 1901: 133). Replace 'York' with 'Kolkata' or 'Yangon', and the statement rings true today. Just under 400 million people currently live in extreme poverty in Asia, even when measured by the old poverty line of PPP$1.25 per day (in 2005 prices). At second glance, Asia therefore holds more cautious lessons. These emerge when we ask what would have been possible, given Asia's economic performance. In addressing the three conjunctures of the orthodox narrative, the remainder of this section expands on a theme that Rolph van der Hoeven (2015) put much emphasis on in his valedictory lecture: the functional distribution of incomes, or how much of the fruits of progress have reached workers in the form of wages.

Conjecture 1: Productivity Growth Leads to Wage Growth

There is ample evidence that countries with higher labour productivity have, on average, also higher wages. This is partly the result of a simple identity in national accounting: labour productivity is usually measured as an economy's value added divided by the number of workers. Average wages can be calculated as an economy's entire wage bill (which is a sub-set of value added in the distribution of income account), divided by the number of wage workers. It follows that, assuming a constant ratio of wages to total value added and a constant share of wage workers in total employment, average wages will be higher. Of course, in reality both ratios vary, but it is still a safe assumption that wages in Singapore must be higher than those in Cambodia – given that labour productivity in Singapore is roughly twenty times higher than in Cambodia.[12] So raising productivity seems to be a good starting point for those who want higher wages. The problem, of course, is that a country's GDP grows relatively slowly and a lot of variation can occur as a country progresses from a least-developed nation to (potentially) high-income status. Therefore, what broadly holds across countries need not hold over time, at least not in the short- or medium-term.

Thailand is a good illustration for this point. As Figure 8.2 shows, the country's key manufacturing sector managed to achieve rapid productivity gains in the decade after the MDGs were adopted, with a compound annual growth rate of nearly 5 per cent. As a result, aggregate labour

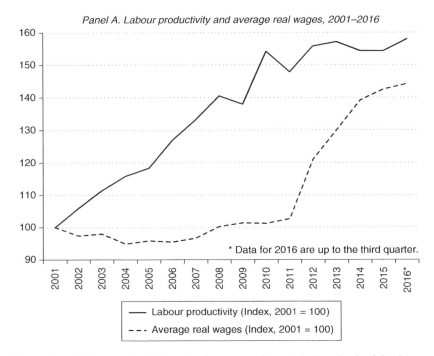

Note: Annual data are calculated as simple averages of quarterly data. Productivity data from the new series (2013 = 100) are linked to the old series based on the ratio of the two series in 2013. Wages refer to government and private employees.

Source: Bank of Thailand (Series EC_EI_029, EC_EI_029_S2, EC_RL_014, EC_RL_014_S2 and EC_EI_027).

Figure 8.2A   Key statistics for Thailand's manufacturing sector

productivity grew by more than 50 per cent from 2001 to 2010 alone. Clearly, this is a highly impressive performance under MDG Indicator 1.4.[13] However, none of these gains reached workers: real wages in Thailand's manufacturing sector stagnated throughout the entire decade, with nominal wage gains outstripping inflation in some years and falling behind in others. Data from Thailand's national accounts confirm that this led to a large decline in the sector's labour share from 47.7 per cent in 1995 to only 31.6 per cent in 2010 (see Figure 8.2, Panel B). Had the labour share indeed held stable since 1995, real wages would have been 50 per cent higher in 2010 than they actually were.

Orthodox explanations for such a divergence usually invoke shifts towards greater capital intensity of production. Hence, the argument runs,

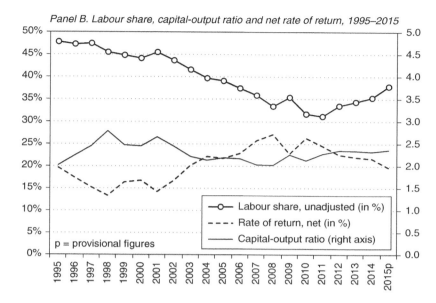

Panel B. Labour share, capital-output ratio and net rate of return, 1995–2015

Note: The labour share is measured as compensation of employees/value added; the net rate of return is measured as net operating surplus (incl. mixed income) / net capital stock at current replacement cost; the capital-output ratio is measured as net capital stock over GDP at factor cost. Hence, a falling ratio represents declining capital intensity.

Source: Thailand National Economic and Social Development Board (NESDB): Capital Stock of Thailand 2015 (Bangkok, n.d.) and NESDB: National Accounts of Thailand 2015 (Bangkok, n.d.).

Figure 8.2B   Key statistics for Thailand's manufacturing sector

it is only fair that the gains from productivity growth accrue to capital. Fortunately, one can put this explanation to a test. The capital-output ratio is the standard indicator for the capital intensity of production. It can be derived by dividing the industry's net capital stock by the value of total output (or GDP at factor cost) so that a rising ratio signals increasing capital intensity. Contrary to the textbook explanation, the data for Thailand's manufacturing sector do not show any evidence for this. If anything, the capital-output ratio fell in the first decade of the new millennium (albeit arguably from a high starting point in the aftermath of the Asian financial crisis). The other striking statistic that can be derived from the national accounts is the net rate of return, or the operating surplus and mixed income that accrues to capital after adjusting for the consumption of fixed capital (hence, *net* and not gross). From an already impressive

16.7 per cent in 2000 it reaches an all-time high of 26.2 per cent in 2010 (see Figure 8.2, Panel B).

In sum, Thailand presents a striking case where, for an entire decade, all the benefits from an impressive productivity performance accrued to capital, and none reached workers. Why have the gains been distributed so unevenly? A key factor is the modest adjustment of minimum wage adjustments during this period, which largely tracked inflation. In the absence of strong trade unions and any meaningful collective bargaining over wages, employers used these as a benchmark for wage adjustments (see Boonyamanond et al., 2013). As a result, Thai workers (and the many migrants in the sector) were not able to capture any gains. Real wages only increased in 2012/13, when the government of Yingluck Shinawatra fulfilled a campaign pledge and raised the minimum wage to 300 Baht per day (approximately US$8).[14] The Thai example therefore presents a puzzle for the orthodox narrative, but supports the heterodox argument that productivity gains by themselves are an insufficient condition for higher wages.

Conjecture 2: Labour Shares are Stable

When productivity growth does not translate into higher real wages, this can – as in the case of Thailand – lead to large shifts in the functional distribution of incomes in favour of capital.[15] As the discussion above has shown, Conjectures 1 and 2 are merely two different ways of looking at the same underlying principle – though traditionally economists have placed greater attention on the analysis of labour shares. One prominent example is Kaldor's (1961) 'stylized fact' of stable labour shares. While this might have held at the time, since the 1990s globalization, the deregulation of labour markets and the 'financialization' of economies have all contributed to shifts in the functional distribution (see Guscina, 2006; ILO, 2012 and 2014). While falling labour shares are well-documented for many advanced economies, Trapp (2015) shows that declining labour shares are also a near-universal phenomenon in developing regions. Among them, East Asia and the Pacific stand out for a sharp decline of 14 percentage points between 1990 and 2011. Does this matter, given the region's stellar record of poverty reduction? Again, the answer will depend on the perspective – and whether the focus is merely on poverty, or also on inequality. Capital incomes are, after all, highly concentrated and shifts in the functional distribution of incomes towards capital therefore tend to be dis-equalizing (see also Atkinson, 2009).

A case in point is China, where income inequality has risen dramatically in the past two decades. According to official data from the National Bureau of Statistics (NBS), the Gini coefficient for disposable incomes

Note: Based on revised flow of funds account (physical transaction), as first published in the China Statistical Yearbook of 2010.

Source: NBS, online database, SYB 2015 (Table 3-27) and SYB 2016 (Table 3-21).

Figure 8.3   Trends in China's labour share, 1992–2014

stood at 0.462 in 2015.[16] This signifies an extremely uneven distribution of incomes, and is a sharp contrast to the more egalitarian distribution before the launch of the market-oriented reforms. China's rising inequality coincides with a remarkable shift in the functional distribution of incomes. As recently as the late 1990s, the labour share had fluctuated in a relatively narrow band between 52 and 53 per cent of GDP. This period of relative stability was followed by one of rapid decline, with a low of 47 per cent recorded in 2011 (see Figure 8.3). However, even this well-known decline in the aggregate labour share somewhat understates the fundamental shift that occurred in the Chinese economy since the turn of the millennium.

A closer look at the data reveals that the labour share has been broadly stable or even growing modestly in the general government and household sectors (see Table 8.1). By contrast, the labour share in the corporate sector (both non-financial corporations and financial institutions) fell dramatically between 2000 and 2010, by some 9.0 percentage points in

Table 8.1   China's labour share by institutional sector, 2000–2014

Institutional sector						Change in percentage points	
	2000	2005	2010	2013	2014	2000 to 2010	2010 to 2014
Total economy	52.7	50.4	47.6	50.9	51.0	−5.2	+3.5
Non-financial Corporations	45.2	38.1	36.2	41.0	41.3	−9.0	+5.1
Financial Institutions	40.3	38.7	31.7	29.4	29.3	−8.5	−2.4
General Government	82.4	84.6	85.1	87.1	85.9	+2.7	+0.7
Households	60.0	66.3	61.0	69.9	69.9	+1.1	+8.9

Note: Based on revised flow of funds account (physical transaction), as first published in the China Statistical Yearbook of 2010.

Source: NBS, online database, SYB 2015 (Table 3-27) and SYB 2016 (Table 3-21).

non-financial corporations and by 8.5 points in their financial counterparts. Given the vast size of China's economy, the numbers involved are truly astonishing: If the labour share in the corporate sector had remained stable at its 2000 level, the annual wage bill would have been 2.3 trillion Yuan higher a decade later (or US$350 billion).[17] While the labour share has since risen, it is still short of its level at the beginning of the millennium, especially in the corporate sector.

Of course, in contrast to the experience of Thailand's manufacturing sector, wages in China have grown rapidly since the turn of the millennium (albeit from a very low starting point). However, few developing countries will manage to replicate China's rapid pace of industrialization, structural transformation and productivity growth. So despite apparent success in raising living standards, the country's experience also holds a more cautious lesson: that productivity growth alone does not guarantee workers a fair share in the fruits of progress.

Conjecture 3: Where Minimum Wages Succeed in Pushing up Wages, they also Destroy Employment

Can policy interventions help to achieve better outcomes where the invisible hand of the market fails, or are such attempts self-defeating? Minimum wages are a particularly controversial policy tool and a core point of the orthodox-heterodox disagreements – though there are some signs of rapprochement. In a paper commissioned by the World Bank,

Betcherman (2014) reviews some 150 studies from developing countries and finds that the impact of minimum wages on employment is usually modest, and can go either way. By contrast, the distributional implications are much more pronounced: minimum wages generally have an equalizing effect among the covered population, but may fail to reach those who are not within their scope. The World Development Report 2013 used this research to argue that a 'plateau' exists where effects that enhance and undermine efficiency exist side by side, and most of the impact of labour market institutions is redistributive. The advice to policy makers was to avoid falling off the 'cliffs' at either extreme (that is, too little or too much regulation) (see World Bank, 2012: 25ff.).

While the theoretical debate is largely settled, it is still worth considering an illustrative example for the impact that minimum wages can have. As suggested by Flyvbjerg (2006), selecting a 'critical' case where the odds are highly stacked against finding a benign outcome is a useful strategy. What would the conditions be under which, from an orthodox perspective, minimum wages should be most damaging? Arguably, the following scenario comes close: Imagine a mature export industry that is subject to intense global competition and dominated by footloose investors and highly price-conscious buyers. Further assume that employers must comply with the minimum wage (which hence has 'bite'), and that the workers do not consume any of the products they produce (and that there are consequently no positive second-order effects on demand). Now introduce a massive shock, say a doubling of the minimum wage within the space of a few years. Surely, the industry would crumble and jobs would be lost?

We are of course talking about Cambodia's garment and footwear sector, where the monthly minimum wage stood at US$61 until the end of April 2013 and, after a series of adjustments and substantial pressure from trade unions, had reached US$128 in January 2015.[18] According to the Better Factories Cambodia (2015: 16), the industry's compliance record remained impeccable throughout this period.[19] Hence, it is no surprise that average wages rose by almost half (with substantial gains even when adjusted for inflation) (see Figure 8.4, Panel A). Perhaps more surprising is that employment continued to expand at break-neck speed and reached an all-time high of 643,000 workers in the fourth quarter of 2015, up by more than a third from 458,000 in the first quarter of 2013 (see Figure 8.4, Panel B).

A plausible (but unproven) hypothesis to explain this finding is that the increase in the minimum wage addressed a market imperfection, namely an employers' cartel that artificially kept wages below their market-clearing level (see Gonzaga et al., 2013). The idea that employers collude to hold down wages is, of course, not new. Adam Smith had noted that '[m]asters

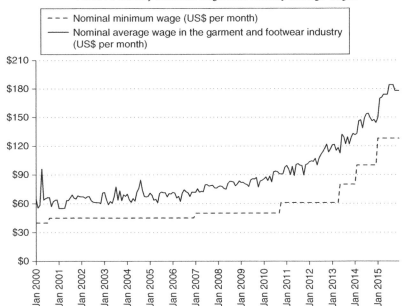

Panel A. Monthly minimum wages and monthly average wages

Note: Data on average wages and the number of workers are based on administrative records from the Ministry of Commerce and cover only factories that hold an export licence.

Source: ILO (2016), based on Ministry of Labour and Vocational Training (minimum wages) and Ministry of Commerce (number of workers).

Figure 8.4A   Monthly minimum wages, average wages and employment in Cambodia's garment and footwear sector, 2000–2015 (nominal US$ and number of workers)

are always and every where in a sort of tacit, but constant and uniform, combination, not to raise the wages of labour above their actual rate' (Smith, 1796 [1776]: I.8.13).[20] The insight of the cartel hypothesis is that minimum wages provide a common wage rate for entry-level workers, and that employers tacitly agree to refrain from competing for workers by offering better conditions and wages – even when they face labour short-ages. This allows employers to keep wages below the point where labour supply and demand would meet, generating large rents for factory owners. Lifting the minimum wage would increase the supply of labour, without significantly reducing effective demand – and hence bring the labour

Panel B. Monthly minimum wages and employment

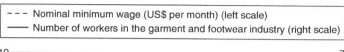

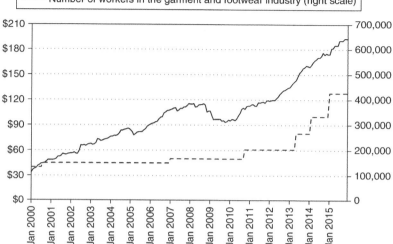

*Figure 8.4B   Monthly minimum wages, average wages and employment
in Cambodia's garment and footwear sector, 2000–2015
(nominal US$ and number of workers)*

market closer to an equilibrium with higher employment and higher wages.
Aside from this, it also redistributes rents from factory owners to workers
(and hence results in a shift in factor shares in favour of labour). Of course,
none of this 'proves' that minimum wages cannot do any harm. But it does
provide evidence that governments can use minimum wages to better the
lot of workers, without any apparent employment losses – even when such
an outcome seems highly unlikely from an orthodox perspective.

THE ROLE OF INSTITUTIONS FOR INCLUSIVE GROWTH

The discussion of these cases does not refute perceived wisdom about
the importance of productivity growth for a long-term increase in living
standards, but it holds two cautious lessons for the link between economic
growth and poverty eradication: First, in the absence of strong labour
market institutions, the orthodox conjecture that productivity growth
translates into higher wages need not hold. In the absence of labour

Narrative for equitable growth based on SDG Goals 8 & 10

Source: Author's interpretation of United Nations (2015).

Figure 8.5   Narrative for equitable growth based on SDG goals 8 and 10

market institutions and strong trade unions that are an effective voice for workers, wages can fall behind productivity growth for extended periods of time, resulting in large shifts in the functional distribution of income. This has adverse effects on inequality, widening the gap between those who have command over productive resources and those who rely on manual labour for their livelihoods. Second, wage-setting mechanisms can help to strengthen or re-establish the link from productivity growth to higher wages. Contrary to orthodox claims, this need not have negative repercussions for employment – even in the case of relatively large minimum wage increases. Hence, there is a compelling case that well-designed labour market institutions can make a significant contribution to achieving greater equity (see Betcherman, 2014).

For the SDGs, this implies that the underlying narrative of goal 8 looks fragile. While the prominence it gives to productivity, employment and labour rights presents major progress on the MDGs, implementing these elements in isolation runs in danger of falling short of the potential they hold for a departure from orthodox development policies. To make a lasting impact on inequality and contribute to just and inclusive societies, policy makers need to look beyond goal 8 and link labour markets to a more complex strategy for equitable growth (see Figure 8.5). Fortunately, the 2030 Agenda contains two crucial elements.

First, goal 10 spells out a commitment to fiscal, wage and social protection policies that reduce inequalities of outcome and achieve faster income growth for the poorest (targets 10.1, 10.3 and 10.4). As argued above, building sound labour market institutions is one core element of such a policy set (Berg, 2015). They range from wage-setting mechanisms that contribute to a more equitable primary distribution of incomes to social security and tax policies. Although their objective is often not primarily redistributive, their aggregate impact can be a much more equitable secondary distribution of disposable incomes (Luebker, 2015).

Second, workers need to have a voice in these institutions through direct participation in wage-setting mechanisms (be it minimum wage fixing or collective bargaining over wages). This requires freedom of association, the fundamental labour right that is not explicitly mentioned in SDG 8. While we cannot ignore its absence, one can argue that it is still implicitly meant: World leaders claim that the 2030 Agenda 'is grounded in the Universal Declaration of Human Rights' (United Nations, 2015: para. 10) and later 'reaffirm the importance of the Universal Declaration of Human Rights' (United Nations, 2015: para. 19). For workers, human rights include the 'right to freedom of peaceful assembly and association' (United Nations, 1948: Art. 20.1) and, even more explicitly, their 'right to form and to join trade unions for the protection of [their] interests' (United Nations, 1948: Art. 23.4). Of course, the Universal Declaration of Human Rights has also established a right on decent wages: 'Everyone who works has the right to just and favourable remuneration ensuring for himself and his family an existence worthy of human dignity, and supplemented, if necessary, by other means of social protection' (United Nations, 1948: Art. 23.3). In a sense, the realization of this right is one of the ultimate objectives of labour market institutions.

CONCLUSIONS: HETERODOX DISCOURSE, ORTHODOX POLICIES?

When the world belatedly noticed that employment and labour issues were entirely absent from the initial set of MDGs, the new target 1B was added to address this oversight. The underlying narrative was straightforward and well within the orthodox frame of development thinking: growing labour productivity, if combined with an expansion of wage employment, should help to end working poverty. By contrast, the 2030 Agenda for Sustainable Development makes ample reference to employment issues – the phrase 'decent work for all' appears no fewer than five times. Goal 8 is devoted to 'Promote sustained, inclusive and sustainable economic growth, full and productive employment and decent work for all' and expands on two familiar themes, productivity and employment, while adding labour rights as a new element. While the proliferation of goals and targets prompts cynics (and a few non-cynics) to dismiss the SDGs as an unattainable wish-list without focus, the more nuanced treatment of labour arguably presents progress.

The problem with goal 8 is that, if taken on its own, it is perfectly compatible with orthodox policy prescriptions. As this chapter argues, these might not deliver on the promise of inclusive economic growth. Their blind spot is labour market institutions. In their absence, productivity growth may not translate into higher wages for workers and hence the formula 'productivity + employment = inclusive growth' does not work its magic. Examples for this abound, including from emerging Asia. The result of such a disconnect between wages and productivity is a shift in the functional distribution of income at the expense of labour, the very opposite of inclusive growth. To achieve a more equitable growth path, heterodox insights need to manifest themselves in policy. Goal 10 provides some useful advice on the role of fiscal, wage and social protection policies to reduce inequalities of outcome and to achieve faster income growth for the poorest. To give workers a voice and a meaningful stake in development, labour rights need to encompass the right to freedom of association – something that the 2030 Agenda only refers to indirectly, by invoking the Universal Declaration of Human Rights.

NOTES

1. The author would like to acknowledge valuable comments from an anonymous peer reviewer, Thomas Rixen and participants at a seminar at the University of Bamberg. All errors remain the sole responsibility of the author. Work on this chapter was supported by the Bamberg Graduate School of Social Sciences (BAGSS) with funds from the German Research Foundation (DFG) under the Excellence Initiative (grant number GSC1024).
2. These give rise to changes in labour shares when, for instance, the share of wage workers in total employment changes. Note that the (unadjusted) labour share should rise as the share of wage workers in total employment grows over the course of development; details are discussed further below.
3. An early account of the structural power asymmetry can be found in Smith (1796 [1776]: I.8.12) who argued that employers, 'upon all ordinary occasions, have the advantage in the dispute [on the level of wages], and force the other into a compliance with their terms'.
4. Data refer to 1999. See World Bank, PovcalNet at http://iresearch.worldbank.org/PovcalNet/index.htm?1. Note that Harold Wilson referred to over 1.5 billion people who lived in 'conditions of acute hunger', so the number had arguably gone up.
5. A/RES/60/1, para. 47.
6. Note that the MDGs do not directly mention wage employment, but aim to (a) increase the share of the working-age population in employment and (b) among those who are employed, reduce the share of those who are own-account workers or contributing family workers. The only practical way to achieve both targets is an expansion of wage

employment (unless the usually very small share of employers in total employment grows significantly).

7.   This is, in part, a mathematical necessity: If incomes of the poorest quintile grew faster than the average over an infinite period of time, the poorest quintile would no longer be the poorest quintile (see Luebker, Smith and Weeks, 2002).

8.   These included UNU-WIDER, the UN's Department for Economic and Social Affairs, the ILO and a few researchers inside the Bank itself.

9.   See the background papers that Deepak Nayyar (2012), Jan Vandemoortele (2012) and Rolph van der Hoeven (2012) prepared for the UN System Task Team.

10.   See the proceedings by the ILO's Committee on Freedom of Association (available online at http://www.ilo.org/public/libdoc/ilo/P/09661/) or the ITUC's survey on the violation of trade union rights (available at http://survey.ituc-csi.org/?lang=en).

11.   See, for example, the 'Global Jobs Pact' as adopted by the International Labour Conference at its Ninety-eighth Session (Geneva, 19 June 2009).

12.   Based on ILO, Key Indicators of the Labour Market, 9th edition.

13.   Note that the productivity growth refers to within-sector gains, that is, they are not driven by the relatively 'easy' wins that can be reaped by shifting labour from low-value added sectors such as subsistence agriculture to the modern sector.

14.   The minimum wage has remained at this level, and prospects that it will be raised under the current military government are slim. See *Bangkok Post*, 'Panel votes to freeze minimum wage through June' (16 November 2015).

15.   If real wages should grow in line with productivity, the labour share should remain roughly stable. There are, however, a few other, technical factors to explain minor changes in labour shares. These include a difference in the deflators used to deflate GDP (implicit GDP deflator) and wages (CPI); changes in employers' social contributions (which are counted towards the labour share, but not towards wages); and changes in the share of wage workers in total employment. Note that Asia has witnessed a rapid increase in the share of wage employment, which should bias trends in the unadjusted labour share upwards.

16.   See NBS, 'China's Economy Realized a Moderate but Stable and Sound Growth in 2015', Press release (19 January 2016).

17.   Counterfactual refers to the year 2010 and compensation of employees, that is, including employers' social contributions.

18.   The minimum wage further increased to US$140 from January 2016 onwards, and to US$153 from January 2017 onwards. All figures exclude bonuses and allowances. Disclosure: In 2014 and 2015, the author (in his capacity as ILO staff) provided advice to the Royal Government of Cambodia on the process and institutions for minimum wage setting, though not on the level of the minimum wage.

19.   Depending on the indicator used, between 97 and 98 per cent of factories were fully compliant with the minimum wage in the latest reporting period.

20.   Interestingly, Smith continued by stating that '[t]o violate this combination is every where a most unpopular action, and a fort of reproach to a master among his neighbours and equals' (Smith, 1796 [1776]: I.8.13).

REFERENCES

Addison, T. and G.A. Cornia (2001) 'Income distribution policies for faster poverty reduction'. WIDER Discussion Paper 2001/93. Helsinki: UNU-WIDER.

Atkinson, A.B. (2009) 'Factor shares: The principal problem of political economy?' *Oxford Review of Economic Policy* 25(1): 3–16.

Behrendt, C. and J. Woodall (2015) 'Pensions and other social security transfers', in J. Berg (ed.) *Labour Markets, Institutions and Inequality. Building Just Societies in the 21st Century*, pp. 242–262. Cheltenham, UK and Northampton, MA, USA: Edward Elgar Publishing.

Belser, P. and U. Rani (2015) 'Minimum wages and inequality', in J. Berg (ed.) *Labour Markets, Institutions and Inequality. Building Just Societies in the 21st Century*, pp. 123–146. Cheltenham, UK and Northampton, MA, USA: Edward Elgar Publishing.

Berg, J. (ed.) (2015) *Labour Markets, Institutions and Inequality. Building Just Societies in the 21st Century*. Cheltenham, UK and Northampton, MA, USA: Edward Elgar Publishing.

Berg, J. and D. Kucera (eds) (2008) *In Defence of Labour Market Institutions. Cultivating Justice in the Developing World*. Basingstoke: Palgrave Macmillan; Geneva: ILO.

Betcherman, G. (2014) 'Labor market regulations: what do we know about their impacts in developing countries?' *World Bank Research Observer* 30: 124–153.

Better Factories Cambodia (2015) *Thirty-second Synthesis Report on Working Conditions in Cambodia's Garment Sector*. Geneva: ILO.

Birdsall, N., D. Ross and R. Sabot (1995) 'Inequality and growth reconsidered: lessons from East Asia', *World Bank Economic Review* 9(3): 477–508.

Boonyamanond, S. et al. (2013) 'Wages, productivity, and the evolution of inequality in Thailand'. Bangkok: ILO (mimeo).

Booth, C. (1902–1903) *Life and Labour of the People in London*, 3rd edition. London: Macmillan.

Chenery, H. et al. (1974) *Redistribution with Growth; Policies to Improve Income Distribution in Developing Countries in the Context of Economic Growth*. Oxford: Oxford University Press.

Cornia, G.A., R. van der Hoeven and T. Mkandawire (eds) (1992) *Africa's Recovery in the 1990s: From Stagnation and Adjustment to Human Development*. New York: St. Martin's Press.

Dagdeviren, H., R. van der Hoeven and J. Weeks (2002) 'Poverty reduction with growth and redistribution', *Development and Change* 33(3): 383–413.

Dollar, D. and A. Kraay (2002) 'Growth is good for the poor', *Journal of Economic Growth* 7(3): 195–225.

Entman, R.M. (1993) 'Framing: toward clarification of a fractured paradigm', *Journal of Communication* 43(4): 51–58.

Flyvbjerg, B. (2006) 'Five misunderstandings about case-study research', *Qualitative Inquiry* 12(2): 219–245.

Freeman, R.B. (2008) 'Labor market institutions around the world'. CEP Discussion Paper No. 844. London: LSE.

Gonzaga. P. et al. (2013) 'Theory of collusion in the labor market'. FEP Working Paper 477. Porto: University of Porto.

Guscina, A. (2006) 'Effects of globalization on labor's share in national income'. IMF Working Paper 06/294. Washington, DC: International Monetary Fund.

Hayter, S. (2015) 'Unions and collective bargaining', in J. Berg (ed.) *Labour Markets, Institutions and Inequality. Building Just Societies in the 21st Century*, pp. 95–122. Cheltenham, UK and Northampton, MA, USA: Edward Elgar Publishing.

ILO (2012) *Global Wage Report 2012/13: Wages and Equitable Growth*. Geneva: ILO.

ILO (2014) *Global Wage Report 2014/15: Wages and Income Inequality*. Geneva: ILO.

ILO (2015) *World Employment and Social Outlook: Trends 2015* (Supporting datasets). Geneva: ILO.

ILO (2016) 'How is Cambodia's minimum wage adjusted?', Cambodian Garment and Footwear Sector Bulletin, Issue 3. Phnom Penh: ILO.

Kaldor, N. (1961) 'Capital Accumulation and Economic Growth', in F.A. Lutz (ed.) *The Theory of Capital*, pp. 177–220. London: Macmillan.

Kraay, A. (2006) 'When is growth pro-poor? Evidence from a panel of countries', *Journal of Development Economics* 80(1): 198–227.

Krämer, H. (2010) 'The alleged stability of the labour share of income in macro-economic theories of income distribution'. Working Paper 11/2010. Dusseldorf: IMK.

Luebker, M. (2015) 'Redistribution policies', in J. Berg (ed.) *Labour Markets, Institutions and Inequality. Building Just Societies in the 21st Century*, pp. 211–241. Cheltenham, UK and Northampton, MA, USA: Edward Elgar Publishing.

Luebker, M., G. Smith and J. Weeks (2002) 'Growth and the poor: a comment on Dollar and Kraay', *Journal of International Development* 14(5): 555–571.

Mayneris, F., S. Poncet and T. Zhang (2014) 'The cleansing effect of minimum wage. minimum wage rules, firm dynamics and aggregate productivity in China'. CEPII Working Paper, No. 2014-16. Paris: CEPII.

Nayyar, D. (2012) 'The MDGs after 2015: Some reflections on the possibilities'. Background Paper prepared for the Expert Group Meeting of the UN System Task Team on the Post-2015 UN Development Agenda, New York (27–29 February).

Ocampo, J.A. and Jomo K.S. (eds) (2007) *Towards Full and Decent Employment*. New York and London: ZED Books.

Okun, A. (1975) *Equality and Efficiency: The Big Trade-off*. Washington: Brookings Institution Press.

Ravallion, M. (2004) 'Pro-poor growth: a primer'. Policy Research Working Paper 15174. Washington, DC: World Bank.

Rixen, T. (2013) 'Why reregulation after the crisis is feeble: shadow banking, off-shore financial centers, and jurisdictional competition', *Regulation & Governance* 7(4): 435–459.

Rowntree, B.S. (1901) *Poverty: A Study of Town Life*. London and New York: Macmillan.

Rowntree, B.S. (1918) *The Human Needs of Labour*. London: Nelson.

Sen, A. (1976) 'Poverty: an ordinal approach to measurement', *Econometrica* 44(2): 219–231.

Shorrocks, A. and R. van der Hoeven (eds) (2004) *Growth, Inequality, and Poverty. Prospects for Pro-poor Economic Development*. UNU-WIDER Studies in Development Economics. Oxford: Oxford University Press.

Smith, A. (1796 [1776]) *An Inquiry into the Nature and Causes of the Wealth of Nations*, 8th edition. London: Strahan, Cadell and Davies.

Trapp, K. (2015) 'Measuring the labour income share of developing countries. Learning from social accounting matrices'. WIDER Working Paper 2015/041. Helsinki: UNU-WIDER.

United Nations (1948) *Universal Declaration of Human Rights*. Resolution 217A (III). Paris: United Nations.

United Nations (2000) *United Nations Millennium Declaration*. Resolution adopted by the General Assembly (A/55/L.2). New York: United Nations.

United Nations (2008) *Official List of MDG Indicators* (effective 15 January 2008). New York: United Nations.

United Nations (2014) *We the Peoples. Celebrating 7 Million Voices*. New York, UN Millennium Campaign.

United Nations (2015) *Transforming our World: the 2030 Agenda for Sustainable Development*. Resolution adopted by the General Assembly on 25 September 2015 (A/RES/70/1). New York: United Nations.

van der Geest, W. and R. van der Hoeven (eds) (1999) *Adjustment Employment and Missing Institutions in Africa: the Experience in Eastern and Southern Africa*. Geneva: ILO; Oxford: James Curry.

van der Hoeven, R. (2012) 'MDGs post 2015: beacons in turbulent times or false lights?'. Background Paper prepared for the Expert Group Meeting of the UN System Task Team on the Post-2015 UN Development Agenda, New York (27–29 February).

van der Hoeven, R. (2015) 'Can the Sustainable Development Goals stem rising income inequality in the world?' Valedictory Lecture, International Institute of Social Studies, The Hague (8 October 2015).

van der Hoeven, R. and C. Saget (2004) 'Labour market institutions and income inequality: what are the new insights after the Washington Consensus?', in G.A. Cornia (ed.) *Inequality, Growth and Poverty in an Era of Liberalisation and Globalisation*, pp. 197–220. Oxford: Oxford University Press.

van der Hoeven, R. and M. Luebker (2007) 'Financial openness and employment: the need for coherent international and national policies', in Jomo K.S. and J.A. Ocampo (eds), *Towards Full and Decent Employment*. New York and London: Zed Books.

Vandemoortele, J. (2012) 'Advancing the Global Development Agenda Post-2015'. Background Paper prepared for the Expert Group Meeting of the UN System Task Team on the Post-2015 UN Development Agenda, New York (27–29 February).

Vandemoortele, J. (2015) 'Tackling inequality is key to the post-MDGs development agenda', *Europe's World*, No. 29 (Spring 2015), http://europesworld.org/issues/spring-2015/ (accessed 20 June 2017).

Wilson, H. (1953) *The War on World Poverty. An Appeal to the Conscience of Mankind*. London: Victor Gollancz.

World Bank (2012) *World Development Report 2013: Jobs*. Washington, DC: World Bank.

World Bank (2015) *World Development Indicators 2015*. Washington, DC: World Bank.

9. Can catch up reduce inequality?

Deepak Nayyar[1]

The past quarter century has witnessed an increase in the share of developing countries not only in world population and world income but also in industrialization and engagement with the world economy. This catch up has been driven by economic growth. But the process is characterized by uneven development and emerging divergences. There is an exclusion of regions, of countries within regions, of regions within countries, and of people, from the process. Yet, catch up on the part of poor countries through rapid growth, even in the aggregate, should increase the possibilities of meaningful development, which improves the well-being of ordinary people, provided there is no countervailing increase in economic inequality.

The object of this chapter is to analyze whether catch up can, and if so how, reduce inequality to realize its potential. In doing so, it formulates two interlinked hypotheses. The ongoing catch up, in terms of faster economic growth, is necessary though not sufficient for reducing economic inequality between and within countries, but it will not be sustainable unless it reduces economic inequality within countries.

The structure of the discussion is as follows. Section 1 sketches the contours of change in the significance of developing countries in the world economy, to emphasize the gathering momentum of this change during the past twenty-five years. Section 2 highlights the uneven nature of outcomes in this process that have excluded geographical spaces – continents, countries within continents, and regions within countries – so that the catch up is concentrated mostly in one continent and a small number of countries. Section 3 seeks to focus on divergences – old and new – that have been associated with an exclusion of people, as a result of which inequality rises and poverty persists. Section 4 addresses the question of whether catch up, driven by economic growth and characterized by unequal outcomes, which has often led to increasing inequality in the past, can reduce inequality in the future.

CHANGING WORLD

The world economy has witnessed profound changes during the past twenty-five years, which would have been difficult to imagine, let alone anticipate, fifty years ago. There has been a dramatic increase in the economic significance of developing countries and significant erosion in the relative importance of industrialized countries. For the purpose of analysis in this chapter, developing countries are made up of Africa, Asia excluding Japan, and Latin America including the Caribbean, while industrialized countries are made up of North America, Western Europe, Japan, Australia and New Zealand. The remaining country-group in the world economy, made up of Eastern Europe and the former USSR, is not considered here. The focus is on the developing world and the industrialized world is simply a point of reference and comparison.

Table 9.1 presents some evidence on changes in the significance of developing countries in the world economy, for selected benchmark years, during the period from 1990 to 2014. It shows that the share of developing countries in world GDP in current prices at market exchange rates jumped from 17.5 percent in 1990 to 37.7 percent in 2014. This increase of more than twenty percentage points was entirely at the expense of industrialized countries whose share in world GDP dropped from 77.8 percent to 57.2 percent over the same period. The share of Eastern Europe and the former USSR in world GDP increased slightly from 4.7 percent in 1990 to 5.1 percent in 2014, although it remained much lower than its share before the collapse of communism, which was almost 10 percent in 1980.[2]

Table 9.1   *Economic significance of developing countries in the world economy (as a percentage of the total for the world)*

	1990	2000	2010	2014
Population	77.0	79.2	80.7	81.5
GDP	17.5	21.6	32.8	37.7
Manufacturing Value Added	17.8	24.7	42.0	47.4
Manufactured Goods Exports	17.9	29.3	40.2	43.8
Merchandise Exports	24.1	31.9	42.1	44.6
Merchandise Imports	22.2	28.8	39.0	42.0

Note: The figures on the share of developing countries in world GDP and manufacturing value added are calculated from national accounts statistics data in current prices at market exchange rates.

Source: United Nations, UNCTAD Stat, based on UN Population Statistics, National Accounts Statistics and International Trade Statistics.

Table 9.2   Growth rates in the world economy by regions and country-groups (percent per annum)

Country-Group	1991–2000	2001–2008	2009–2014	1991–2014
		GDP		
Asia	6.0	7.5	6.1	6.2
Africa	2.7	5.7	3.4	4.2
Latin America	3.1	4.2	3.4	3.1
Developing Countries	4.7	6.5	5.4	5.2
Industrialized Countries	2.7	2.2	1.7	2.0
World	3.0	3.4	2.9	2.8
		GDP per capita		
Asia	4.5	6.3	5.0	5.0
Africa	0.3	3.3	0.9	1.8
Latin America	1.4	3.0	2.3	1.7
Developing Countries	3.1	5.1	4.0	3.7
Industrialized Countries	2.1	1.5	1.3	1.4
World	1.6	2.2	1.7	1.6

Notes:
(a) The growth rates for each of the country-groups and the world have been calculated from data on GDP and GDP per capita in 2005 US Dollars.
(b) The average annual growth rates for each of the periods and for the entire period have been calculated by fitting a semi-log linear regression equation $L_n Y = a + bt$ and estimating the value of b.

Source: United Nations, UNCTAD Stat, based on UN National Accounts Statistics.

Differences in GDP growth rates underlie the rising share of developing countries and the falling share of industrialized countries in world GDP. Table 9.2 compares their growth performance during 1991–2014 divided further into three sub-periods: 1991–2000, 2001–2008 and 2009–2014, as the global economic crisis led to a sharp slowdown in growth after 2008. For the period as a whole, from 1991 to 2014, the GDP growth rate in developing countries at 5.2 percent per annum was two-and-a-half times that in industrialized countries at 2 percent per annum. The table also shows that this difference was far greater after the turn of the century. There was a distinct slowdown in growth in industrialized countries, juxtaposed with an acceleration of growth in developing countries at 6.5 percent per annum during 2001–2008 and, despite the massive downturn in the world economy, it was as high as 5.4 percent per annum during 2009–2014. In fact, GDP growth rates in developing countries were three times the GDP growth rates in industrialized countries not only during 2001–2008, before the global financial crisis, but also during 2009–2014, in the Great Recession that followed in its aftermath.[3]

As population growth rates in the developing world slowed down, this impressive GDP growth translated into a rapid growth of GDP per capita. During 1991–2014, GDP per capita growth in developing countries was 3.7 percent per annum, which was more than two-and-a-half times that in industrialized countries at 1.4 percent per annum and more than double that in the world economy at 1.6 percent per annum. This difference was greater after the turn of the century. In developing countries, growth in GDP per capita was 5.1 percent per annum during 2001–2008 and 4 percent per annum during 2009–2014, as compared with 1.5 percent per annum and 1.3 percent per annum respectively in the industrialized countries, or 2.2 percent per annum and 1.7 percent per annum respectively in the world economy.

Consequently, for developing countries as a group, the divergence in per capita incomes in relation to industrialized countries came to an end.[4] The beginnings of a modest convergence in per capita incomes became discernible in the 1990s, which gathered some pace in the 2000s (Nayyar, 2013). However, it would not be correct to describe this as convergence in any meaningful sense of the word. The difference in income levels is so large that, even in 2014, GDP per capita in current prices at market exchange rates for developing countries was just about 11 percent of that in industrialized countries (Table 9.3). Yet, it is worth noting that there was a significant convergence of per capita income in relation to the world as a whole. GDP per capita, in current prices at market exchange rates, in developing countries as a proportion of that in the world economy increased from 23 percent in 1990 to 46 percent in 2014 (Table 9.3 and Figure 9.1).

In addition, there was a significant catch up in industrialization for the developing world as a whole beginning around 1950 that gathered further momentum in the early 1970s after a period of learning to industrialize (Nayyar, 2013). The transformation was striking during the period under review. This emerges clearly from the evidence presented in Table 9.1. The share of developing countries in world manufacturing value added increased by almost thirty percentage points from 18 percent in 1990 to 47 percent in 2014. Similarly, the share of developing countries in world exports of manufactured goods rose from 18 percent in 1990 to 44 percent in 2014, which suggests that their manufacturing sector also became competitive in world markets. The increase in these shares was more rapid after the turn of the century.

The same trends are mirrored in the engagement of developing countries with the world economy. Table 9.1 shows that, between 1990 and 2014,

Table 9.3   Divergence and convergence in GDP per capita between LDCs,
the Next-14, BRICS, Developing Countries, Industrialized
Countries and the world economy: 1990–2014

| (US dollars in current prices at market exchange rates) | | | |
	1990	2000	2010	2014
Least Developed Countries	301	282	743	988
The Next-14	966	1597	4368	5761
of which BRICS	*561*	*959*	*3613*	*5011*
Other Developing Countries	1373	1827	4197	5411
Developing Countries	964	1465	3787	4934
Industrialized Countries	19329	25599	38683	46873
WORLD	4191	5426	9237	10660

Note: The country-group 'Other Developing Countries' is Developing Countries excluding
the Next-14 and the LDCs. The Next-14 are Argentina, Brazil, Chile, China, Egypt, India,
Indonesia, South Korea, Malaysia, Mexico, South Africa, Taiwan, Thailand and Turkey.
The BRICS are Brazil, India, China and South Africa.

Source: United Nations, UN National Accounts Statistics and Population Statistics.

the share of developing countries in world merchandise exports rose from
24 percent to 45 percent, while their share in world merchandise imports
rose from 22 percent to 42 percent. Once again, this change gathered pace
after 2000. The story was similar in other forms of interaction with the
outside world (Nayyar, 2013, 2016). It extended to trade in services, foreign
direct investment, whether inflows or outflows, and international financial
markets. International migration was, possibly, the most significant form
of engagement with the world economy, reflected in the rising share of
developing countries in the stock of international migrants, cross-border
movements of people, whether emigration, guest workers, illegal migrants
or professional persons, and remittances from migrants in the world
economy (Nayyar, 2008, 2013).

UNEQUAL OUTCOMES

The structural transformation in the world economy over the past twenty-
five years, associated with a dramatic increase in the relative importance of
developing countries, was distributed in a very unequal manner and there
was an exclusion of geographical spaces from this process.

The catch up was concentrated in Asia, one of the three continents,

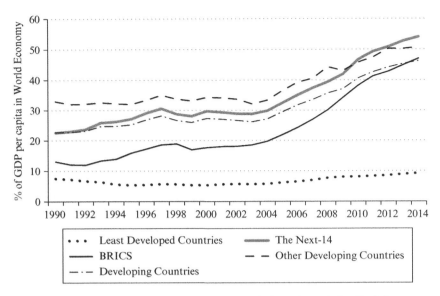

Source: United Nations, UN National Accounts Statistics and Population Statistics.

Figure 9.1 *GDP per capita in LDCs, the Next-14, BRICS and Developing Countries as a percentage of GDP per capita in the world: 1990–2014*

while the significance of Latin America saw modest change and that of Africa experienced a stagnation or decline. However, development was uneven not only across continents but also between countries within continents. There was a high degree of concentration among a few: China, India, Indonesia, Malaysia, South Korea, Taiwan, Thailand and Turkey in Asia; Argentina, Brazil, Chile and Mexico in Latin America; and Egypt and South Africa in Africa. In fact, the economic significance of these countries, termed the Next-14, in the developing world was overwhelming in terms of their size, reflected in population and GDP, their industrialization, reflected in industrial production and manufactured exports, and their engagement with the world economy, reflected in trade, investment and migration (Nayyar, 2013). In the Next-14, too, there was a further concentration in an even smaller subset of countries – Brazil, India, China and South Africa – described as the BRICS (Nayyar, 2016).

It should come as no surprise that there was, in addition, an exclusion of regions within these countries that led the catch up process, so that the distribution of benefits from their rapid economic growth was unequal. At the other end of the spectrum, there were the Least Developed Countries (LDCs), located mostly in sub-Saharan Africa, South Asia, South-East Asia and the Pacific, as many as 48 in number, which were largely excluded and left behind. Indeed, disparate outcomes in development across geographical space are striking, whether continents or country-groups in the developing world, or even regions within countries.

Among continents, Asia led the process in terms of economic growth, industrialization, and engagement with the world economy. Between 1990 and 2014, Asia accounted for 84 percent of the total increase in the share of developing countries in world GDP, while Latin America accounted for 15 percent and Africa for a mere 1 percent. Similarly, Asia contributed more than 90 percent of the total increase in the share of developing countries in world manufacturing value added and world manufactured exports, and around 80 percent of that in world merchandise trade. The contribution of Latin America to the increased share of developing countries in the world economy in these macroeconomic aggregates was modest, while the contribution of Africa was negligible.[5]

The differences in the comparative growth performance of the three continents, GDP and GDP per capita in constant 1990 US dollars, high-lighted by Table 9.2, are just as striking, with Asia far ahead although there was an improvement in the growth performance of both Latin America and Africa after 2000. During 1991–2014, GDP growth in Asia was 6.2 percent per annum, as compared with 3.1 percent per annum in Latin America and 4.2 percent per annum in Africa. Consequently, between 1990 and 2014, the share of Asia in world GDP in current prices at market exchange rates rose from 10 percent to 27 percent, while that of Latin America increased from 5 percent to 8 percent (partly a recovery to earlier levels before the lost decade of the 1980s), but that of Africa remained in the range of 2.5–3 percent.[6] Given different population growth rates in each of these regions, differences in GDP per capita growth were even more pronounced. During 1991–2014, growth in GDP per capita was 5 percent per annum in Asia, 1.7 percent per annum in Latin America and 1.8 percent per annum in Africa (Table 9.2). Consequently, per capita income in Asia witnessed a significant convergence in relation to per capita income of the world, while Latin America stayed roughly where it was because its initial per capita income levels were much higher, but per capita income in Africa witnessed a divergence (Nayyar, 2013).

Among country-groups in the developing world, the Next-14 was the counterpart of Asia among continents. Between 1990 and 2014, there was a striking increase in the economic significance of the Next-14 in the world economy. Their share in world GDP rose from 12 percent to 28 percent, in world manufacturing value added from 14 percent to 39 percent, and in world merchandise trade from 12 percent to 26 percent, although their share in world population remained unchanged at about 50 percent (Nayyar, 2017). Consequently, the Next-14 accounted for 77 percent of the total increase in the share of developing countries in world GDP, 85 percent of that in world manufacturing value added, and 70 percent of that in world merchandise trade.

The growth performance of the Next-14 was just as impressive as that of Asia. During 1991–2014, in terms of constant 2005 US dollars, their GDP growth at 5.5 percent per annum was somewhat better than that of all developing countries at 5.2 percent per annum but distinctly better than that of industrialized countries at 2 percent per annum and that of the world economy at 2.8 percent per annum. Similarly, during 1991–2014, their GDP per capita growth, in real terms, was 4.4 percent per annum, as compared with 3.7 percent per annum for all developing countries, 1.4 percent per annum for industrialized countries, and 1.6 percent per annum for the world economy (Nayyar, 2017). This was an important factor underlying the leading role of the Next-14 in the catch up process.

It needs to be said that there was enormous diversity among, and significant differences between the countries that made up the Next-14 (Nayyar, 2013). The BRICS were an important and leading subset of the Next-14 (Nayyar, 2016). Between 1990 and 2014, their share in world GDP rose from 6 percent to 19 percent, in world manufacturing value added from 6 percent to 29 percent, in world merchandise trade from 4 percent to 15 percent, although their share in world population remained about the same in the range of 40 percent. The BRICS accounted for accounted for 66 percent of the total increase in the share of developing countries in world GDP, 75 percent of that in world manufacturing value added, and 58 percent of that in world merchandise trade. The growth performance of BRICS was even better than that of the Next-14. During 1991–2014, real GDP growth was 7 percent per annum and real GDP per capita growth was 5.9 percent per annum, both of which were 1.5 percentage points higher than the corresponding figures for the Next-14.[7]

It is worth noting that China was the most important part of the BRICS story. Yet, it was not the whole story. There was more to BRICS than China. BRICS were the most important part of the Next-14 tale. But there was far more to the Next-14 than BRICS. The Next-14 were the most important part of the growing significance of developing countries. Yet, there was more to the developing world than the Next-14. It would seem that the catch up process was characterized by a concentration at each level. But there was also a significant dispersion across levels in this hierarchy of country-groups.[8]

Beyond such concentration, there was also an exclusion of regions within countries, particularly in the Next-14 that lead the catch up process. Regional inequalities and economic disparities increased significantly everywhere (Nayyar, 2013). There are obvious examples. In Brazil, regional inequalities between the northeast and south, in particular Sao Paulo, increased significantly during periods of rapid economic growth. There is an increase in economic disparities between the south and the north in Mexico, as states in the south such as Chiapas and Oaxaca are significantly poorer while states in the north are more industrialized and developed which is partly a function of geographical proximity to the United States. In Indonesia, the economic gap between Java and the other islands is much wider. The economic disparities between coastal China in the east and the hinterland in the west are much greater than ever before. In India, the regions in the west and the south that already have a lead have left other regions in the north and the east behind. These examples can be multiplied beyond the Next-14 across countries in the developing world. This is neither surprising nor altogether new. Regions that are better endowed with natural resources, physical infrastructure, skilled labor or educated people, experience rapid economic growth, while disadvantaged regions lag behind, through a cumulative causation that creates market-driven virtuous circles or vicious circles.

Such exclusion of geographical spaces extends to countries. The LDCs provide a most striking illustration.[9] The number of LDCs has doubled from 24 in the early 1970s to 48 in the early 2010s. Of these, 10 are small island economies and 13 are landlocked countries. In 2010, the share of LDCs in world output was less than 0.9 percent, lower than it was in the mid-1970s. In fact, in 2010, the assets of the 20 richest people in the world were more than the combined GDP of all LDCs. This reality is daunting, even if a comparison of assets (stock) with income (flow) is inappropriate. Yet LDCs, with 833 million people in 2010, accounted for 12 percent of world population. In current prices at market exchange rates, the average GDP per capita in LDCs in 2010 was less than one-fifth of that in developing countries and less than one-fiftieth of that in industrialized countries. Economic development has simply not created social opportunities for most people in LDCs.

Indeed, at the end of the first decade of the twenty-first century, social indicators of development in LDCs were much worse than the average for the developing world. Adult literacy was less than 60 percent as compared with 80 percent in developing countries. Life expectancy at birth was 51 years as compared with 60 years in developing countries. Infant mortality rates were 78 per 1000 births as compared with 48 per 1000 births in developing countries. Gross enrolment ratios in tertiary education were less than 6 percent as compared with 21 percent in developing countries. Of the total population, 38 percent did not have access to safe drinking water as compared with 16 percent for developing countries. The situation in LDCs is distinctly worse than the average in developing countries.

DIVERGENCES: OLD AND NEW

The pace of economic growth in the developing world, since 1990, has been much faster than it was earlier during the second half of the twentieth century. But the distribution of benefits from increases in output and income has been most unequal across continents and countries. Even so, it is important to consider the impact of this catch up process on economic inequality between countries and between people in the world, as also on economic inequality within countries.

Inequality between Countries

There are two dimensions of international economic inequality: income distribution between countries and income distribution between people in the world. Measures of the former assume that income distribution within countries is perfectly equal and use per capita income in each country, weighted by its population, to determine inter-country inequality in the world. Measures of the latter are based on actual incomes of individuals irrespective of the countries where they live, to determine inter-personal inequality in the world. The most common measure for income distribution between countries or people is the Gini coefficient.

Available evidence shows that the population-weighted international inequality between countries during the period 1950–1990 remained high, with a Gini coefficient in the range of 55, but declined during the period 1990–2010 (Milanovic, 2005; Nayyar, 2013; Bourguignon, 2015). The observed trend is almost entirely attributable to the increase in per capita income in two countries, China and India, with large populations. Some other countries in Asia, even if their populations were not so large, also witnessed an increase in their per capita incomes. Thus, it is plausible to suggest that catch up was the underlying factor. However, the impact is perhaps overstated in these estimates. GDP per capita in China and India increased much more in PPP terms than it did at market exchange rates. And PPP adjustment for China and India is disproportionately large in comparison with industrialized countries. If China and India are excluded, population-weighted inequality does not register a decline, although the exclusion of China makes much more difference than the exclusion of India. In this context, it is interesting to note that the substitution of provinces in China and states in India for the two largest countries changes the picture. The growing inter-regional inequality in China and India has a discernible impact on population-weighted international inequality. If the provinces of China and the states of India are treated as countries, the population-weighted Gini coefficient of international inequality, so defined, reveals a significant increase after 1980 (Milanovic, 2005).

In fact, there can be little doubt that this dimension of international inequality is still largely attributable to the income gap between rich and poor countries, even if it did not widen after 1980 and may have narrowed after 2000 for the latter taken together. For such analysis, it is appropriate to use the Theil coefficient. This inequality measure, which is weighted for the size of population in each country, also considers only inequality between, and not within, countries. Its advantage as compared to other inequality measures, such as the Gini coefficient, is that it can be decomposed and has the useful property of being additive for the components. Evidence available on the Theil coefficient of world inequality in 1980 and 2000, based on Maddison PPP statistics, shows that, throughout the period, more than 85 percent of the population-weighted inequality between countries in the world was attributable to inequality between regions. This was, in turn, largely on account of the income gap between industrialized and developing countries. In fact, the decomposition of the Theil coefficient of international inequality, by region, for 1980 and 2000 shows that the contribution of industrialized countries to overall inequality between countries in the world was greater than what was attributable to regions (United Nations, 2006; Nayyar, 2013). Clearly, this is an old divergence that persists.

Even so, international inequality between countries in the developing world was quite significant. However, between 1980 and 2000, the Theil coefficient of developing world inequality, once again based on Maddison PPP statistics, decreased from 36 to 23, although if China is excluded it increased from 27 to 31 (Nayyar, 2013). But this evidence does not capture the emerging new divergences, driven by the catch up process, of inter-country inequality among developing countries. The reality is brought out clearly by Table 9.3, which sets out statistics on GDP per capita, in current prices at market exchange rates, for the LDCs, the Next-14, the BRICS, developing countries, industrialized countries and the world, for selected benchmark years, during the period 1990–2014. It shows that there was one striking divergence for LDCs and one striking convergence for the Next-14. The trends emerge even more clearly from Figure 9.1, which plots time-series data on GDP per capita levels in each of the country-groups as a percentage of GDP per capita in the world economy (perhaps the most appropriate denominator to normalize absolute values, spanning a wide range, for a meaningful comparison). Per capita income in the LDCs diverged from the rest. Per capita income in the Next-14, which was at the same level as all developing countries in 1990, converged to the level in other developing countries (that included the oil-exporting economies) by the mid-2000s, to widen the gap with both country-groups after catching up. It is worth noting that, in 1970, per capita income for all the country-groups in Figure 9.1 was roughly the same (Nayyar, 2013). Obviously, catch up was associated with rising inter-country inequality in the developing world.

Global inequality among people, the other dimension of international inequality, was much higher than inequality between countries. During the period 1950–1990, the Gini coefficient of income distribution between people in the world remained almost unchanged in the range of 65 (Bourguignon and Morrisson, 2002; Milanovic, 2005; Nayyar, 2013). Clearly, income distribution among people was more unequal than income distribution between countries in the world economy. This is not surprising because measures of inter-country inequality assume that income distribution within countries is perfectly equal.

It is reasonable to ask whether catch up, driven by rapid economic growth in the developing world, has had any effect on inter-personal inequality in the world. This is a point of debate. Some recent estimates (Bourguignon, 2015) suggest that, during the period 1990–2010, there has been a reduction in global inequality among people, as the Gini coefficient measuring world income distribution has declined significantly from 70 to 62. Indeed, Bourguignon (2015) invokes this trend to describe 1990 as a historic turning point in the evolution of global inequality, which increased steadily beginning in 1820 and has persisted at high levels.[10] This claim is open to question and the decline might be deceptive for several reasons.

First, as stated earlier, GDP per capita in China and India, or elsewhere in the developing world, increased much more in PPP terms than it did at market exchange rates. And such PPP adjustments are disproportionately large. The problem is accentuated because the changes in the methodology of World Bank PPP estimates lead to large, sometimes inexplicable, increases in income for some countries (Chang, 2010). All this could, and probably does, affect measures of income distribution. Second, even if the PPP problem is set aside, the data used are mostly from household surveys on expenditure that measure consumption inequality, which is always lower than income inequality because the rich save while the poor do not. In any case, household surveys tend to underestimate the income of the rich. Third, these estimates certainly do not capture the incomes of the top 1 percent or 0.1 percent, the super-rich or ultra-rich, whose share in national income has risen disproportionately over the past quarter century (Atkinson, Piketty and Saez, 2010; Atkinson, 2015). Fourth, available evidence suggests there was a sharp increase in economic inequality between people within countries (Milanovic, 2005; Palma, 2011; Stiglitz, 2012; Piketty, 2014; Atkinson, 2015) almost everywhere. Surely, this trend is bound to have exercised an influence on inter-personal inequality, even if there was some reduction in inter-country inequality, in the world.

Inequality within Countries

The logical next step is to examine what happened to economic inequality between people within developing countries during the period since 1990. This issue also has two dimensions: the incidence of absolute poverty and the distribution of income between people.

There are millions of people in the developing world living in absolute poverty. This is not new. The crucial question is whether or not catch up made things better for the poor. In the absence of evidence on well-being of the poor, measurement of poverty is the only alternative. The headcount measure, which estimates the proportion of the population or the number of poor below a specified poverty line, is the most widely used because it is the simplest to estimate and to understand. Of course, the methodological difficulties associated with it are considerable, ranging from choosing poverty lines, through finding appropriate price indices for adjusting poverty lines to inflation over time, to using sample data on household consumer expenditure or family incomes from surveys, for estimates at a macro level. Each is a source of endless debate. Such exercises, which count the poor, are either national estimates or World Bank estimates. There can be little doubt that national estimates are better and more robust in terms of methodology and database, although even these are often much debated on points of disagreement. World Bank estimates are simply not as good in terms of their methodology or statistical foundations.[11] However, World Bank estimates are the only possible source for inter-country comparisons over time and are used here to sketch the contours of a global picture.

These estimates use two poverty lines, which are $1.25 and $2 per day in 2005 PPP.[12] The first is the mean of the poverty lines in terms of con-sumption per capita in the poorest 15 countries of the world, whereas the second is the median poverty line for developing countries as a group. Thus, it is plausible to suggest that those who live below the poverty line of PPP$1.25 per day are the perennial poor who are probably unable to reach the critical minimum even in terms of nutrition, while those who live below the poverty line of PPP$2 per day are the vulnerable poor who might have been able to reach the critical minimum in terms of food and clothing plus some basic needs but not appropriate shelter or adequate healthcare. Clearly, the population between the two poverty lines is vulnerable to any

Table 9.4   Number and proportion of the poor in the developing world

REGION	Number in millions				Proportion in percentages			
	Below PPP$1.25 per day		Below PPP$2 per day		Below PPP$1.25 per day		Below PPP$2 per day	
	1990	2011	1990	2011	1990	2011	1990	2011
East Asia and the Pacific	926	161	1334	459	56.2	7.9	81.0	22.7
of which China	*683*	*84*	*961*	*250*	*60.2*	*6.3*	*84.6*	*18.6*
South Asia	617	399	959	979	53.8	24.5	83.6	60.1
of which India	*446*	*301*	*718*	*739*	*51.4*	*24.7*	*82.6*	*60.5*
Sub-Saharan Africa	290	416	389	617	56.5	46.9	76.0	69.5
Middle East and North Africa	13	5	53	39	5.8	1.7	23.5	11.6
Latin America and the Caribbean	53	28	97	55	12.2	4.6	22.4	9.3
Eastern Europe and Central Asia	9	2	32	10	1.9	0.5	6.9	2.2
TOTAL	1908	1011	2864	2159	43.1	17.0	64.6	36.3

Note: The poverty lines of PPP$1.25 and PPP $2 per day are in PPP 2005 US dollars.

Source: World Bank, PovcalNet Database.

shock such as a bad harvest, high inflation, employment cuts, or an illness in the family, which could push them down deeper into poverty.

Table 9.4 sets out these estimates, in terms of the proportion of the population and the number of the poor, below the two poverty lines, disaggregated for geographical regions in the developing world, for 1990 and 2011, in order to keep the data within manageable proportions.[13] The proportion of people in developing countries who lived below PPP$1.25 per day dropped from 43 percent to 17 percent, while the proportion of people who lived below PPP$2 per day also dropped from 65 percent to 36 percent. The progress was slower in reducing the number of poor people. The number of people who lived below PPP$1.25 per day dropped from 1.9 billion to 1 billion, while the number of people who lived below PPP$2 per day dropped from 2.9 billion to 2.2 billion.

The evidence in Table 9.4 also shows that poverty is concentrated in three regions of the developing world: East Asia (largely China), South Asia (mostly India) and sub-Saharan Africa. In other regions, the percentages were low and the numbers were small. Between 1990 and 2011, the proportion of people below PPP$1.25 per day declined sharply by 48 percentage points in East Asia, attributable mostly to China, significantly by 29 percentage points in South Asia, attributable mostly to India, and only modestly by 10 percentage points in sub-Saharan Africa. However, progress was far less impressive in terms of reducing numbers. For both poverty lines, China was the exception. India reduced the number below PPP$1.25 by almost 150 million people but made no progress with the number below PPP$2 per day. In sub-Saharan Africa, the number of poor below PPP$1.25 per day increased by 126 million, while the number of people below PPP$2 per day went up by 228 million. Consequently, between 1990 and 2011, the number of people in the developing world between the two poverty lines, the vulnerable poor, increased by 200 million from 0.95 billion to 1.15 billion.

In absolute terms, in 2011, the number of poor people below the poverty line of PPP$2 per day remained large even in China and India, at almost 1 billion, as also in the rest of Asia at around 0.5 billion. It is surprising that poverty persisted to this degree in Asia despite its rapid economic growth, rising share of world income and catch up in industrialization, particularly when China and India were an integral part of that process. In sub-Saharan Africa, in 2011, the number of people living below PPP$2 per day was 0.6 billion. This is not surprising given the economic performance of Africa during 1990–2014, reflected in the marginal increase in its share of world GDP and the modest growth in GDP per capita per annum. It would seem that catch up, driven by rapid economic growth, helped reduce the incidence of absolute poverty in Asia, although not as much as it could have possibly because of rising inequality, whereas absolute poverty persisted at high levels in Africa, possibly because much slower economic growth meant that it was not part of the catch up process.

The distribution of income between people, the other dimension of inequality within countries, is just as important. But it is exceedingly difficult to find systematic or complete evidence on income distribution in the developing world. The problem lies partly in statistics at the national level, which make international comparisons even more difficult, particularly for country-groups or regions. Yet, it is important to sketch a picture, even if it is a rough approximation, of what happened to inequality within countries in the catch up process driven by rapid growth. For this purpose, Table 9.5 puts together evidence on changes in income distribution, measured in terms of Gini coefficients, in the Next-14, for selected years during 1990–2010 and thereafter.

It reveals both similarities and differences. In Argentina, Brazil, Chile and Mexico, inequality was high to start with, declined after 2000, but remained higher than in most of the Next-14. South Africa was worse

Table 9.5   Income distribution changes in the Next-14: 1990–2010 (Gini coefficients)

Country	Circa 1990	Circa 2000	Circa 2005	Circa 2010	Latest Data
Argentina	43.1	48.0	47.0	42	41 (2011)
Brazil	60.5	58.8	53.7	52	
Chile	55.7	54.0	50.9	50.8	50.1 (2011)
China	34.6	39.0	48.7	48.1	47.4 (2012)
Egypt	31.9	37.8	32.1	31	
India	29.6	31.7	36.8	36.8	
Indonesia	32.8	31.0	39.4	38	39 (2012)
South Korea	34.9	37.2	32.6	31	31.1 (2011)
Malaysia	46.1	49.9	46.0	46.2	40.1 (2014)
Mexico	49.0	52.0	49.0	45.0	
South Africa	63.0	57.8	67.4	69.4	69.4 (2011)
Taiwan	31.2	32.6	34.0	34.2	33.8 (2012)
Thailand	42.9	43.1	42.4	40.8	
Turkey	46.5	46.0	44.8	40.2	40 (2013)

Notes:
The headings for columns in this table are *circa* 1990, 2000, 2005 and 2010 because data on Gini coefficients in the specified years are not necessarily available for all countries, so that the figures are for the closest possible year. In the column *circa* 1990, the figure on Turkey is for 1987, on Malaysia and Mexico for 1989, on South Korea for 1992 and on Egypt for 1991. In the column *circa* 2000, the figure on Malaysia is for 1997, on South Korea for 1998, on India and Indonesia for 1999, on Brazil for 2001 and on Turkey for 2002. In the column *circa* 2005, the figures on Chile, China, South Africa, Thailand, South Korea and Turkey are for 2006, and on Egypt, India and Malaysia for 2004. In the column *circa* 2010, the figures on Brazil, Chile and Thailand are for 2009, and on South Africa for 2011. Gini coefficients are based on nationally representative household surveys, except for Argentina, where the sample relies on the 28 largest cities. The Gini coefficients for Argentina, Brazil, Chile, China, South Korea, Malaysia, Mexico, South Africa, Taiwan and Turkey are based on per capita disposable income, whereas the Gini coefficients for Egypt, India, Indonesia and Thailand are based on per capita expenditure.

Source: UNU-WIDER, World Income Inequality Database, Version 3.3.

as its already high inequality of incomes increased continuously and by a large proportion. China, India and Indonesia were characterized by a low, or moderate, inequality in 1990, which increased significantly thereafter. It must be noted that the Gini coefficients in India and Indonesia, which measure consumption inequality, definitely underestimate income inequality. Other estimates of income inequality show that, in 2010, the Gini coefficient was more than 50 in China and just a little less than 50 in India (Atkinson, 2015). In Malaysia and Turkey, the Gini coefficients were high in 1990 but declined modestly after 2000. In Egypt and Thailand, the Gini coefficients rose from 1990 to 2000 and fell thereafter but these measure consumption inequality so that income inequality in Thailand could have been close to Latin American levels. During 1990–2010, the Gini coefficient in South Korea decreased from 35 to 31 (though it rose to 37 in 2000) while that in Taiwan increased from 31 to 34 but income inequality was moderate in both.

In the Next-14, which led the process of catch up, income inequality increased significantly in some countries where it was low to start with, and remained at high levels in other countries even if it decreased from higher initial levels, although South Korea and Taiwan do not quite conform to this generalization, perhaps because their initial income distributions were more equal and they were somewhat ahead of the others in catching up.[14] But it needs to be stressed that the Next-14 were neither exceptions nor unusual in this era, as income inequality was driven up by markets and globalization almost everywhere. In fact, research on the subject (Cornia and Kiiski, 2001; Bourguignon and Morrisson, 2002; Milanovic 2005; Palma, 2011; Piketty, 2014; Atkinson, 2015) suggests that, even if inequality levels differ across countries, there is a global trend of rising income inequality between people within countries, including industrialized countries, transition economies and other developing countries, where economic growth was not rapid but slow. This era was also associated with rising inequality within countries attributable to a sharp increase in the shares of the top 1 percent, and top 0.1 percent, of the population in national income, so that a disproportionately large part of increments in income accrued to the super-rich and ultra-rich (Atkinson and Piketty, 2010; Atkinson, Piketty and Saez, 2010; Stiglitz, 2012; Piketty, 2014; Atkinson, 2015).

CATCH UP AND ECONOMIC INEQUALITY

It is now time to address the basic question posed in this chapter. Is it possible for the catch up process, driven by economic growth in the developing world, to reduce economic inequality between countries and among people? If so, how? The answer must draw upon past experience to consider future prospects. The discussion that follows begins with two propositions and goes on to formulate two hypotheses.

The propositions are simple enough. First, economic growth matters and is necessary but not sufficient for bringing about a reduction in inequality. Second, there is a triangular relationship between growth, inequality and poverty, which can and does shape outcomes in development.

The hypotheses are also straightforward. First, catch up, driven by economic growth, is enabling, hence essential, for reducing inequality between countries in the world and between people within countries, although it may not have done so in the past. Second, in a longer-term perspective, catch up is unsustainable in the future unless it is associated with, or brings about, a reduction in inequality.

Growth matters because it is cumulative. If real GDP growth is 7 percent per annum national income doubles in ten years and if it is 10 percent per annum national income doubles in seven years. Similarly, if real GDP per capita growth is 5 percent per annum per capita income doubles in fourteen years, and if it is 7 percent per annum per capita income doubles in ten years. Of course, the complexity of economic growth cannot be reduced to the arithmetic of compound growth rates, just as the dynamics of income distribution cannot be reduced to arithmetic means. In retrospect, however, the cumulative impact of growth on GDP or GDP per capita is an irrefutable fact. Yet, it is important to recognize that the transformation of economic growth into meaningful development, which improves the well-being of people, is neither automatic nor assured. Hence, economic growth while necessary cannot be sufficient.

All the same, economic growth is enabling or permissive, even if it is not causal, because there is a triangular relationship between growth, inequality and poverty. The extent to which economic growth, for any given rate of growth, translates into poverty reduction depends upon what happens to economic inequality. If there is no change in economic inequality, increments in output or income accrue to different segments (fractile-groups) of the population in exactly the same proportion as the initial income distribution. Thus, a much larger proportion of the increment in income accrues to the rich who are a relatively small proportion of the population while a much smaller proportion of the increment in income accrues to the poor who are a relatively large proportion of the population. It follows that economic growth translates into a less than proportionate poverty reduction. It is only if economic growth is associated with a reduction in economic inequality that it would translate into a more than proportionate poverty reduction; indeed, reduced inequality could also reduce poverty in the future if it stimulates growth.

However, a reduction in inequality would be very difficult at low growth rates for potential losers have both voice and influence in polity and economy. It would be much more feasible if growth rates are high, especially if these lead to commensurate employment creation. Therefore, catch up, associated with higher growth rates, is essential for reducing inequality in the future, even if it has not done so in the past. This is because rapid economic growth has a potential for doing so, if it can create employment, and insofar as it can open up possibilities of some redistribution of income in favor of the bottom 40 percent, if the increment in aggregate income is large enough not to hurt the top 10 percent in absolute terms.

How did catch up in the developing world, driven by rapid growth during the past twenty-five years, affect inequality between countries in the world, between people in the world, and between people within countries? It is always difficult to attribute cause-and-effect because outcomes are shaped by so many factors. Even so, this chapter suggests some lessons from past experience.

Catch up did lead to a modest reduction in inter-country inequality between 1990 and 2010. This was probably less than it appears because population-weighted measures, which assume that income distribution within countries is perfectly equal, do reflect the rapid growth in PPP-GDP per capita in two countries – China and India – with large populations. However, even in terms of GDP per capita in market prices and current exchange rates, there was a narrowing of the gap with the world economy. This was not so vis-à-vis industrialized countries; yet, for developing countries as a group, divergence stopped although there was little convergence. But this process was associated with increasing inequality between countries in the developing world, since catch up was concentrated in one continent, Asia, and a few countries, the Next-14.

Global inequality among people, which remained unchanged at high levels during the period 1950–1990, some estimates suggest, diminished during the period 1990–2010. This reduction in inter-personal inequality between people in the world might also be overstated for reasons explained earlier. All the same, if income distribution between people in the world became less unequal, catch up was clearly an important underlying factor. A historical perspective highlights its significance. The Great Divergence that began *circa* 1820 led to a widening gap between rich and poor people in the world until *circa* 1970 (Nayyar, 2013). In the absence of catch up, this inequality might have persisted at high levels or risen further.

The story of income inequality between people within countries is different. Evidence available, even if incomplete, suggests that income distribution between people worsened almost everywhere – whether industrialized countries, transition economies or developing countries – from 1990 to 2010 in the age of markets and globalization. Of course, this was not necessarily a consequence of rapid economic growth, since growth rates in industrialized countries and transition economies were much lower than earlier. The outcome in developing countries was mixed. It had two dimensions. For one, there was a significant reduction in absolute poverty, clearly visible in Asia, which would not have been possible without rapid economic growth in the catch up process. For another, income inequality between people increased in most countries, with few exceptions, so that poverty persisted in Asia despite rapid economic growth, while poverty intensified in sub-Saharan Africa possible because slower growth was juxtaposed with rising inequality. Obviously, for any given rate of growth, if inequality had risen less or not at all, catch up could have reduced poverty further. It is also clear that, for any given level of inequality, if rates of growth had been lower and catch up had been slower, poverty reduction would have been less than it was.

In sum, during the period since 1990, catch up driven by rapid growth probably led to a modest reduction in economic inequality between countries and between people in the world although it created new divergences between countries in the developing world, while it led to a significant increase in economic inequality between people within countries although it brought about a significant reduction in absolute poverty in countries that experienced rapid growth. The counterfactual is important. In the absence of catch up, outcomes might have been worse.

It must be recognized that linear extrapolations of the past 25 years, which expect more of the same to continue, are not appropriate for thinking about the next 25 years. The prospects of catch up on the part of developing countries in the world economy will depend not only on how the Next-14 fare in times to come but also on whether this process spreads to other countries in the developing world. The leaders in this process, the Next-14, can sustain their growth in the future only by ensuring that the benefits of catch up are distributed in a far more equal manner between people and regions within countries, so that the exclusions that have characterized development outcomes so far do not persist. The followers in this process, low-income or even middle-income countries, can provide an impetus to their growth as latecomers if it does not exclude regions and includes more people.

Development is about creating production capabilities in economies and ensuring the well-being of people in countries. Economic growth is simply a means to this end. And there are two obvious pitfalls. In the long run, economic growth might not be sustainable. And, it might not be transformed into meaningful development, if it does not improve the living conditions of people. In the pursuit of development, poverty eradication, employment creation, and inclusive growth are an imperative. For one, these are constitutive as essential objectives of development. For another, these are instrumental as the primary means of bringing about development.[15] This is the only sustainable way forward for developing countries because it would enable them to mobilize their most abundant resource, people, for the purpose of development. The same people who constitute resources on the supply side provide markets on the demand side.

This interaction can reinforce the process of economic growth through a cumulative causation (Nayyar, 2014).

This requires a creative interaction between the state and the market, beyond the predominance of the market model in the process of development. It is in part about regulating markets and in part about inclusive growth. For a similar context, but at a different time, Polanyi (1944) analyzed what he characterized as the 'Great Transformation' in Europe. In doing so, he described a double-movement: the first from a pre-capitalist system to a market driven industrialization in the nineteenth century; the second from the predominance of the market model to a more inclusive world in which the state played a corrective, regulatory, role. This transformation, which began in the early twentieth century, was complete by the mid-twentieth century. But it did not last long. There was a resurgence of the market model beginning in the late 1970s. Hence, the present situation in developing countries is similar to the pre-transformation situation in Europe (Stewart, 2007). Such a Great Transformation in the developing world in the early twenty-first century, similar to the Great Transformation in the industrialized world in the early twentieth century, could deepen and widen the catch up process (Nayyar, 2013).

The two interlinked hypotheses, together, bring the argument in this chapter to closure. Catch up through economic growth is necessary for reducing inequality, even if outcomes in the recent past have been mixed. But the catch up process itself, driven by rapid economic growth is not sustainable in the future, unless it creates inclusive societies that do not exclude people and regions within countries from the process. The conclusion can be stated in two short sentences. Catch up can reduce inequality. If it does not, there will be no catch up.

NOTES

1. Emeritus Professor of Economics, Jawaharlal Nehru University, New Delhi 110065, India. I would like to thank Peter van Bergeijk and Rolph van der Hoeven for persuading me to think about this issue, and Atul Sanganeria for valuable research assistance.
2. The share of industrialized countries, and Eastern Europe plus the former USSR, in world GDP, has been calculated from UNCTAD Stat based on UN National Accounts Statistics.
3. For an analysis of the economic resilience of developing countries in the aftermath of the financial crisis and the Great Recession, see Nayyar (2011).
4. For a discussion, with supporting evidence, see Nayyar (2013).
5. The contribution of Asia, as also Latin America and Africa, to the increase in the share of developing countries in each of these macroeconomic aggregates is calculated from United Nations statistics cited as sources for Table 9.1.
6. The shares of the three continents in world GDP at current prices and market exchange rates are calculated from UNCTAD Stat based on UN National Accounts Statistics.
7. The figures on BRICS, cited in this paragraph, are from Nayyar (2017).

8. For a detailed discussion on the relative importance of China in BRICS, of BRICS in the Next-14, and of the Next-14 in the developing world, see Nayyar (2016 and 2017).
9. The statistics on LDCs cited in this paragraph and the next are essentially obtained from UNCTAD (2011). Some are from earlier annual issues of the UNCTAD Report on *Least Developed Countries*. The Forbes list of 'The World Billionaires' reports that, in 2010, the net worth of the top 20 billionaires in the world was $634 billion. In 2010, the total GDP of all LDCs was $614 billion. See also, Nayyar (2013).
10. This has been described as the Great Divergence (Pomeranz, 2000). For further evidence and analysis, see Bourguignon and Morrisson (2002) and Nayyar (2013).
11. The issues in the debate about World Bank estimates of poverty are discussed at some length in Nayyar (2013). See also, Kaplinsky (2005) and Pogge and Reddy (2010). These poverty estimates of the World Bank are presented and analyzed at some length in Chen and Ravallion (2012).
12. The latest series of World Bank estimates use poverty lines of $1.90 and $3.10 per day in 2011 PPP. However, this new series is not used here because it creates problems of comparability with earlier years while its latest estimate is for 2012.
13. These estimates for the number of people and proportion of the population below the poverty lines of $1.25 and $2 per day in PPP 2005, for ten selected years during the period 1981–2008, are reported and discussed in Nayyar (2013).
14. It is worth noting that, as compared with 1990, the Gini coefficient for South Korea was higher at 38.6 in 1980, while that for Taiwan was lower at 27.7 in 1981. Clearly, income distribution became more equal in South Korea and more unequal in Taiwan.
15. This argument is similar to Amartya Sen's conception of development as freedom. Sen (1999) argues that development is about expanding real freedoms that people enjoy for their well-being, social opportunities and political rights. Such freedoms are not just constitutive as the primary ends of development. Such freedoms are also instrumental as the principal means of attaining development.

REFERENCES

Atkinson, Anthony B. (2015). *Inequality: What Can be Done?*, Cambridge, MA: Harvard University Press.

Atkinson, A.B. and T. Piketty (eds) (2010). *Top Incomes: A Global Perspective*, Oxford: Oxford University Press.

Atkinson, A.B., T. Piketty and E. Saez (2010). 'Top Incomes in the Long Run of History', in A.B. Atkinson and T. Piketty (eds) *Top Incomes: A Global Perspective*, Oxford: Oxford University Press, pp. 664–759.

Bourguignon, Francois (2015). *The Globalization of Inequality*, Princeton: Princeton University Press.

Bourguignon, Francois and Christian Morrisson (2002). 'The Size Distribution of Income among World Citizens: 1820–1992', *American Economic Review*, 92: 727–744.

Chang, Ha-Joon (2010). *23 Things They Don't Tell You about Capitalism*, New York: Bloomsbury Press.

Chen, Shaohua and Martin Ravallion (2012). 'More Relatively-Poor People in a Less Absolutely-Poor World', Policy Research Working Paper 6114, Washington, DC: The World Bank.

Cornia, G. Andrea and Sampsa Kiiski (2001). 'Trends in Income Distribution in the Post-World War II Period: Evidence and Interpretation' WIDER Discussion Paper 89, Helsinki: UNU-WIDER.

Kaplinsky, Raphael (2005). *Globalization, Poverty and Inequality*, Cambridge: Polity Press.

Milanovic, Branko (2005). *Worlds Apart: Measuring International and Global Inequality*, Princeton: Princeton University Press.

Nayyar, Deepak (2008). International Migration and Economic Development in Joseph Stiglitz and Narcis Serra (eds) *The Washington Consensus Reconsidered: Towards a New Global Governance*, Oxford: Oxford University Press, pp. 277–305.

Nayyar, Deepak (2011). 'The Financial Crisis, the Great Recession and the Developing World', *Global Policy*, 2: 20–32.

Nayyar, Deepak (2013). *Catch Up: Developing Countries in the World Economy*, Oxford: Oxford University Press.

Nayyar, Deepak (2014). 'Why Employment Matters: Reviving Growth and Reducing Inequality', *International Labour Review*, 153: 351–364.

Nayyar, Deepak (2016). 'BRICS, Developing Countries and Global Governance', *Third World Quarterly*, 37: 575–591.

Nayyar, Deepak (2017). 'BRICS, Emerging Markets and the World Economy', in P. Anand, F. Comim, S. Fennel and R. Weiss (eds) *Oxford Handbook on BRICS*, Oxford: Oxford University Press, forthcoming.

Palma, J. Gabriel (2011). 'Homogeneous Middles vs. Heterogeneous Tails, and the End of the Inverted-U: It's All About the Share of the Rich', *Development and Change*, 42: 87–153.

Piketty, Thomas (2014). *Capital in the Twenty-First Century*, Cambridge, MA: The Belknap Press, Harvard University Press.

Pogge, Thomas and Sanjay Reddy (2010). 'How Not to Count the Poor', in Sudhir Anand, Paul Segal and Joseph E. Stiglitz (eds) *Debates on the Measurement of Global Poverty*, Oxford: Oxford University Press, pp. 42–85.

Polanyi, Karl (1944). *The Great Transformation: The Political and Economic Origins of Our Times*, Boston: Beacon Press.

Pomeranz, Kenneth (2000). *The Great Divergence: China, Europe and the Making of the Modern World Economy*, Princeton: Princeton University Press.

Sen, Amartya (1999). *Development as Freedom*, New York: Alfred E. Knopf.

Stewart, Frances (2007). 'Do We Need a 'New Great Transformation'? Is One Likely?' in George Mavrotas and Anthony Shorrocks (eds) *Advancing Development: Core Themes in Global Economics,* London: Palgrave Macmillan, pp. 614–639.

Stiglitz, Joseph E. (2012). *The Price of Inequality*, New York: W.W. Norton.

UNCTAD (2011). *The Least Developed Countries 2011 Report*, New York and Geneva: United Nations.

United Nations (2006). *Diverging Growth and Development, World Economic and Social Survey 2006*, New York: United Nations.

10. Can the SDGs stem rising income inequality in the world?[1]

Rolph van der Hoeven

INTRODUCTION

This chapter firstly argues that income inequality has been treated inter-mittently in international settings over the 50 years, including in the Millennium Development Goals. However, continuing globalization and the financial crises of 2008 have put income inequality more in the centre of academic and political attention. Concern for income inequality is not sufficient, and the second part of the chapter discusses how national and international policies affect various forms of income inequality. It gives special attention to the functional income inequality, the distribution of income between labour and capital and the growing income share of the top 1 per cent income earners. It then argues and documents that income inequality has been only weakly included in the SDGs and that additional measures and political efforts are needed to effectively stem growing income inequality.

Inequality in International Settings

The beginning of the 1970s saw an increasing interest in income inequality, also for developing countries. But not everywhere: For example the text of first Development Decade of the United Nations (1960–1970) was very weak on income inequality.[2] Yet, more and more scholars and activists raised their voices then on growing inequality and enduring poverty, especially in Latin American. Prebisch (1970) advocated reduction of inequality and argued that reducing inequality would not hamper growth and economic progress, and showed that less income inequality could lead to a more balanced growth, through which poverty could reduce faster. The International Labour Organization (ILO) carried out in the 1970s various country analyses on employment and inequality and put the issue of unacceptable high levels for inequality on the international agenda. It was even the major recommendation of ILO policy advice for

Colombia. The ideas gathered by ILO and research groups in various countries resulted in 1974 in the publication *Redistribution from Growth* by the Institute of Development Studies in Sussex (Chenery et al., 1974, which documented for several countries growing inequality and emphasized practical redistribution policies). Adelman (1979) brought the idea of redistribution from growth further to *Redistribution before Growth*, based on successful development patterns in Taiwan and Korea.[3] The attention to greater equality in the mid-1970s also led to the so-called basic needs approach to development. It became a focus in various development institutes like IDS and ISS, and a lead concern for ILO. The logic was as follows. If the satisfaction of basic needs is a main objective of development, then more attention to redistribution is warranted in order to arrive faster at providing basic needs (Hopkins and van der Hoeven, 1983).

The basic needs approach, however, was not everywhere accepted. For some, the basic needs approach focused too much on the poorest developing countries, and gave too little attention to international measures to foster national economic growth (van der Hoeven, 1988). Basic needs were thus interpreted as a distraction from the 1970s debate on a New International Economic Order (NIEO) that envisaged reforms in the international relations so that developing countries could grow faster. This fear became stronger when the World Bank became interested in the basic needs approach, however, more as a social planning instrument without redistributive elements than as a strategy for large structural changes within countries and between countries. Furthermore structural adjustment programmes (SAPs) started to dominate in various circles' development thinking and financing. After two oil crises in the 1970s and an increase in foreign debt in many developing countries – caused by the abundance of petrodollars on the world market – and after the debt crisis of Mexico in 1982, the World Bank and the IMF introduced these programmes, with a focus on budgetary cuts, liberalization of markets and active promotion of exports, aiming at stimulating growth and at strengthening capacity in developing countries to repay debts in foreign currency (Addison, 2002; Chapter 7 by Addison in this volume). Attention to social problems and domestic income inequality in these programmes moved to the background.

The middle and late 1980s saw a countermovement. Critics (national politicians, NGOs, scientists from the South and the North and some organizations in the UN system itself) saw the SAPs, because of their liberal economic policy, as a major cause for increasing inequality and other social problems, especially in those countries that were obliged to take part in these programmes. By the end of the 1980s criticism of the structural adjustment programmes increased as these programmes did not lead to accelerated economic growth and reduction in debt; their prime objectives. It took until the middle of the 1990s before more social objectives of development gained general traction again. In the early 1990s the UNDP launched its annual *Human Development Report* asking for more attention to human development and also acting as a challenge to the already existing World Development Reports of the World Bank. The UN itself organized a number of World Summits on development issues, of which the Social Summit in Copenhagen in 1995 (World Summit for Social Development) gave policy recommendations for poverty reduction, employment and social inclusion and contained explicit recommendations for the reduction of political, legal, economic and social factors that promote or maintain inequality in income.

Millennium Development Goals and Inequality

The results of the renewed attention to social issues led to preparations for the UN Millennium Summit in 2000 and to the subsequent formulation of the Millennium Development Goals, in which a 50 per cent reduction of poverty and improving several social targets at the global level were among the 8 goals (see Appendix 1). In preparing an ILO contribution to the MDGs Luebker (2002) carried out a thought experiment on inequality: what if all *developing* countries would have in the year 2000 an inequality level, which was the lowest they had seen since the Second World War. The outcome of this thought experiment was that *the number of poor people in 2000 could have been one-third less if countries would have a level of inequality equal to what they would have had in the recent past*. A second thought experiment added another facet, namely that a country with moderate inequality would grow faster than a country with greater inequality. Under this scenario the number of poor could have been reduced by almost 40 per cent.

The end of the 1990s also saw growing globalization. Globalization is characterized by greater integration in terms of trade and capital flows, made possible by new technologies but more so by international conventions and agreements liberalizing the rules governing external markets. The Economic Research Institute of the United Nations (UNU-WIDER) started at the end of the 1990s a large research programme on inequality, growth, poverty and globalization. It looked first at what it labelled the old explanatory factors of inequality (land inequality, poor education, poor infrastructure, urban bias) and found that, while these still explained the *level* of inequality, these could not explain well the *rise* in inequality. The main causes of the *rise* in national income inequality were the liberalization of international trade and especially of capital markets, the significantly increased financialization of national economies and of international relations, technological change, and the growing restriction put on traditional labour market institutions that had led to greater inequality between unskilled and skilled workers (Cornia, 2004; Shorrocks and van der Hoeven, 2004). Despite these and various other analyses, the MDGs did not include reducing national income disparity in the targets for poverty reduction, and, for that matter, did not include reducing national inequality in other targets, such as those for education and health (Vandemoortele, 2011). Around 2005 a large number of reports from, among others, the UN, the World Bank, UNDP and ILO, appeared which all called for a reduction of rising or high income inequality, based on extensive research and data collections in this field. The validity of the Kuznets curve (which argued that during a process of development income inequality would rise and thereafter would decline – hence there would be no need for special attention) was rejected and valid arguments were put forward that a more equal distribution of income and assets did not have to lead to a decrease in economic growth. The financial crisis of 2008 and its after-effects strengthened the case for specific policies to stem growing income inequality as incomes of different groups in different country groupings were affected by the crisis. (Table 10.1), but few drastic measures were taken instead (van der Hoeven, 2010).

In effect, the poorer segments in the developed countries faced a triple whammy: they did not profit from globalization, they were hardest hit in terms of unemployment and are since bearing the consequences of fiscal tightening following the massive stimulus and bank bail-outs. The situation for developing countries though is more complex. The growth path of the emerging developing economies shows similar movements to those of developed countries, but of less intensity and these economies were thus less affected by the crisis. However, except for some Latin American countries[4] (Chapter 6 by Cornia in this volume), the growing inequality which was building up or being reinforced is not yet being halted, and wage shares in most emerging market economies are still declining, with a negative effect on domestic demand. The poorer developing countries, mainly in Africa, were less affected as their banking system was less developed, but still suffered from slower exports proceeds, remittances and lower aid levels.

After the financial crisis in 2008, the more traditional financial and economic circles sounded the alarm bell, fearing that large and rising income inequalities could affect the foundations of the free-market system. These fears thus confirmed what earlier research had shown: *Globalization, at least the unrestricted globalization that we see now, and income equality are clearly at odds with each other* (Gunther and van der Hoeven, 2004; van der Hoeven 2010; Vos 2010; Bourguignon, 2015).

Table 10.1   Effects of financial crisis on various socio-economic groups in different country groupings

	Precrisis	Crisis	Postcrisis stimulus	Postcrisis fiscal austerity
Developed countries				
Capital owners	++	–	++	+
Skilled workers	++	–	+	–
Unskilled workers	–	–	+	–
Excluded	–	0	0	–
Emerging developing countries				
Captial owners	++	+	++	+
Skilled workers	++	–	+	+
Unskilled workers	+	–	+	–
Peasants	–	–	+	–
Poor developing countries				
Captial owners	+	0	+	+
Skilled workers	+	–	+	–
Unskilled workers	–	–	+	–
Peasants	–	0	+	–

Source: van Bergeijk, de Haan and van der Hoeven (2011: 13).

Drivers of Income Inequality

In order to see what measures could halt growing income inequality it is useful to look in more detail at what the drivers of income inequality are. The above paragraphs dealt mainly with income inequality within countries. But should we not have a more cosmopolitan approach, especially given the strong growth of several emerging economies (Chapter 9 by Nayyar in this volume), and rather look at inequality in the world? Several authors have done so in detail, for example, Milanovic (2012a, 2012b, 2016) and van Bergeijk (2013). See Figure 10.1.

If we treat each country as a unit (Concept 1), average incomes across countries have actually become more unequal until 2000 with a slight decline thereafter. However, if countries are weighted only by the size of the population (Concept 2) incomes across the world become more equal. But if we take incomes of all households individually into account (Concept 3 for which much less data are available) the Gini Index of global income inequality is around 0.7, much higher than the level of income inequality found within any individual country. Despite the con-

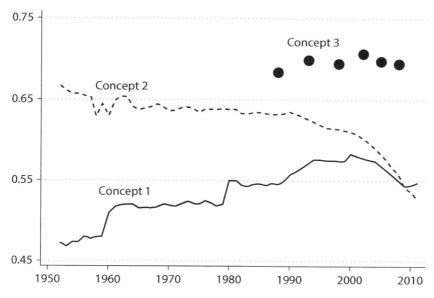

Note: See text for explanation.

Source: Based on Milanovic (2012b) Table 2, page 6.

Figure 10.1   *Gini index of global income inequality according to three
different concepts of global income inequality*

vergence in world income of some big emerging countries, rising income
inequalities within these countries resulted in overall global inequality
declining only slightly after some increase during the globalization era
from the mid-1980s to the early 2000s (Milanovic, 2012a).[5] It remains
therefore important to consider national income inequality.

Regarding national income inequality, the classical economists paid
attention mainly to the distribution of income between labour and capital,
the main factors of production: factor income or functional inequality.
This distinction between labour and capital income drove the great
classical debates for many years. In the post-Second World War period,
however, less attention was given to this type of inequality, as neoclassical
production functions often assumed a constant capital share under the
assumption that wage increases follow productivity increases. Attention
shifted to personal income or household income distribution. One can
interpret household income distribution in three ways:

- *Primary* income distribution: the distribution of household incomes consisting of the (sometimes cumulated) different factor incomes in each household, before taxes and subsidies as determined by markets and market institutions.
- *Secondary* income distribution: the distribution of household incomes after deduction of taxes and inclusion of transfer payments (that is, as determined by fiscal policies).
- *Tertiary* income distribution: the distribution of household incomes when imputed benefits from public expenditure are added to household income after taxes and subsidies. This interpretation of household income is particularly relevant for developing countries as different services and government services are often provided for free or below market prices.

Most policy discussions on inequality though focus on secondary household income distribution (take home pay, rents, interest earnings and profits after taxes). However attention is shifting back to factor income distribution.[6] Daudey and Garcia-Penalosa (2007) argue that the distribution of personal or household income depends on three factors: the distribution of labour endowments, the distribution of capital endowments, and the way in which aggregate output is shared between the two production factors. The factor distribution of income is a statistically significant determinant of the personal distribution of income:[7] a larger labour share is statistically associated with a lower Gini index of personal incomes. It is therefore important to also (re-)consider the factor distribution of income. The focus on factor income inequality points to the importance of better understanding the changing position of labour in the production process in order to correctly interpret inequality trends, as labour has been losing ground relative to capital over the past 20 years (ILO, 2011). Furthermore, experience has shown that it is not possible to reduce primary household income inequality without addressing how incomes are generated in the production process and how this affects factor income inequality (van der Hoeven, 2011). Atkinson (2009) argues convincingly that there are at least three reasons to pay again greater attention to factor income distribution:

- To make a link between incomes at the macroeconomic level (national accounts) and incomes at the level of the household.
- To help understand inequality in the personal distribution of income.
- To address the social justice concerns with the fairness of different returns to different sources of income.

Also Glyn (2009) argues that factor income distribution matters to people for at least two reasons. First, despite broader access to capital among households, wealth, and especially high-yielding wealth, is still extremely unevenly distributed as Thomas Piketty (2014) has reminded us so eloquently. Therefore the observed redistribution from labour to property income contributes still significantly to increasing household income inequality. Second, the fact that profits may be rising much faster than wages conflicts with widely held views of social justice and fairness. Trapp (2015) has argued that dynamics in the factor income distribution are of particular relevance for developing countries, especially in their effort to fight poverty. Regressive redistribution of factors and their remuneration will be felt strongly in developing countries, due to weak social safety nets and limited access to capital by the poor. The main asset of the poor certainly is labour. As such, the labour income share can serve as an indicator in designing policies for social protection and tax systems as these usually target the factor income distribution (minimum wage policies, tax concessions for investments, and so on). It is therefore important to be more explicit about the drivers of factor income distribution, as well as the drivers of primary, secondary and tertiary household income distribution and the relation between these. There are many drivers that affect the different types of income distribution. One can distinguish between drivers that are largely exogenous (outside the purview of domestic policy) and endogenous drivers (that is, drivers that are mainly determined by domestic policy). However, a clear line is difficult to draw, because even drivers that are typically considered to be exogenous or autonomous are often the outcome of policy actions in the past or the outcome of a domestic political decision to create international institutions (for example the creation of the WTO to establish trade liberalization or the decision to invest in technical progress). With increased globalization, exogenous drivers gain in importance. As a consequence more is expected from national policy drivers to counteract the effect of the more exogenous drivers. Table 10.2 shows the interactions between the various exogenous and endogenous drivers and the various types of income distribution.

The crosses in Table 10.2 indicate were the effects of these various drivers are strongest. We see that exogenous factors (globalization) affect mainly factor income and primary household income distribution (upper left quadrant of Table 10.2), while endogenous drivers affect both factor income and various types of household income distribution (lower left and right hand quadrants).

Table 10.2   Interaction between main drivers and various types of income distribution

Distribution type Drivers	Factor income distribution	Wage distribution	Primary household income distribution	Secondary household income distribution	Tertiary household income distribution
Exogenous Drivers					
1.Trade globalization	X	X	X		
2.Financial globalization	X	X	X		
3.Technical change	X	X	X		
Endogenous Drivers					
4.Macroeconomic policies	X	X	X		
5.Labour market policies	X	X	X	X	
6.Wealth inequality	X	X	X		
7.Fiscal policies: taxation and transfers	X		X	X	X
8.Govt expenditure					X

Source: Based on UNDP (2013) Table 3.8.

Globalization and Factor Income Inequality

The decline in labour income shares during a phase of globalization is not limited to specific sectors but is an economy-wide phenomenon. Rodriguez and Yayadev (2010) investigated, by means of a large panel dataset for 135 developed and developing countries, whether the secular decline in labour income shares is due to the decline of the labour income share in particular sectors or whether the decline in labour income share is economy-wide. By matching national economy-wide results with results for the labour income share at the 3 digit industry level they were able to conclude that the declines in labour income shares are primarily driven by decreases in intra-sector labour shares opposed to movements in activity towards sectors with lower labour income shares. *This suggests that the decline in labour shares is driven by economy wide phenomena and therefore, national policies rather than industry specific policies are needed to reverse it.*

The downward trend of the labour income share is even more pronounced in many emerging and developing countries, with considerable declines in Asia and North Africa and more stable, but still declining, labour income shares in Latin America (ILO, 2011).[8] The ILO (2013) and Stockhammer (2013) have used an enlarged panel dataset encompassing developed, developing and emerging economies to investigate the drivers of declining labour income shares. The average of labour shares in a group of 16 developing and emerging economies declined from around 62 per cent of GDP in the early 1990s to 58 per cent just before the crisis. These results confirm an earlier observation (Diwan, 1999) that currency crises are associated with sharp declines in the labour income share, reiterating that the cost of financial instability affects labour disproportionally. More recent analyses (Stockhammer, 2013; ILO, 2013) find decline of the welfare state and weakening of labour market institutions in addition to financialization, globalization and technical change as drivers of factor income inequality.

The decline of the labour income share in developing countries is the more worrying as, according to past patterns of development, the labour income shares in developing countries should actually rise with increasing per capita GDP (Figure 10.2).

More recent data confirm the trend of a declining labour income share

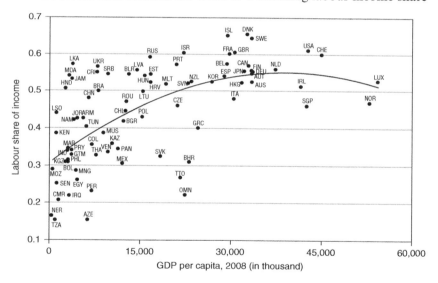

Note: The labour share of income is measured as the ratio of compensation of employees to GDP at factor cost in 2008. GDP at factor cost is measured as GDP at market prices, minus the difference between taxes, less subsidies for production and imports.

Source: ILO (2014) Figure 8.2 page 153.

Figure 10.2   The unadjusted labour income share and GDP per capita in 2008

observed before the crisis of 2008. In a recent study, using an augmented dataset (distinguishing labour income share in the corporate sector and in the whole economy), Karabarbounis, and Neiman (2015) found that the global corporate labour share has exhibited a relatively steady downward trend, from a level of roughly 64 per cent, reaching about 59 per cent at the end of the period, while labour's share of the overall economy also declined globally from 58 per cent to 53 per cent. Trapp (2015) used an innovative way to determine changes in the labour share in developing countries, by collecting social accounting matrices of a large number of countries to estimate labour income shares in these countries. Her finding confirms the other analyses mentioned above of a downward trend of the labour income share in most developing regions (Figure 10.3). East Asia and the Pacific is the region that experienced the fastest decrease (on average 14 percentage points since 1990), closely followed by Eastern Europe and

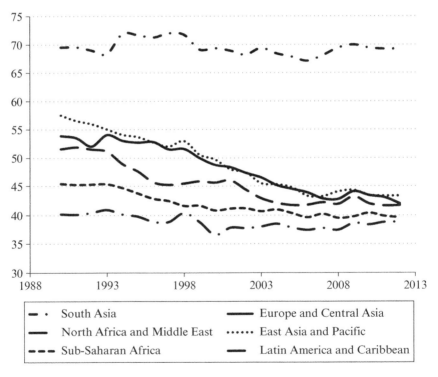

Source: Trapp (2015) Figure 6, page 16.

Figure 10.3   Labour income share by region, 1990–2011

Central Asia (both about 11 percentage points), and Latin America and the Caribbean (both about 10 percentage points). A considerable decline also occurred in sub-Saharan Africa, where labour income shares fell by 6 percentage points between 1990 and 2011. Exceptions to the downward trend are in South Asia, the Middle East, and North Africa, where labour income shares fluctuated, but on average remained stable (note that labour income shares in these regions actually should have increased, as mentioned earlier, given the positive growth in GDP in these regions).

The last two sets of analyses range until 2011/2012, extend well beyond the financial crisis and its immediate aftermath. *It is clear from these analyses that the decline of the labour share has not halted or been reversed after the financial crisis, and also does not attest to the sometimes-heard thesis that the financial crisis hit capital owners harder than ordinary workers and their families.*

The Increasing Share of Top Income Earners

Furthermore the share of the top 1 per cent of income earners is increasing in many countries, a consequence of the declining labour share and of greater inequality between wages themselves. If the labour income of the top 1 per cent of income earners were excluded nationwide, the decline in the labour income share would probably have been even greater than what we observed in Figure 10.4. This reflects the sharp increase, especially in

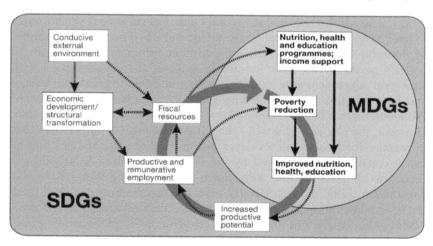

Source: UNCTAD (2014), Chart 22, page 50.

Figure 10.4 Context of the SDGs

English-speaking developed countries, of wage and salaries (including bonuses and exercised stock options) of top executives, who now cohabit with capital owners at the top of the income hierarchy (Atkinson, Piketty and Saez, 2011). The proportion of wage earnings in the top segments of household income also increased, to various degrees, in other countries including Japan, the Netherlands, Canada, Italy, Spain and the United Kingdom – though not in Sweden, Finland or Australia (Atkinson, Piketty and Saez, 2011). Data for the share of the top 1 per cent income in developing countries are much scarcer, but for 11 developing countries, for which data are available, a similar trend as in developed countries can be observed.[9] The share of the 1 per cent top income group in Colombia reaches 20 per cent, a level similar to that in the USA. It is increasing also for ten out of eleven developing countries in the sample.

Millennium Development Goals and Sustainable Development Goals

Can the Sustainable Development Goals stem this growing income inequality? The 17 Sustainable Development Goals (see Appendix 2) adopted in September 2015 came into force as of 1 January 2016 and are the successors of the Millennium Development Goals (MDGs) which were adopted in 1991 and whose target date is the end of 2015.

In understanding the making of the SDGs, it is useful to reflect how the MDGs came about. An enthusiastic group in the secretariat of the UN developed these on the basis of the UN Millennium Summit declaration of 2000.[10] The MDGs reflected the wish of many development practitioners to have, at a global level, clear goals and measurable outcomes of a number of desirable development challenges, without proscribing a fixed set of policies, as this would have led, in the wake of the dissatisfaction with structural adjustment policies of the 1980s and 1990s, to great controversy and to a rejection of an otherwise generally accepted policy document (Vandemoortele, 2011; Chapter 3 by Vandemoortele in this volume). However, the absence of a well-founded development theory meant that in practice for most countries development policies remained business as usual, considerably influenced by the Poverty Reduction Strategies, the successor of the Structural Adjustment Policies of the World Bank. As Saith (2006: 1189) puts it: 'Poverty reduction is somehow detached from the constraints imposed by structural inequalities and anti-poor and anti-labour policy biases. The answer is held to lie in the simple equation: external assistance + technological fixes + good local governance = poverty reduction'.

UNCTAD (2014) argues that the MDG approach was essentially a linear one, focusing mainly on human and some environmental development goals and programmes, targeted directly at meeting those goals. By focusing on outcome goals, to the exclusion of the means for achieving them, the MDGs encouraged reliance on specific programmes aimed at improving the targeted indicators that were mostly financed by Official Development Assistance (ODA). Ensuring sustainability depends, however, critically on reversing vicious circles of development, in which especially many least developed countries find themselves (UNCTAD, 2014). Economic development has thus a major role to play in achieving human development goals, and a still more critical role in sustaining advances in human development over the long term. *Employment is a critical linkage in this process, especially when it is accompanied by rising labour productivity* (Nayyar, 2013). An economic development process is needed that creates productive and remunerative jobs allowing people to generate the income needed to escape poverty, while also generating the public revenues needed to finance health services and education. This in turn *requires an international economic system that supports such development processes.* If the post-2015 agenda is to be successful in achieving the adopted SDGs, it needs to encompass all of the elements presented in Figure 10.4: *economic transformation, employment creation, the generation of fiscal resources* and *a favorable global economic environment*, also called *structural transformation*, a necessary condition for long-term growth of per capita income (Ocampo, Rada and Taylor, 2009). Indeed:

> [I]t is associated with two types of dynamic efficiency, accelerating the growth of productivity, output and employment over time. The first is a Schumpeterian efficiency effect, whereby those sectors with the highest rates of productivity growth and capacity expansion lead the innovation process and drive productivity gains. The second is a Keynesian efficiency effect, whereby the pattern of specialization shifts towards sectors that benefit from faster growth of domestic and external demand, generating positive impacts on output and employment. These two types of efficiency generally go hand in hand, as the more knowledge-intensive sectors also tend to face stronger domestic demand growth in the long run, and tend to be more competitive in international markets. (UNCTAD, 2014)

UNCTAD (2014) found that in the case of the LDCs overall growth rates closely reflect sectorial changes in employment: economic growth is negatively correlated with the share of agriculture in employment, but positively correlated with the shares of industry and services, a clear case of structural transformation. Moreover, *the LDCs that have experienced the greatest structural transformation are also those that have made the greatest progress towards attaining the MDGs.* Also, economic growth has been much more strongly correlated with MDG performance in countries with above-average structural transformation than those with less structural transformation.

The 2014 LDC report of UNCTAD considered two critical aspects of human development: poverty (MDG 1) and enrolment in primary education (MDG 2). It found a strong and positive association between structural change and progress in halving poverty: countries that achieved faster transformation performed better in terms of poverty reduction than those where transformation was slower. Asian LDCs such as Bhutan, Cambodia and Nepal, which have experienced rapid transformation of their economic structures over the past two decades, have also been among the highest achievers in reducing poverty. A similar result holds for educational attainment: progress in primary school enrolment appears to be strongly associated with structural transformation. UNCTAD (2014) finds this pattern generally replicated across other MDG targets, suggesting a significant positive association between structural change and the average progress across all the MDG targets.

So there is ample justification for including goals on transformative economic policies and outcomes. The political climate for doing so has also changed now that the Bretton Woods institutions are losing their monopoly in development financing (attested by the recent establishments of a BRIC bank and the Asian Infrastructure Investment Bank, AIV, 2014) the fear of Northern dictated structural adjustment programmes is declining and hence development policies, based on the experience of structural transformation, which some of the successful emerging countries underwent, can lead to an international acceptance of a development agenda which is built around more Southern oriented structuralist development strategies. Goals on structural transformation and sustainable growth then do become relevant: First, because the MDGs, in which these goals did not figure, did not spur efforts on structural transformation, which they should have, and second, because countries that performed better on structural transformation, also did better in achieving the MDG goals.

Hence it is logical that in the preparation of the SDGs more attention was given to issues of sustainable growth and structural transformation. Actually, the list of SDGs reflects much more the principles and aspirations of the Millennium Declaration of 2000, and represents therefore a more integrated approach to development, in which economic, social and ecological concerns are more balanced. They contain, as Mkandawire (2004) formulated, a possible agenda for transformative social policies. If we classify the 17 goals as social, economic, environmental or general (an exercise which is open to multiple interpretations, as some goals can be typified by more than one term) we arrive at five social goals, five environment goals, three economic goals and four general goals.[11] This classification does also point to a rather balanced set of goals.

Inequality and Sustainable Development Goals

Various authors (van der Hoeven, 2010; Vandemoortele, 2011; Melaned, 2012) have argued that the MDGs, by emphasizing targets at a global level (and more and more also at a national level), have ignored the inequalities that averages conceal. They suggest therefore that attention to inequality is imperative in any formulation of the SDGs and that targets for all SDGs should be broken down for different socioeconomic classes or for different income groups. These argumentations have been strengthened by recent analyses that conclude that greater equality and more equal access to government services will contribute to improved and sustained development in general (Wilkinson and Pickett, 2010). However, for a workable set of SDGs it is not only necessary to make the various impacts on poorer groups more visible and to suggest corrective measures in terms of public and development aid expenditures, but also to analyse and take action on what kind of economic or social processes are causing these enormous (often growing) inequalities.

In the evaluation of the results of the MDGs it became clear that the lack of any reference to inequality was a great oversight in the MDGs. This mistake was exacerbated by the fact that currently most poor people, defined as those living on less than $1.25 a day, do not live any more in low income countries (Sumner, 2012: Chapter 5 by Edward and Sumner in this volume). Various scholars and activists have come to the conclusion that tackling inequality is actually a greater challenge than tackling poverty. During the preparation of the SDGs, a group of about 90 concerned scholars urged in an open letter[12] to the Secretary of the High-Level Panel of Eminent Persons on the Post 2015 Development Agenda that the SDGs should take inequality on board in all its aspects and adopt as a goal the reduction of the Palma ratio, which indicates how much more the income of the 10 per cent richest is, compared to the 40 per cent poorest. As Palma (2011) has elaborated this ratio not only gives a better picture of inequality, but also can shed light on the specific situation of the middle class. Palma (2011) correctly argued that *differences in inequality are less an outcome of technical factors and more the result of the political process, where norms and habits determine the degree of inequality and where the attitude of the middle class plays an important role.*

Which measures are necessary to stem the growing inequality? For this it is useful to return to Table 10.2, which distinguishes between exogenous and endogenous drivers of inequality. The literature has shown that domestic policies can have a great effect on inequality (Dagdeviren, van der Hoeven and Weeks, 2004; Luebker, 2015). Figure 10.5 gives the degree of redistribution in countries at different levels of GDP per capita. There is

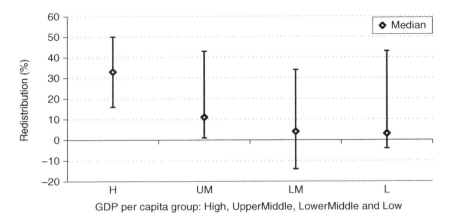

Source: Based on UNDP (2013), Figure 3.13.

Figure 10.5   The degree of redistribution in the late 2000s by GDP per capita group

great variation in all income groups. High income countries are on average better able to reduce primary or market income inequality, but we notice also for all income categories, huge variations in this reduction of primary inequality. National institutions and national policies can therefore play an important role in reducing primary or market outcome inequality. Moreover, the degree of inequality reduction from primary to secondary distribution does not seem to be related to the level of initial primary or market outcome inequality.

To what extent do the SDGs take income inequality and redistribution into account? The most direct reference to inequality is in goal 10: reduce inequality within and between countries. However the targets related to domestic (within) inequality are rather weak. The first target states: *By 2030, progressively achieve and sustain the growth of the bottom 40 per cent of the population at a rate higher than the national average,* followed by targets calling to promote inclusion, and ensure equal opportunity, amongst others by eliminating discriminatory laws. Another target is to adopt policies, especially fiscal, wage and social protection policies and progressively achieve greater equality. The formulations of these targets reflect the difficulty among the negotiators behind the SDGs to come to clear statements on inequality. *The only time-bound target* (target 10.1: rate of income growth of bottom 40 per cent faster than national average) *is rather vague and completely misses the fact that increases in inequality are especially created at the top end of the income scale.* One can only deplore that the modest suggestion of the Palma ratio as an indicator of inequality, which is sensitive to more that proportionate increases at the top income scale, has not been taking into account in the current SDGs.

The other targets of goal 10 are calling for more policy attention to national inequality (targets 10.2–10.4) and to systemic issue of the international financial, trade and migratory system (targets 10.5–10.10). Regarding the latter, it might be instructive to analyse the outcome of the conference on Financing for Development (FfD), a preparatory conference for the SDGs. Although the outcome document of the FfD conference, the Addis Ababa Action Agenda, mentions several concerns on growing inequality and urges national governments to increase fiscal resources, that can be used to counteract the growing income inequality stemming from globalization (see also Bourguignon, 2015), it fails to recommend fundamental changes in the International Financial System which could increase the fiscal capacity of developing countries to finance redistributive policies. First, various developed countries prevented recommendations on changing the current global financial architecture in the Addis Ababa Action Agenda. A change would have led to less volatility in foreign flows and hence less need for developing countries to hold costly foreign reserves to face growing volatility. With less volatility, these foreign reserves could have been used by developing countries for national investment. Nobel prize laureate Joseph Stiglitz has calculated that the effect of using foreign reserves for domestic investment in developing countries would have been a bigger contribution to the financing of the MDGs than current development aid.[13] Second, recommendations to set up an international tax body to stem the illicit outflow of resources from developing countries through tax treaties and transfer pricing and so on, which would have greatly increased the fiscal situation in developing countries, were not accepted, as developed countries wanted to keep the discussion and measures on tax issues under the auspices of the OECD, an organization dominated by Western developed countries. Third, sensible proposals to set up a Sovereign Debt Reduction Mechanism, the adoption of which would have avoided unregulated and ad hoc debt rescheduling, were not accepted, putting yet another strain on the fiscal situation in developing countries (AIV, 2014; Vos, Chapter 4 in this volume).

So on a first reading one could say that the SDGs and the Addis Ababa Action Agenda, in the way they have been currently formulated, will not be able to stem the growing inequality in the World. This is rather worrying: Chapter 5 by Edward and Sumner in this volume shows, using various simulation models, that growing inequality is a major impediment to drastically reducing poverty and that continuing or growing income inequality levels invalidate most of the optimistic projections on reducing poverty. Vandemoortele in Chapter 3 in this volume argues therefore that, in the current economic and social context, *the key global challenge is extreme inequality*. Not dealing effectively with inequality will undermine the major trust of the SDGs for greater transformation and universality as Jolly, Chapter 2 in this volume, argues.

Thus while the SDGs provide statements to reduce income inequality, the targets and indicators provided give, prima facie, insufficient weight to reducing income inequality. However, another important element in the preparation of the SDGs was the active involvement of civil society. Civil society and some governments have now achieved that the SDGs are embedded in the Human Rights Declaration and in the other international instruments relating to human rights and international law, although not in all labour rights as Luebker, Chapter 8 in this volume, has pointed out. Furthermore the 2030 Agenda for Sustainable Development stated that a follow-up and review process should be an integral part of the SDGs. The follow-up and review process could thus become an important instrument to reduce extreme inequalities and to strengthen international and national policies to achieve that. However current indications of the review process do not stem for optimistic reading regarding reducing income inequality. The rather weak target on reducing income inequality, as indicated above (*by 2030, progressively achieve and sustain the growth of the bottom 40 per cent of the population at a rate higher than the national average*) has been included in the verifiable sets of indicators developed by the UN Statistical Commission[14] and no other strong indicators, besides the wage share in national income, have been added to the list of indicators. But it is interesting to note that the first review of the SDGs by the Secretary-General of the UN to the High Level Political Forum in July 2016 casts doubts on target 10.1 and the indicator thereof of reducing income inequality. *Target 10.1 seeks to ensure that income growth among the poorest 40 per cent of the population in every country is more rapid than its national average. This was true in 56 of 94 countries with data available from 2007 to 2012. However, this does not necessarily imply greater prosperity, since nine of those countries experienced negative growth rates over that period.*[15]

However these review processes will not only be informed by governments and international agencies, but also by civil society. It is also these processes that one must rely on to put issues of inequality at the forefront of development policy. At various passages in the SDGs and in the Addis Ababa Action Agenda many lofty words have been said about reducing inequality. Active involvement of civil society can thus call governments and the UN system to task on growing national and international income inequalities and demand national and international policies to counteract these.

These strong pleas for a more political approach resonate well with Palma (2011), and several chapters in this book (Jolly, Chapter 2; Vandemoortele, Chapter 3; Luebker, Chapter 8). Thus both civic action and political pressure are needed to demand policies and measures which go beyond the formulation of some of the current time-bound targets in the SDGs, and which follow the general discourse of the SDGs and the Post-2015 Development Agenda. This might then lead to a global social contract between citizens within countries and between nation states on an effective partnership for inclusive development (van der Hoeven, 2011; Ghosh, 2015; Chapter 8 by Luebker in this volume). Elements of such a global Social Contract should include first, the *right to development* especially the economic, social and cultural rights and the basic elements thereof in the form of non-discrimination, participation and accountability. Second, the contract should include *the introduction of a global social floor*, which is financially possible, but where currently political will is lacking. Third, *a revitalized form of global governance*, where the coherence, at national and international level between social, economic and environmental sustainable policies, is strengthened allowing developing countries to strive for necessary structural transformation. This could take the form of a Global Economic Coordination Council. Deliberations at and resolution of the council need not only to be based on current statistics of GDP and other economic phenomena, but also need to include alternative measures. The review mechanism of the SDGs could provide a framework for this, but whether it would depends on much more than currently is agreed upon.

NOTES

1. This is a revised version of my valedictory address (http://www.iss.nl/fileadmin/ASSETS/iss/Documents/Academic_publications/Valedictory_Lecture_8_October_2015.pdf). I would like to thank Peter van Bergeijk, Jan Willem Gunning and an anonymous reviewer for useful comments on an earlier version.
2. 'It is true that the General Assembly resolution lays down a precise quantitative target only for the increase in aggregate incomes, and that there is no similar quantitative target for changes in income distribution. We can, however, take it for granted that the 5 per cent growth target established by the resolution also implies that the increment in income thus achieved should be wisely used for the benefit of the poorer sections of the population and should result in a degree of social progress which is at least in "balance" with the rise in aggregate national income' (Meier, 1971: 54).
3. Adelman argued that redistributing factors of production (land, better education, investment capital) before these would become scarce in a strong growth phase of the development process, and thus would command higher wages and prices, would be a superior way to achieve a more equal income distribution during the course of development. This idea was similar to Tinbergen (1975), who explained inequality as a race between technological progress and education. If technological progress grew faster than education, those who could master technological progress could receive larger rents than those who could not, leading to higher income inequality.

4. The commodity crash has clearly exposed the growth model of some Latin American countries like Brazil. Although the 2008 financial crash did affect these countries less, they are now in crisis. Some emerging countries were thus later than other countries affected by an unstable international environment. See also Saad Filho (2015).

5. Bourguignon (2015) arrives at similar high levels. According to his figures the decline in world inequality started in the 1990s, somewhat earlier than Milanovic indicates. See Chapter 9 by Nayyar in this volume for a discussion on the figures provided by Bourguignon (2015).

6. The IMF (Jaumotte and Tytell, 2007) investigated the effect of globalization on the labour income share in developed countries as did the OECD (Bassanini and Manfredi, 2012) while UNDP (Rodriguez and Yayadev, 2010) and ILO (2011) carried out several analyses on a broader set of data encompassing all countries in the world.

7. Other variables used are manufacturing share, GDP per capita, openness, civil liberties and human capital.

8. In Latin America the increase in factor income inequality was compensated by a decline in household income inequality through fiscal policies, income transfers and minimum wage increases (Chapter 6 by Cornia in this volume; Lustig 2015).

9. The World Top Income Database. http://topincomes.g-mond.parisschoolofeconomics. eu (accessed 4 August 2016).

10. These were based on early conceptualization of development goals by the OECD and drew on the Millennium Declaration, accepted by all Heads of State at the Millennium Summit of the UN in September 2000. The Declaration itself has a longer and higher set of aspirations, and should not be confused with the very specific and time-bound set of indicators which comprise the 8 MDGs and 21 targets through which progress towards the MDGs are measured (Melaned, 2012: 4).

11. See Appendix 2 for all 17 SDGs; 5 Social Goals (SDG 1, 2, 3, 4, 6), 5 Environmental Goals (SDG 7, 12, 13, 14, 15), 3 Economic Goals (SDG 8, 9 and 10), 4 General Goals (SDG 5, 11, 16, 17).

12. http://www.post2015hlp.org/wp-content/uploads/2013/03/Dr-Homi-Kharas.pdf.

13. 'Developing countries earn at most 1 to 2 per cent in real return on their foreign reserves. They could invest these reserves locally with returns up to 10 to 15 per cent. Assuming a difference of 10 per cent between domestic and foreign returns, the opportunity cost of holding reserves is quite high, well in excess of $300 billion per year – more than 2 per cent of GDP. The total opportunity cost of reserves is roughly equal to the amount of funds needed by developing countries to finance necessary investments to meet the MDGs'(Stiglitz, 2006: 249).

14. See UN Statistical Commission : http://unstats.un.org/sdgs/indicators/database/ (accessed 3 August 2016).

15. Para 73 of *Progress towards the Sustainable Development Goals Report of the Secretary-General* UN High-level Political Forum on Sustainable Development, convened under the auspices of the Economic and Social Council, 3 June 2016 document number E/2016/75*.

REFERENCES

Addison, T. (2002) 'Structural adjustment', in R. Clarke, C. Kirkpatrick and C. Polidano (eds) *Handbook on Development Policy and Management*, Cheltenham, UK and Northampton, MA, USA: Edward Elgar Publishing, Chapter 5, pp. 42–50.

Adelman, I. (1979) 'Redistribution before growth', in Institute of Social Studies, *Development of Societies: The Next Twenty-Five Years*, Den Haag: Martinus Nijhoff, pp. 160–176.

AIV (Advisory Council on International Affairs) (2014) *Improving Global Financial Cohesion, The Importance of a Coherent International Economic and Financial Architecture*, Advisory Report 89, The Hague.

Atkinson, A.B. (2009) 'Factor shares: the principal problem of political economy?', *Oxford Review of Economic Policy*, 25(1): 3–16.

Atkinson, A.B., T. Piketty and E. Saez (2011) 'Top incomes in the long run of history', *Journal of Economic Literature*, 49(1): 3–71.

Bassanini, A. and T. Manfredi (2012) 'Capital's grabbing hand? a cross-country/cross-industry analysis of the decline of the labour share', OECD Social, Employment and Migration Working Papers, No. 133. Paris: OECD Publishing.

Bourguignon, F. (2015) *The Globalization of Inequality*, Princeton: Princeton University Press.

Chenery, H. et al. (1974) *Redistribution with Growth*, Oxford: Oxford University Press.

Cornia, Giovanni A. (ed.) (2004) *Inequality, Growth and Poverty in an Era of Liberalization and Globalization*, Oxford: Oxford University Press.

Dagdeviren, H., R. van der Hoeven and J. Weeks (2004) 'Redistribution does matter: growth and redistribution for poverty reduction', Chapter 7 in A. Shorrocks and R. van der Hoeven (eds), *Growth, Inequality, and Poverty: Prospects for Pro-poor Economic Development*, Oxford: Oxford University Press, pp. 125–153.

Daudey, E. and C. Garcia-Penalosa (2007) 'The personal and the factor distribution of income in a cross-section of countries', *Journal of Development Studies*, 43(5): 812–829.

Diwan, Ishac (1999) *Labor Shares and Financial Crises*. Mimeo, Washington, DC: World Bank.

Ghosh J. (2015) 'Beyond the Millennium Development Goals: a southern perspective on a global new deal', *Journal of International Development*, 27, 320–329.

Glyn, A. (2009) 'Functional distribution and inequality', in W. Salverda, B. Nolan and T.M. Smeeding (eds) *The Oxford Handbook of Economic Inequality*, Oxford: Oxford University Press, pp. 101–126.

Gunther, B. and R. van der Hoeven (2004) 'The social dimension of globalization: a review of the literature', *International Labour Review*, 143(1–2), 7–43.

Hopkins, M. and R. van der Hoeven (1983) *Basic Needs in Development Planning*, Aldershot: Gower Publishing.

ILO (2011) *World of Work Report 2011: Income Inequalities in the Age of Financial Globalization*, Geneva: ILO.

ILO (2013) *Global Wage Report 2012/13: Wage and Equitable Growth*, Geneva: ILO.

ILO (2014) *World of Work Report 2014*, Geneva: ILO.

Jaumotte, F. and I. Tytell (2007) 'How has the globalization of labor affected the labor income share in advanced countries?', IMF WP/07/298, Washington: IMF.

Karabarbounis, L. and B. Neiman (2015) 'The global decline of the labor share', *The Quarterly Journal of Economics*, 61–103.

Luebker, M. (2002) 'Assessing the impact of past distributional shifts on global poverty levels', Employment Paper 2002–37, Geneva: ILO.

Luebker, M. (2015) 'Redistribution policies', in J. Berg (ed.) *Labour Markets, Institutions and Inequality. Building Just Societies in the 21st Century*, Cheltenham, UK and Northampton, MA, USA: Edward Elgar Publishing, pp. 211–241.

Lustig, N. (2015) 'Income redistribution and poverty reduction in Latin America: the role of social spending and taxation in achieving development goals',

Development Journal – Society For International Development, 57(3–4) (Double Issue), September.

Meier, G.M. (1971) *Leading Issues in Development* (2nd edition), Oxford: Oxford University Press.

Melaned, C. (2012) *After 2015: Contexts, Politics and Processes for a Post 2015 Global Agreement on Development*, London, ODI:

Milanovic, B. (2012a) 'Global inequality recalculated and updated: the effect of new PPP estimates on global inequality and 2005 estimates', *Journal of Economic Inequality*, 10(1), 1–18.

Milanovic, B. (2012b) 'Global inequality by the numbers: in history and now an overview', Policy Research Working Paper 6259, Washington, DC: World Bank.

Milanovic, B. (2016) *Global Inequality, a New Approach for the Age of Globalization*, Cambridge, MA: Belknap Press of Harvard University Press.

Mkandawire, T. (ed.) (2004) *Social Policy in a Development Context*, Basingstoke: Palgrave Macmillan.

Nayyar, D. (2013) 'The Millennium Development Goals beyond 2015: old frameworks and new constructs', *Journal of Human Development and Capabilities*, 14(3), 371–392.

Ocampo, J.A., C. Rada and L. Taylor (2009) *Growth and Policy in Developing Countries: A Structuralist Approach*, New York: Columbia University Press.

Palma, J.G. (2011) 'Homogeneous middles vs. heterogeneous tails, and the end of the "inverted-u": it's all about the share of the rich', *Development and Change*, 42, 87–153.

Piketty, T. (2014) *Capital in the Twenty-First Century*, Cambridge: Harvard University Press.

Prebisch, R. (1970) Change and Development – Latin America's Great Task: Report Submitted To The Inter-American Development Bank, New York: Praeger.

Rodriguez, F. and A. Yayadev (2010) 'The declining labor share of income', Human Development Reports Research Paper 2010/36, New York: UNDP.

Saad Filho, Alfredo (2015) 'Social policy for mature neoliberalism: the Bolsa Família Programme in Brazil', *Development and Change*, 46(6), 1227–1252.

Saith, A. (2006) 'From universal values to Millennium Development Goals: lost in translation', *Development and Change*, 37(6), 1167–1199.

Shorrocks, A. and R. van der Hoeven (eds) (2004) *Growth, Inequality, and Poverty: Prospects for Pro poor Economic Development*, Oxford: Oxford University Press.

Stiglitz, J. (2006) *Making Globalization Work*, New York: W.W. Norton and Company.

Stockhammer, E. (2013) 'Why have wage shares fallen? A panel analysis of the determinants of functional income distribution', Conditions of Work and Employment Series No. 35, Geneva: ILO.

Sumner, A. (2012) 'Where do the poor live? A new update', IDS Working Paper 2012-339, IDS, Sussex.

Tinbergen, J. (1975) *Income Distribution, Analysis and Policies*, Amsterdam: North Holland.

Trapp, K. (2015) 'Measuring the labour income share of developing countries', WIDER Working Paper 2015/041, UNU-WIDER, Helsinki.

UNCTAD (2014) 'The least developed countries report 2014, growth with structural transformation: a post 2015 development agenda', Geneva: UNCTAD.

UNDP (2013) *Humanity Divided: Confronting Inequality in Developing Countries*, New York: UNDP.

van Bergeijk, P.A.G. (2013) *Earth Economics*, Cheltenham, UK and Northampton, MA, USA: Edward Elgar Publishing.

van Bergeijk, P.A.G, A. de Haan and R. van der Hoeven (eds) (2011) *The Financial Crisis and Developing Countries, A Global Multidisciplinary Perspective*, Cheltenham, UK and Northampton, MA, USA: Edward Elgar Publishing.

van der Hoeven, R. (1988) *Planning for Basic Needs: A Soft Option or a Solid Policy, A Basic Needs Simulation Model Applied to Kenya*, Aldershot: Gower Publishing.

van der Hoeven, R. (2010) 'Income inequality and employment revisited: can one make sense of economic policy?', *Journal of Human Development and Capabilities*, 11(1).

van der Hoeven, R. (ed.) (2011) *Employment, Inequality and Globalization: A Continuous Concern*, London: Routledge.

Vandemoortele, J. (2011) 'The MDG story: intention denied', *Development and Change*, 42, 1–21.

Vos, R.P. (2010) 'The crisis of globalization as an opportunity to create a fairer world', *Journal of Human Development and Capabilities*, 11(1).

Wilkinson, R. and K. Pickett (2010) *The Spirit Level. Why Equality is Better for Everyone*, London: Penguin Books.

APPENDIX 1 MILLENNIUM DEVELOPMENT GOALS (MDGs), AS FORMULATED IN 2000

1. Eradicate extreme poverty and hunger.
2. Achieve universal primary education.
3. Promote gender equality and empower women.
4. Reduce child mortality.
5. Improve maternal health.
6. Combat HIV/AIDS, malaria and other diseases.
7. Ensure environmental sustainability.
8. Develop a global partnership for development.

APPENDIX 2 SUSTAINABLE DEVELOPMENT GOALS (SDGs), AS FORMULATED IN 2015

1. End poverty in all its forms everywhere.
2. End hunger, achieve food security and improve nutrition and promote sustainable agriculture.
3. Ensure healthy lives and promote well-being for all at all ages.
4. Ensure inclusive and equitable education and promote life-long learning opportunities for all.
5. Achieve gender equality and empower women and girls.
6. Ensure availability and sustainable management of water and sanitation for all.
7. Ensure access to affordable, reliable sustainable and modern energy for all.
8. Promote sustained, inclusive and sustainable economic growth, full and productive employment and decent work for all.
9. Build resilient infrastructure, promote inclusive and sustainable industrialization and foster innovation.
10. Reduce inequality within and among countries.
11. Make cities and human settlements inclusive, safe and sustainable.
12. Ensure sustainable consumption and production patterns.
13. Take urgent action to combat climate change and its impacts.
14. Conserve and sustainably use the oceans, seas and marine resources for sustainable development.
15. Protect, restore and promote sustainable use of terrestrial ecosystems, sustainably manage forests, combat desertification and halt land degradation and biodiversity loss.
16. Promote peaceful and inclusive societies, provide access to justice

for all, and build effective, accountable and inclusive institutions at all levels.
17. Strengthen the means of implementation and revitalize the global partnership for sustainable development.

Index

Printed and bound by CPI Group (UK) Ltd, Croydon, CR0 4YY

23/04/2025

14660962-0003